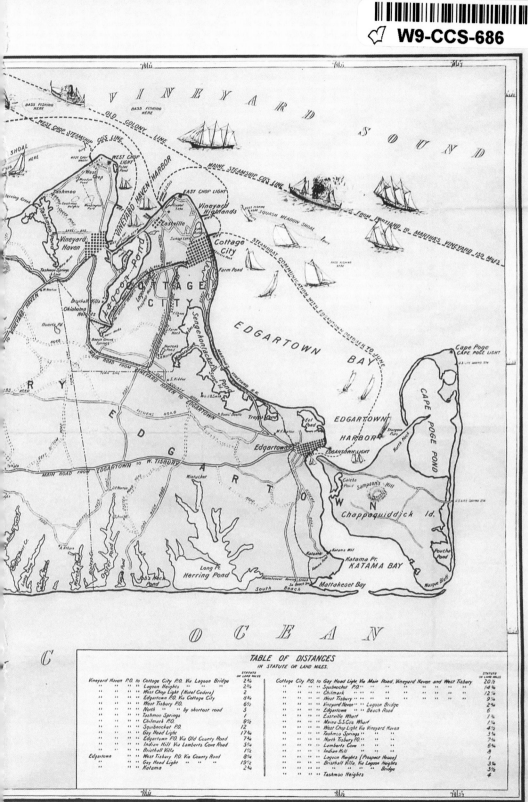

TABLE OF DISTANCES
IN STATUTE OR LAND MILES.

	STATUTE OR LAND MILES			STATUTE OR LAND MILES
Vineyard Haven P.O. to Cottage City P.O. Via Lagoon Bridge	2½	Cottage City P.O. to Gay Head Light, Via Main Road, Vineyard Haven and West Tisbury	20½
" " " Lagoon Heights	2¾	" " " Squibnocket P.O.	14½
" " " West Chop Light (Hotel Cedars)	2	" " " Chilmark	12½
" " " Edgartown P.O. Via Cottage City	8½	" " " West Tisbury	9½
" " " West Tisbury P.O.	6½	" " " Vineyard Haven " Lagoon Bridge	2½
" " " North " by shortest road	5	" " " Edgartown " Beach Road	6
" " " Tashmoo Springs	1	" " " Eastville Wharf	1½
" " " Chilmark P.O.	9½	" " " Maine S.S.Cos Wharf	1¼
" " " Squibnocket P.O.	12	" " " West Chop Light Via Vineyard Haven	4½
" " " Gay Head Light	17¾	" " " Tashmoo Springs	3¼
" " " Edgartown P.O. Via Old County Road	7¾	" " " North Tisbury P.O.	7¼
" " " Indian Hill Via Lamberts Cove Road	5¼	" " " Lamberts Cove	6¼
" " " Bristhall Villa	1½	" " " Indian Hill	8
Edgartown " West Tisbury P.O. Via County Road	8¼	" " " Lagoon Heights (Prospect House)	1
" " " Gay Head Light " " "	19½	" " " Bristhall Villa, Via Lagoon Heights	3¼
" " " Katama	2¼	" " " " " Bridge	3½
		" " " Tashmoo Heights	4

Casting into the Light

Casting into the Light

TALES OF A FISHING LIFE

Janet Messineo

PANTHEON BOOKS, NEW YORK

*Grateful acknowledgment is made to Conrad Neumann for permission
to reprint "Bass Fishing at Squibnocket" by Conrad Neumann.
Reprinted by permission of Conrad Neumann.*

Library of Congress Cataloging-in-Publication Data
Name: Messineo, Janet, author.
Title: Casting into the light : tales of a fishing life / Janet Messineo.
Description: New York : Pantheon Books, 2019. Includes
bibliographical references and index.
Identifiers: LCCN 2018052725. ISBN 9781524747640
(hardcover : alk. paper). ISBN 9781524747657 (ebook).
Subjects: LCSH: Messineo, Janet. Women fishers—Massachusetts—
Biography. Surf casting—Massachusetts. Surf fishing—
Massachusetts.
Classification: LCC SH415.M47 A3 2019 | DDC 799.109744—
dc23 | LC record available at lccn.loc.gov/2018052725

www.pantheonbooks.com

Jacket photograph by Ben Scott
Jacket design by Deb Wood

Printed in the United States of America

First Edition
2 4 6 8 9 7 5 3 1

To the Wednesday Writers Group (WWG), to Lisa Belcastro, Connie Berry, Stephen Caliri, Matthew Fielder, Cat Finch, Dan Meaney, Cynthia Riggs, and Nancy Wood, who encouraged me to keep writing

Contents

A Note from the Author

Alone, in the darkness, the hunt for a trophy striped bass keeps me awake during the hours when I should be home tucked safely in my warm bed.

As the years have passed, I've realized that fishing is not all about keeping every fish that I catch. Fishing for this beautiful creature has taught me a profound respect for all of nature. I've observed the striped bass go into decline and have learned that nothing is inexhaustible. I now do my part in conserving the fish I once longed to possess. Many times after I've landed a striped bass, I pause to admire its magnificent beauty, then I release it back into the surf and wish it well as it swims off to live another day.

Casting into the Light

I

—

The Hook

STRIPED BASS, *Morone saxatilis,* are the most prized migratory game fish in the Northeast. They have earned respect from anglers because of their powerful fighting strength, beauty, and deliciousness as table fare. They can live for at least forty years and have been known to weigh up to one hundred pounds, although fish more than fifty pounds are scarce. They can grow to more than fifty inches in length. They have a massive strong head and their sides are silver with seven dark longitudinal lines including the lateral line. The striped bass spends most of its adult life in the ocean, migrating north and south seasonally. It ascends to freshwater in the estuaries to spawn in the spring. The juveniles remain in freshwater for a few years before entering the ocean to begin their lifelong annual migration.

In New England, the striped bass has been a valued resource since the region was first settled in the 1600s. The early settlers described the bass as being in immense abundance. One of the first public schools in America was established in Plymouth Colony in 1670 with income from the striped bass fisheries. Today in New England this species is still a highly valued resource.

Pilot's Landing, Aquinnah, 2014

On Martha's Vineyard, the saltwater fishing season starts in April and runs through November. When the water temperature drops to below forty-five degrees, the striped bass migrate south, following their forage to warmer waters. When the spring water temperatures rise above fifty-five degrees, they return to Vineyard waters.

I enjoy fishing for many species, but striped bass are the fish that first captivated my interest, especially because they are so difficult to find since they are primarily nocturnal feeders. They have a reputation of being finicky and clever fighters. Under the cover of darkness, they will trap bait up against jetties or in between fields of large boulders near the shoreline. Once hooked, they have been known to rub their mouths against the rocks to cut your line. A bluefish is more likely to feed during the daylight hours and in open waters. Bluefish ferociously shake their heads and jump into the air trying to free themselves from a hook. They give the fisherman a hearty tussle; they feel more like fighting a fish of muscle, but not much brain.

A fifty-pound striped bass from the surf has been the dream of many obsessed surf anglers for generations.

———

I was packing up my gear after a day of fishing for bluefish. Early that morning I had driven my 1979 International Scout from Katama Beach on Martha's Vineyard to Wasque Point on Chappaquiddick Island, over a three-mile barrier beach that connects the two islands.

A woman who looked to be about fifty years old, alone in her four-wheel-drive vehicle, stopped for a chat with one of the fishermen I was standing with at the Wasque Rip. To me, she was elderly. She told us she was heading out to Cape Poge for the night to fish for striped bass. From where we stood, Cape Poge is another seven miles of desolate beach driving on rough-cut roads through the dunes, and before the 1980s there was no beach management at night. It's a barrier beach, Cape Poge bay on one side, Nantucket Sound on the other. I stood wide-eyed.

I was impressed that all she had with her was her fishing gear, a thermos of coffee, and a sandwich. It was unusual to see any woman fishing on the beach. The idea of spending the night alone on a desolate beach in search of striped bass filled me with anxiety. A shiver of fear ran down my spine, but at the same time I felt excitement and got an adrenaline surge. At that moment, I wanted to be her.

Becoming a respected surf fisherman has been a challenge. My first memories are vague, but I remember wanting to become a great fisherman—not a woman fisherman, separated by gender, but just a respected fisherman. I knew that I was as capable as any man of catching and landing a large fish. It took many years to prove to myself and to the male-dominated fishing community that I could make this come true. I've had many scary nights alone on the beach in search of a huge creature that I longed to know. As I think back over four decades, I'm not sure why I didn't give up after being frightened half out of my wits. I've learned that giving up is not something I do.

During the off-season, from December until mid-April, I live a normal life. I work, clean the house and cook dinners, walk the dog, pay my bills, and take care of everyday business. Come April, the first time I get my fishing rod out of its winter storage and stand in the surf up to my thighs to cast, I exhale. It feels as though I have been holding my breath for the last five months. My posture changes, my face relaxes, most of the aches and pains in my body melt away. I feel serene, focused, and safe. I'm home.

It's the meditative place similar to where gardeners go when they kneel in the dirt and dig their fingers in the soil. People who crochet or make quilts go to that place as they sit for hours and sew thousands of tiny stitches. Musicians get lost in the chords and notes, golfers know that place of peace when they chase a little white ball around the greens. My doctor told me that when he skis he no longer thinks of all his responsibilities and his mind becomes calm and quiet.

For me, it's fishing. Standing in the surf, casting my lure toward the horizon, I feel like I am the woman I'm meant to be. As I watch the sun rise or set, rain or shine, all those important thoughts that have been occupying my mind become trivial. I feel small under the light of the moon and a ceiling of bright stars. When I'm fishing, I feel alive and right-size. After four decades, fishing is not something I do, it is part of my being. It's who I am. My life becomes meaningful and I feel part of my surroundings.

I never thought about fishing from a boat. I worked as a waitress for twenty years and then as a fish taxidermist for the next thirty, and on my wages, purchasing a boat was out of the question. When I first got interested in surf fishing, buying a rod and a few lures was challenging enough.

In 1912, Charles Church caught an International Game Fish Association (IGFA) world-record striped bass weighing seventy-three pounds off of Cuttyhunk Island, Massachusetts. In 1967, Charlie Cinto, from Plymouth, Massachusetts, tied that record. Both fish were taken from a boat in the waters around Cuttyhunk. In 1981, fourteen years later, another seventy-three-pound striped bass caught from a beach on Cape Cod by Tony Stetzko Jr. tied that record.

Al McReynolds from New Jersey broke all those records in 1982 with a seventy-eight-pound, eight-ounce striped bass caught from a jetty in Atlantic City, New Jersey. That fish held until Greg Myerson caught an eighty-one-pound, fourteen-ounce striped bass in 2011 from his boat in Westbrook, Connecticut. Greg's fish is the current world-record striped bass.

I know that as a surfcaster my odds of ever seeing a fish close to

The Origins of Angling, Dame Juliana
Berners fishing, 1496

sixty or seventy pounds are slim, but stories like these keep me hoping because you never know when the fish of a lifetime might come to you.

Striped bass have caused fishermen to become obsessed. Here on Martha's Vineyard, anglers, visiting and resident, have tragically lost their lives while fishing for stripers. We have lost more than a few men who drowned walking into the ocean in chest waders with no belt. Waders are necessary apparel for a surf fisherman, especially in the early spring or late fall when the water temperature is below sixty degrees. A tight belt around the waist keeps water from entering your waders. Without a belt, if a big wave hits you or you step into a deep hole and your waders fill with water, you can lose your footing and get pulled into the surf. Boat anglers have met their demise when unexpected weather and rough seas became too challenging for the size of their boat.

Once hooked, the striped bass becomes a hard-fighting, clever opponent. It can take a lifetime to become a proficient striped bass fisherman. Each spring and then again in the late fall, fishermen all along the coast from Maryland to Maine arm themselves with rods in hand, hoping to connect with a school of migrating striped bass.

Women, who are generally physically smaller than men, have been perceived as weaker as well, and thus not capable of handling large fish without the aid of a male. Up until the early 1990s, another challenge for women had been that most foul-weather clothing was designed and manufactured to fit men. I struggled for years wearing waders that were much too big for me.

Women have been noted in the sports fishing world for a long time. The first known work on the sport of fishing, an essay published in 1496 called *The Treatise of Fishing with an Angle,* is said to have been written by a woman, Dame Juliana Berners, a nun in England, although there is some controversy about whether she really existed.

Since the days of Dame Juliana, many women have knocked on the door to be accepted into the recreational fishing world, but upon entering have faced many challenges. I can only imagine what it felt like for Dame Juliana, standing in a stream fly fishing, wearing the garb of a fifteenth-century nun.

2

My Beginning

I RAN AWAY FROM HOME three times when I was eleven years old. It was springtime, and I remember feeling as if I couldn't stand living with my family one more minute. I was daydreaming at my desk during school hours when spring was blooming, and I could hear the birds in the trees in the schoolyard. I imagined that I could build a little shack in the woods and live among the creatures of the forest.

The first time I attempted to leave, I walked the railroad tracks heading north. The Boston-to-Maine line ran through Salem, New Hampshire. I put an extra set of clothes in a bag and set off with a couple of dollars that I had saved from my fifty-cents-a-week allowance. Where was I going? I didn't care. The cops picked me up as it was getting dark.

The last time, I left with my childhood friend Ruthie. I had found a partner in crime. She said she knew of a barn that we could stay in. I thought that sounded perfect. After school, she took me to the big old barn. We climbed a ladder and settled onto some bales of hay in the loft. I was free and on my own. I felt no fear. I felt safe and happy.

Then it started to get colder and it started to snow. We were having one of those late spring storms. Ruthie started to cry. She wanted to go home. I didn't. As the night grew colder and darker, she begged me to go back home. I reluctantly gave in. I was angry with her, but knew she would tell where I was, so I had no choice but to leave with her. We went to her house and turned ourselves in. I have no idea how I got home, but the police were at the house when I got there.

The only thing I recollect is that the police and my parents said, "If you run away one more time, you will get locked up in 'girls' school.' I didn't know what 'girls' school' was, but I knew that the bad girl down the street was sent there and I never saw her again. I didn't know what kind of bad thing she did, either. I made up my mind to stay put until I could legally leave when I turned eighteen.

When I found alcohol at fifteen and marijuana at seventeen, I could run away without going anywhere. The need to escape was the deep-down feeling I had from a young age. Many years later fishing became my escape.

My journey began as the daughter of mill workers. My father's family emigrated from Sicily to Ellis Island with Lawrence, Massachusetts, as their destination. Lawrence is where they worked in the textile mills and where they remained for their whole lives.

When my dad was young he worked at the Rockingham horse racetrack in Salem, New Hampshire. He started as an exercise boy and later became a jockey. He traveled with the racetrack. After World War II began, he left the track and joined the Army. While stationed in England during the war, he met his bride-to-be, my mom, Sybil Saxelby.

When the war ended, my dad returned to America on a troopship. His young sixteen-year-old wife, with my brother, Paul, who was born in England, were transported on a massive ship, the *Alexandria,* with hundreds of other English war brides and their babies. My parents were reunited in New York City and then traveled to Lawrence. Not long after they settled in a three-story tenement building on High Street, I was born.

Jobs were scarce in Lawrence at that time. Most of the mills had shut down or moved to the South. My dad had become a family man—no more riding the horses—so, like his family before him, he went to work in the textile mill. They had no car, and he walked from our apartment back and forth to work each day.

He didn't have a high school education, but he enrolled in classes offered by the Veterans Administration, training to become a dental assistant. He thought this was an opportunity for him since he had been a medic in the Army. But he found out that without the proper education, there wasn't enough money in that field at that time for him to be able to support a family.

His uncle Joe, who worked in a jewelry store, taught him to repair watches. Then in around 1953, Western Electric opened a factory in Lawrence and hired him right away. There were lines of people wanting to work, so he was lucky to get a job. For the rest of his career days he worked at Western Electric. Once my brother, Paul, and I started school, my mom was also hired by Western. He worked the day shift, she the night shift.

While I was growing up, my brother and my father were the sportsmen in our family. They had few opportunities to fish, but they never missed a chance to cast into a river or brook or, on rare occasions, to go deep-sea fishing with drop lines for cod or flounder. During summer vacation, we would sometimes rent a little apartment, together with family and friends, and spend a couple of weeks by the ocean.

I can remember following my dad and Paul out to the Black Rocks at Salisbury Beach. I watched them cast from the jetty while I searched for shells and crabs in between the rocks.

I have memories of playing around the rivers near my childhood homes. When I was three we moved into a veterans' housing project, where we stayed until I was eight. It was an improvement from the cramped third-floor rooms on High Street, which were hot in the summer and cold in the winter. Paul and I now had a bedroom to share and my parents had their own room. The project was a fun place to grow up. Except for the "Ragga Man." He was an old man who drove a horse and carriage through the projects collecting rags. He would yell, "Ragga man, ragga man!" They told us children that if we did not behave, we would be given to the ragga man. Terrifying.

The Shawsheen River ran by our neighborhood. The dozens of

buildings were inhabited by veterans and their war brides from all over the world. We always had lots of other children to play with.

When we moved over the Massachusetts border into New Hampshire, the Spicket River became our new playground. In those days, probably because I was a girl, I was neither encouraged nor discouraged from fishing. My mom told me that I was usually around the periphery looking for interesting bugs or creepy-crawlies to keep me entertained. I tagged along with my brother, much to his dismay, trying to catch anything that I could fool with a worm and a bobber. I spent most of my time trying to free my hook from the debris that littered the river bottom. Paul was always much more successful than I was.

As a teenager, like most of the young people from the Lawrence-Salem area, I got my first job at Rockingham racetrack. I worked in the concession stands selling jumbo hot dogs for thirty-five cents each—not as glamorous as my dad's job riding the horses. I saved my money and bought an Epiphone acoustic guitar. Once I turned seventeen, I followed the family tradition and got a job working in a factory, the Blue Bonnet Shoe Company. I was a box-toe girl: I glued the reinforcements into the toe of each shoe. I worked after school and on weekends. It was a steadier job than working seasonally at the racetrack.

We were fortunate teenagers in Salem. The ballroom on the reservoir at Canobie Lake amusement park held record hops every Friday evening. Each week during the summer months we got to hear all the up-and-coming rock-and-roll stars. Little Stevie Wonder, then sixteen years old, playing "Fingertips" on his harmonica, and Sonny and Cher singing "I Got You Babe" wearing raccoon vests, and the Shirelles singing "Will You Still Love Me Tomorrow." I heard the Beach Boys, Jerry Lee Lewis, the Temptations, and too many to list of the Motown groups. I was a regular, when I was not grounded for disobeying family rules.

I wanted to go to the Maine College of Art in Portland, but my parents said that they would not fund art school. I came from a time when most women were not supported to pursue a career to become *something* but rather to get enough education to get a job to meet a man who had a high-paying job and could support his wife and children. It was the mid-'60s and most of the girls in my class went on to be secretaries, nurses, or teachers. Artist was not an acceptable career choice.

At seventeen years of age, after graduating from high school in 1965, in the evenings after work I attended three months of private art school in Lawrence. I paid for the classes with the wages I had saved from working at the shoe factory. My instructor was an accomplished artist, but his teaching style was old school, and I felt I was being suffocated. He was a realist and had no tolerance for any works that went off in another direction. If I had been more mature, I might have been able to learn from him, but I was rebellious and couldn't fit into his interpretation of art. I left home when I turned eighteen and got an apartment in Lawrence, not far from my job at the shoe factory.

I always felt that my shoe shop job was temporary. One of the women who worked across from me on the conveyor belt had been employed in that factory for many years. She worked on one of the heavy sewing machines and her mother worked right next to her. She won a trip in a raffle to some exotic island that the factory sponsored. Instead of taking the vacation, she cashed it in for the money. It was a turning point for me. I thought, "This is not the life for me. If I don't leave now, I might be here forever!" I walked up to the time clock, punched out, and never returned.

My dad got me a job at IT&T, International Telephone & Telegraph. They produced specialty components for the aerospace, transportation, and industrial markets. It was a big step up from the shoe shop, but I knew that working in factories was not the path for me.

Shortly after I turned eighteen, I left my family in New Hampshire and my job at IT&T, with no more than an extra change of clothes in my knapsack, my raccoon vest—like the one Cher wore—and my guitar. It was early spring, and I was suffering again with the urge to run.

Cape Cod was my destination. Much to my parents' disapproval, instead of continuing my education so I could become a teacher or a secretary, I was drawn to the artistic beatnik community that had piqued my curiosity during a family vacation in Provincetown in 1960. My vision was to set up an easel with a canvas on the sidewalk and to wear a beret on my disheveled head of long curly hair. I loved the smell of oil paints. I wasn't even dreaming about fishing rods. I wanted to be a beatnik.

It was early spring in Provincetown, and after a month or so, I found more drama than art in the streets, and I didn't meet anyone with similar goals. I left, thumb out, and headed for Hyannis. I met two guys from Southbridge, Michael and Bernie, who shared my love of guitar playing. One day, while we were sitting in a park in the center of town playing our guitars and singing Bob Dylan and Woody Guthrie songs, they asked me if I wanted to go to Martha's Vineyard.

"What's Martha's Vineyard?" I asked.

They said, "It's an island!"

Being from a small mill town, I pictured palm trees, monkeys, and bananas. That sounded fascinating to me. Once again, I grabbed my guitar and knapsack and hopped on the back of Bernie's Vespa. We headed for the ferry in Woods Hole that brought us to the island of Martha's Vineyard.

I soon learned that the Vineyard is not a tropical island with monkeys and bananas. The streets are lined with privet hedges, oak trees, and all the typical New England greenery. I imagined a small ferryboat that could carry only a few people at a time. I was surprised when we entered the port at Woods Hole and a huge white ship came into view. This fleet of ferries owned by the Steamship Authority transported huge trucks, cars, and hundreds of passengers to and from Martha's Vineyard each day.

It was 1966 when I rode off the boat on the back of that Vespa scooter wearing my raccoon vest, short-short cutoff jeans, and lace-up leather sandals. I felt like I had come home.

It took no time at all before I was surrounded by a community of artists and liberal-minded young, adventurous friends. We called our way of life "being on the skids." I had not a care in the world. I was elated to be living on my own. I enjoyed mid-'60s island life, being young and feeling carefree. The Vineyard was a safe place for me to let loose the free spirit that was bursting from my seams.

That entire summer was full of adventure, mostly on the island. I did make a couple of short trips off-island, but I always made my way back. The Vineyard had become my home base.

The summer was coming to an end and I didn't understand why suddenly most of my friends were leaving—going home, going to college, or going somewhere else. I didn't want to go anywhere else. I didn't really have anywhere else to go. Going back to my parents' home was not an option. This was a safe environment for a naive eighteen-year-old girl and I wanted to stay.

By September, most of the friends I had made had left the island. It was starting to get cold and sleeping under skiffs on the beach or under the Vineyard Haven drawbridge was not as comfortable as it had been in July. Maybe it was time to look for work.

One day I was wandering around Oak Bluffs Harbor. That's what I did every day: I wandered, waiting to see what adventures would find me. That day what found me was a job.

The boat was the *Marsh Wind.* I think the captain's name was Paul Dunn. It was a head boat, sometimes called a party boat. Once or twice a day the boat was hired to take people out to fish with drop lines and bait. I was hired to bait the hooks and take the fish off them for the clients. I cleaned up the gear and swabbed the deck after each group of fishermen was finished for the day. My pay was two dollars a day and a cot to sleep in on the boat. I loved it. This was my first fishing job.

I was called a tomboy as a child. I never minded getting my hands dirty and felt more at home in my brother's hand-me-down jeans than in a dress. I would rather dig worms and climb trees than play with dolls. Working on a fishing boat suited me. I had no problem preparing the bait by chopping squid into small pieces and taking a wiggling fish off a hook for the clients. My hands were bloody and covered with fish slime. I loved it.

I was getting to know some of the island locals who spent time on the harbor. One day, a good friend of the owner of the *Marsh Wind,* George Lawrence, asked me if I needed a place to stay. He offered me a room in his house in exchange for taking care of his two boys and doing some light housekeeping. I jumped at the offer. My job on the *Marsh Wind* was coming to an end as the fishing season subsided.

George's house was an old Victorian home on Penacook Avenue in Oak Bluffs. The boys, Cliffy and Eddie, were thirteen and fifteen. The family was from Medford, Massachusetts, and George wanted to get his teenage boys out of the city. His wife and other children stayed in Medford.

I loved living in the quaint town of Oak Bluffs. Circuit Avenue, the main street, which had been bustling with tourists eating ice cream and searching for the perfect trinket in the gift shops, was now empty. The music that could be heard coming from the restaurants and barrooms had gone silent, and I could hear the dried leaves that had fallen from the trees blowing across the road in the wind. It was late October and the island was deserted. Most of the homes were boarded up for the winter. I walked among the gingerbread-type houses hidden one block behind Circuit Avenue. This cluster of bright-colored Victorian cottages surrounds a tabernacle built in 1879. In the summer it holds weekly interdenominational services and hosts cultural events. Oak Bluffs now felt like a ghost town, especially after six in the evening. The island people would say, "They roll up the sidewalks after Labor Day."

I had a few close friends my age. One was Laurie Miller and the other Nick Kempf. Laurie was an artist and Nick a blues harp player, astrologer, and seriously into the occult. Nicky was living in his grandmother's second-floor apartment on Circuit Avenue above the Lemon Tree store. We spent our days listening to or playing music, doing art projects, and talking to spirits on the Ouija board. Life was good. I had a bed to sleep in, a little food in my belly, and living with the Lawrence family was peaceful and drama-free.

One afternoon when I was with the guys at Nicky's grandmother's apartment, there was a knock at the door. A police officer asked if I was there.

Everyone knew me as "Mess," short for my last name, Messineo.

It seemed like everyone had nicknames in those days. My friends had started calling me Mess at an early age, and it stuck for the next forty years. No one on the Vineyard knew my real name. The officer asked me to step outside. I followed him down the stairs and onto the street.

The officer asked me if I could produce ten dollars. I had no money, so I said, "No."

He said, "You are breaking the law. You're a vagrant." He gave me a choice: "Either you leave the island, or you go to jail."

He wouldn't let me go back to talk to Nicky and Laurie.

I said, "I guess I'll have to leave."

He drove me to George's house. Unfortunately, no one was there. It was in the afternoon; the Lawrence boys were in school and George was off-island. I didn't know how to get in touch with him. I grabbed my guitar, packed my knapsack, got back into the police cruiser, and was driven to the ferry terminal in Vineyard Haven.

By then it was late afternoon. It was fall, so the sun was low and it was getting dark. The officer locked me in the police cruiser and went into the ferry terminal to buy me a ticket.

Then we sat. In the off-season in 1966, they didn't run many boats. We sat and waited for awhile longer. I don't remember talking to him. We just waited for the boat.

Finally, he asked, "Do I need to wait here with you or will you take the next boat?" It must have been his dinnertime.

I started to cry. I said, "Of course I am going to leave. I have nowhere to go and I don't want to go to jail."

He gave me the boat ticket and left. By that time, it was dark.

I must have known a telephone number for Nicky or Laurie, and apparently I had a dime to make a call. Somehow, I got in touch with my friends. I was crying and told them I was being thrown off the island. I told them that the cop had told me that if I didn't leave he was going to put me in jail. They told me to stay right where I was and wait for them.

I stood in the dark, alone and crying. The ferry docked, unloaded, loaded, and left once more. I hid in the shadows of the terminal.

Finally, a small truck pulled up with Laurie and his older brother,

Allan Miller. Allan rolled down his window and said, "Get in." I was wailing now, saying, "No, I can't—they're going to throw me in jail."

"They *can't* do that," he said. "He is a town cop and he transported you over the town line." I got into his vehicle. Allan started driving toward Oak Bluffs. "We're going back to the police station to talk to them," he said.

I was screaming, "No, no, they'll throw me in jail!" I was shaking all the way to the Oak Bluffs police station.

Luck was with me. The police station was closed for the night and no one was there.

Allan said, "You can stay with me and my wife."

We drove back to Vineyard Haven, up State Road to West Tisbury, then we turned down a long dirt road, passing a tiny wooden chapel built in 1680 by a minister, Thomas Mayhew Jr. The Christiantown chapel's purpose was to Christianize the indigenous peoples, the Wampanoag tribe. We continued down the bumpy dirt road until we came to the Miller family home.

Allan had built a beautiful house deep in the woods and I felt safe there. I met his wife, Bonnie, and their two toddlers, Andrew and Tina. The house smelled of fresh-cut lumber and was spacious and creatively decorated. I stayed with them for a few weeks until another adventure came my way.

About thirty years later, as I was telling my "getting deported" story I realized that it made no sense for the police to seek me out. Why didn't they come to George's house to get me when everyone was home? How did they know that I didn't have any money? For that matter, how did they know I was at Nicky's grandmother's apartment?

How was I a vagrant? I had a place to live, after all. But I was young, and I believed them when they said I had to leave the Vineyard.

It was 1966 and I was a young white girl living with a black man and his two sons. I now imagine the town fathers sitting around a big table saying, "This cannot happen in our town. We have a teenage white girl living with a black family. How are we going to get her out of here?"

I'll never know the real story. George passed away many years ago. Cliffy and Eddie found me again about ten years later. We reconnected, but they were young, like me, and were just as oblivious to what happened that day. They have grown into handsome, productive adult men who, being well over six feet tall, tower over my five-foot frame. They refer to me as their sister.

Now I wonder what would have happened if I had taken the boat that day. What if I had left the Vineyard? I can imagine myself alone in Woods Hole in the late fall, on a dark evening, confused, with no money and nowhere to go, waiting for an adventure to find me. I don't see any positive ending to that story. I am ever indebted to Allan Miller for rescuing me on that cold, dark evening and I'm grateful that I stayed safe on the Vineyard.

The following summer I met and married my first husband, Richard Lesko, nicknamed Butch. He was working as a lifeguard at Owen Park Beach, a small public beach on Vineyard Haven Harbor, a short walk from Main Street and adjacent to the Steamship Authority. Protected by a large breakwater so that it stays calm, Owen Park is a popular beach for parents to bring their little children for a swim as they sit and watch the ferries travel back and forth from the mainland.

Our ideas were different from our parents' expectations. The times were changing, and we felt like we were a part of something exciting, political, important.

In the winter of 1968, we left the Vineyard in a '61 Plymouth Valiant bound for California with our rescue dog Freckles and two friends, Frank Atkinson and David Boyd. Some LSD dealers from California had come to the Vineyard and inspired us to take the trip. They invited us to stay with them on a commune.

We headed west to *experience* some off-island adventures. I don't remember too much about our trip cross-country. We did pick up a couple of guys who were hitchhiking in Virginia, hoping that they had some money. They didn't, but they stayed with us all the way to California.

Now we had six people and a dog and not much money. We barely

Holding Fix, Butch with Freckles, Haight-Ashbury, 1968

ate anything, drove all day, and then slept sitting up side by side, all the way to the West Coast.

Once we crossed the California border, we headed north to meet up with friends and try communal living. It was called Holiday Commune, in the town of Felton, near Santa Cruz, a peaceful rural place with a large main house and small shared cabins along a rambling river. It was okay for a while, but it wasn't too long before we packed our few belongings and Freckles and drove to San Francisco.

We found a room to rent in a second-floor shared apartment on the corner of Haight and Ashbury, right in the center of the drug culture.

Our landlord's dog had a litter of black Lab mutt puppies, so of course we fell in love with one. We named him Fix. We stayed in that room, with our two dogs, for about six months. Then we wanted to get out of the city, so we got enough money together to buy a tent and we hitchhiked down to below Big Sur. There was a huge three-day festival on the beach, off Route 1, at Lime Kiln Creek. After the music ended and everyone left, we hiked about two miles into the redwood forest. There we set up camp and enjoyed living among the redwood trees on the edge of a rushing river.

After almost three months, in which we lived on not much else but brown rice and a whole lot of peace and serenity, the forest rangers found us squatting. We were told to leave. The rangers told us, "You're really lucky that we are the ones that found you. Pig hunting season is about to begin, and you would not want to be found by that group." I can only imagine!

We went back to San Francisco, where we worked odd jobs for a few more months to get plane fare back to the East Coast. I cooked for an elderly woman each day and Butch got temporary labor jobs when he could. My parents, reluctantly, took us into their home in Salem until we could get on our own feet, dogs and all.

We found a small three-room cottage for fifteen dollars a week, and we rented out one of the rooms to a single man for five dollars. We squirreled away all the money we earned. We bought a VW bus just in time for the Woodstock music festival in Bethel, New York, and managed to save enough money to buy forty acres of land in Milton, New Hampshire, for eight thousand dollars. We were attempting to build a log cabin while growing our own food and residing in a tipi for two years from May until October. We moved into an apartment

"Ah, but I was so much older then . . ."   Our tipi, Milton, New Hampshire, 1970

Butch, third from left, and me, right, at a Sunday flea market in Derry, New Hampshire, with friends, trying to make money to buy land, 1969

in Lowell, Massachusetts, the first year. I left to come back to the Vineyard after the second year.

As time moved on, our back-to-the-land lifestyle was wearing me out. I was twenty-four years old and the Vineyard was calling to me. The idea of sitting in the sun on a beach, listening to music, dancing, and maybe even going bowling was seeping into my dreams.

I returned to the island in 1972, without a husband.

Until I could find a place of my own, I stayed with my friends Donna and Eddie Montesion in Edgartown. I helped take care of their two little girls, Missy and Martha. It took a while to get the smoke odor from the tipi fire out of my hair and clothes, but it didn't take long to get accustomed to island life.

One sunny day, we all piled into Eddie's Toyota Land Cruiser and headed for Chappaquiddick. It was my first ride onto Norton Point Beach. The access on the south shore of Chappaquiddick Island, Norton Point is a narrow three-mile barrier beach that passes by Katama swimming beach and connects Martha's Vineyard to Chappaquiddick. It is only accessible by four-wheel-drive vehicle.

Eddie let some of the air out of his tires so the Land Cruiser wouldn't sink into the sand. I realized immediately that we were not driving on a solid road. Our bodies gently swayed in rhythm to the bumps in the trail. The soft tires carried the vehicle as if the Toyota was riding on puffy clouds. We laughed as we bumped our heads on the ceiling when Eddie hit a couple of deep holes. We bounced down the soft trail between Katama Bay and the south shore of islands. I was somewhat anxious; I wasn't used to being miles from any civilization. We passed only a couple of other vehicles and it looked like a desert, devoid of stores or service stations.

Once we arrived, Donna and I spread out blankets and beach chairs and sat chatting, soaking up sunshine, and watching the girls play in the sand. We could hear the squawking seagulls and screaming terns flying overhead. The tiny shorebirds were running back and forth, pecking in the sand on the edge of the water.

Then Eddie grabbed his fishing rod, ran to the edge of the surf, and started casting a tiny shiny lure into the water. After only a few casts, he hooked something. We jumped up from our beach chairs and gathered around him with anticipation to see what was on the end of his hook. As it came out of the water and landed on the beach at our feet it looked like a little tuna fish. Eddie said it was a bonito. I had never seen such a beautiful fish. It was about two feet long and its back was a shiny bright green. Its belly was the purest white, and in the sunlight, I could see a rainbow of subtle iridescent colors.

I stood looking toward the horizon and out over miles of ocean and wondering how he did that. Why had he suddenly decided that some fish were swimming close by? He later told me that the birds were diving, indicating that some fish were feeding close to shore. It was a magical moment and I wanted to learn how to do that.

Eddie filleted the fish, cooked it on the grill, and we all shared it for lunch on the beach. I still smile when I think of that day. After living in a tipi in the woods of New Hampshire for a couple of summers, growing our own food, and attempting to build a log cabin, I thought, "This has to be island life at its best."

Fishing in the rivers with a bobber and a worm when I was a child couldn't compare to this day on the ocean. I am sure *that* was the moment that inspired me to want to fish from the surf. I wanted to do that, and I had talked for years about wanting to buy a four-wheel-drive vehicle.

I had no interest in wanting to fish from a boat. I knew owning my own boat was not a reality, but the simplicity of fishing from the beach felt like something I could accomplish and maybe even do well someday. A few more years passed before I began my quest to become a shore fisherman.

3

The Journey Begins

THE BLACK DOG TAVERN was designed in 1970 by Robert Douglas, captain of the Martha's Vineyard tall ships the *Shenandoah* and
the *Alabama*. Allan Miller, the carpenter who rescued me from being
deported, and a handful of local carpenters were the builders. The
Black Dog sits on a waterfront property owned by Captain Douglas
on Vineyard Haven Harbor. Allan managed the tavern for the first
five years.

Before the Black Dog, the Vineyard was lacking any good, whole-
some year-round restaurants. When I was in my teens, in the winter,
Butch and I would go to Brickman's bowling alley, sit at the counter,
and order a packaged blueberry muffin and a teacup and saucer of
coffee. The island needed a place where one could sit and enjoy a fresh
cup of coffee, an oversized sandwich made with homemade bread,
and a piece of homemade pie.

Captain Bob Douglas changed the Vineyard restaurant scene
forever—big heavy mugs of steaming hot, fresh coffee, french fries
made from freshly cut potatoes, bakery-fresh pies, breads, and pastries, and home-cooked food served in front of a huge fireplace in

Mess Apron made by Woodchips

a post-and-beam dining area that was designed to look as if it had been built in the 1700s.

When I first returned from my New Hampshire tipi days, until a position came open in the tavern for a waitress, Allan hired me to work in the Black Dog Bakery on Beach Road right near the Vineyard Haven ferry dock, in front of the tavern.

In January 1972, I moved from being a baker to the tavern on Vineyard Haven Harbor and became a Black Dog waitress. We were able to wear our own clothes and not a typical waitress uniform. I designed my own apron that I modified from a carpenter's bib apron. I embroidered the bibs with flowers and other designs. Arnold Brown and his wife, Edie, liked them so much, they asked if they could produce them in their shop, Woodchips Designers. They named them the "Mess Apron" after my nickname and sold them to the public. I still have one.

It took a few years for some of the townspeople to accept the tavern. They felt like they were being invaded by hippies, and it was rumored that they thought they might be drugged if they ate there.

Unlike the long lines of today, some winter evenings we barely had any customers.

The Black Dog was a meeting place for many talented island musicians and artists. One evening a group of musicians from Long Island, New York, were performing in the tavern dining room. They played a ukulele, a saxophone, and guitars and sang original three-part harmonies. They called themselves Mr. Timothy Charles Duane, aka TCD.

I looked across the restaurant and locked eyes with Duane Giese-mann. A few months later we were in love. He left his band behind in New York and moved to the island. Shortly afterward, the rest of the band members and their families also moved to the Vineyard.

For four years, we lived in a cozy second-floor two-room apartment on Beach Road in Vineyard Haven, a short walk from the Black Dog. The Lagoon was our backyard, where we watched shellfish-ermen scalloping in the fall and were entertained watching people learning to sail in small rented sailboats in the summer. We could see Vineyard Haven Harbor and watch the ferries come and go through our kitchen window on the other side of the apartment.

Remembering that day on the beach with the Montesions, and now living surrounded by the ocean, I had an idea that we should learn to fish. I bought an inexpensive department-store two-piece rod and reel for Duane for a birthday gift. We lived near the Lagoon Pond drawbridge, where the water flows in and out of the Lagoon. We had noticed people fishing there so one cloudy afternoon we decided to give it a try.

It started to rain. Hard. Duane and I looked at each other, shrugging our shoulders, confused. Were we supposed to leave or keep fishing? Were we supposed to go home? Finally, I could hear my mother's voice saying, "Not enough sense to get out of the rain!" We reeled our line in and headed for our warm and dry home, never to fish together again.

Duane's passion was his music. He was done with fishing, but I still wanted to learn. I went down to the bridge and tried to fish on my own a few times. After getting my feet drenched, I realized I needed boots, so I bought a pair of hip boots. I also bought a few hooks and sinkers. I was not successful, but it seemed to me that patience and technique, rather than physical strength, were what it took to become a successful surf fisherman. I felt like I was ready for the challenge.

After school hours, Allan Miller's children spent a lot of time at the Black Dog Tavern with their dad. When his son Andrew was about nine years old he taught me how to make my first squid jig. He showed me how to cut a round wooden clothespin, paint it white, and attach a three-prong treble hook to the bottom. I spent most of my spare time, after waitressing a dinner shift, fishing from the piers in front of the Black Dog on the harbor. I would tie my handmade jig onto a line on a small lightweight rod and jig it up and down off the lighted docks at night. It wasn't long before a squid would grab it. I would jig up a bucket of squid to use for bait. Switching to my bigger rod, I would attach a whole squid onto my hook and throw it into the harbor. Occasionally a fish would take my bait, but, being inexperienced, I was not often successful at landing it. The harbor is full of boats and moorings, and as soon as a fish took my bait it would swim around an obstacle and my line would break.

Dick Curwell was the drummer in a local jazz band, and a well-known local fisherman. Before I was married to Butch, I was dating the band's piano player, Johnny Cassel. Dick and I had become close friends.

One day I followed him out to the end of the jetty at Anthier's Bridge in Edgartown.* He reluctantly gave me a pittance of advice on how to catch a striped bass. I could sense that he didn't want me hanging around disturbing his concentration, but he did tell me a Rebel was a good lure. I went and bought one. Luke's Tackle Shop was just down the road from my apartment on Beach Road in Vineyard Haven. I was in awe of all the attractive gear I saw hanging on the walls. I looked with envy at the lures that dangled on the inside of the buckets that all the fishermen carried onto the beach. I thought they had to be rich to own that many lures. At that time, a lure cost between three and six dollars, and on waitress wages that was expen-

---

* Anthier's Bridge, on the Oak Bluffs—Edgartown Beach Road, better known as the Big Bridge, is often called the Jaws Bridge because it was featured in the Spielberg movie.

sive. I hoped to someday have a bucket full of lures just like the real fishermen, but that one-ounce Rebel was my first.

Whenever I was around guys who fished, I asked if they would take me sometime. "Please take me," I would beg. "I promise I won't be scared or cry." A woman surfcasting from the beach was still a rare sight at that time, and trying to break into a sport that was considered a "man thing" was difficult. I was looked upon as an intruder. Since I was a petite woman, I suppose they thought I did not have the strength or fortitude. I wanted to prove them wrong. I knew I could catch big fish from the beach if someone would give me a chance and teach me.

I know now that fishing requires more than patience. I had to endure eerie sounds and shadows in the darkness, harsh winds, and at times torrential rains. I was pushed around by the waves and for a long time not sure what was tugging on the end of my line. Hooking on to something mysterious was terrifying. When I fished by myself, I wanted to catch something, but at the same time, I thought, "What if it pulls me into the water over my head? Maybe it would yank my fishing rod out of my hand. What would I do with a big fish once I landed it? How would I take the hook out of its mouth?"

In 1976, I left the Black Dog Tavern and got a job waitressing at a Greek restaurant called Helios, co-owned by Bill Prokos and Lucia Evans. Helios started in Edgartown as a Greek take-out restaurant, but later moved to State Road in Vineyard Haven in a building owned by the singer-songwriter James Taylor. They now had space for a sit-down restaurant. The back of the building was an old garage called Nobnocket. In 1974, it was converted into rooms that were rented to local artists so that they would have an inexpensive place to create. It was called the Art Workers Guild. Many well-known artists of today began their careers there. The metal sculptor Travis Tuck created his work there, as did Julia Mitchell the weaver and Rez Williams the oil painter.

My boss, Bill Prokos, loved to fish, and he once took a group of us Helios workers to Chappaquiddick on a fishing adventure. One of the waitresses, Claire Thatcher, let us stay overnight at her house on Chappy. We had a spaghetti dinner and a few drinks that evening,

My first time fishing on Chappaquiddick, before I had any proper fishing attire. An early morning in the spring of 1977.

and to my surprise Bill woke us up before the sun rose and we all went to a beach. Once again, I have no memory of catching fish, but I do remember being both excited and cold.

One day in Luke's Tackle Shop, I overheard one man telling another that the town had cut an opening from the Edgartown Great Pond to the ocean and that the bass were *in*.

When the Edgartown, West Tisbury, Oyster, and Chilmark Great Ponds' water levels get too high, a cut is made in the barrier beach to open the ponds and let them drain into the ocean when the tide is going out. This is sometimes done by hand with shovels, but more often with a bulldozer. The ponds get too high when we have many rainstorms and the pond water gets too acidic. This is not healthy for the shellfish. Opening the ponds allows ocean water to come in when the tide turns, raising the salinity level.

This was before I owned my own four-wheel-drive vehicle, and hitchhiking was a common way of getting around the island. A wait-ress friend, Cathy Weiss, who loved to fish, picked me up at my house at four in the morning, and we drove to Katama Beach on the south side of the island beyond Edgartown. She did not have a four-wheel drive either, so we left the car in the parking lot and hitchhiked down South Beach to the pond opening. I'm sure we did not catch any fish that day, but hitchhiking on the beach became a way for me to follow the fishermen. Cathy was not able to join me after that first time because she had a young daughter at home who needed her.

One morning I was following the fishermen down to Edgartown Pond opening. As I trekked down the beach, thumb out, trying to get a ride with rod in hand, armed with my one-ounce Rebel lure, a local fisherman motioned for me to hop on the bed of his pickup truck. He gave me a ride all the way to the pond opening. It is about a mile of bumpy over-sand driving. When we reached our destination, I jumped off the truck bed and was on my own.

There were close to a dozen fishermen lined up catching large striped bass. I watched as the fishermen cast their lures so far out into the water that they became invisible by the time they landed. Their rods were bending almost in half as they pulled huge bass out of the surf and onto the beach, one after another. This was the first-ever bass blitz that I witnessed—when a large pod of fish drive baitfish on the beach and get into a feeding frenzy. Wide-eyed, I stared at all those beautiful big striped bass lying on the beach. At that time twenty-eight- to thirty-two-pound bass were a typical day's catch.

My heart was pounding as I tried to match their casts so that I could reach the feeding fish. I didn't understand why I couldn't cast my little one-ounce Rebel more than four feet into the crashing surf. I cringed when my out-of-control line was taken by the wind, crossed their lines, and interfered with the other fishermen landing their fish. Although I was trying not to make eye contact, I felt they were scowling at me.

In a final attempt to cast my lure out far enough for a fish to find it, I whipped my fishing rod as hard as I could and *snap!* My little Rebel broke from my line, sailed into the ocean, and was gone. It was a while before I understood that with a fifteen-knot southwest wind in your face, it is impossible to cast a one-ounce lure any distance into the surf. I am sure that the other fishermen were relieved to see the back of my baggy waders as I walked down the beach toward home, hitchhiking, empty-handed.

4

Not a Clue and a Conger

I HAD BEEN TOLD THAT striped bass are basically nocturnal feeders and that I should fish at night if I wanted to catch any. When I went to some of the great fishing spots I had heard about, I rarely found anyone else fishing. The beaches were desolate. "If there are so many fish here," I wondered, "where are all the fishermen?"

I hadn't yet learned that the tides can help determine the best times to catch fish. I once again felt the paradox. I wanted to catch a fish, but I was terrified of what might be on the end of my line!

Before the early 1980s a commercial license was not required to sell fish locally to restaurants and markets. Not only was catching fish a recreational sport, but it could also bring in money. I later realized that money was one of the reasons why recreational fishermen guarded not only their fishing spots but also their techniques.

Squibnocket is on the south side of the Vineyard in Chilmark. We call it up-island although it is in a southerly direction from the down-island towns of Vineyard Haven and Oak Bluffs. The surf can have some of the largest waves found around the island, especially during a southerly storm. This attracts not only fishermen in search of large striped bass but also surfers looking to ride a big wave. The beach is rocky, and the ocean is scattered with large boulders. It can be a treacherous fishing spot on a stormy night.

One evening I decided to fish Squibnocket, alone once more. It was a chilly but windless evening. Before I owned a small headlamp for night fishing, I had an enormous flashlight strung on a rope around my neck. I bought my first Plano tackle box. It was a small plastic handheld box, with one compartment on the top with sections for lures and a large space under that for my pliers and a knife, a rag to wipe my hands, and some extra hooks and leaders. It doubled as an uncomfortable seat.

I left my car in the parking lot and climbed down the big rocks that protected the parking area from the surf. Once I got my footing on the front beach, I tossed my line, hook, and weight with the chunk of squid that I was using for bait into the dark, toward the ocean. Once my weight held on the bottom and my bait was secured, I squatted down on my tackle box, gazing up at the stars.

My rod bent, and I felt a tug. I jumped from my little perch, I set the hook! I was ON! Oh my God! I could feel the heavy weight of a fish and I was imagining a big striped bass. I knew that this was a big fish that was bending my rod and resisting coming onto the beach. I was pumped, knees knocking, heart pounding. As I got this heavy, mysterious creature close to the beach, I realized that something didn't feel quite right. I aimed my trusty flashlight into the dark at the edge of the surf—and saw a long, dark, ugly snakelike creature. It was a huge conger eel, well over six feet in length and as big around as my thigh, with a mouth full of razor-sharp teeth snapping at me.

Now what was I to do? I was alone in the dark with a conger eel.

I managed to pull it out of the surf and drag it onto the beach. I tugged and tugged to get my hook free from those fierce jaws, but to no avail. I even tried standing on it to give myself some leverage, but its snakelike body was too round and slippery to stand on. My hands were shaking, and my knees were weak with fear. I finally decided to cut my line and leave the hook stuck in that strong jaw. I packed up my gear as fast as I could and ran like hell to my car, leaving my catch behind. One would think that would discourage me, but the excitement inspired me to go fishing more often.

West Chop is a residential peninsula on the north end of the island a short drive from the town of Vineyard Haven. It is surrounded on the east side by Vineyard Haven Harbor and on the north and west sides by the Vineyard Sound. Many large summer homes sit on the top of the bluff facing Woods Hole. One is owned by the Singer family. Before a "fisherman's path" was put in between the road and the private beach, the fishermen walked through the Singers' property to the steep set of stairs that lead to a long jetty. We call it Singer's jetty. The West Chop rip holds many species of fish and is a popular fishing spot either from the jetty or from a boat.

One night I was fishing on the end of Singer's jetty. This night there was a small crescent moon, but it was still a dark night and, as usual, I was alone.

I was startled by a noise behind me. I looked toward the beach. A skunk was waddling down the jetty, heading right for me.

I was trapped at the end of the jetty! I looked at the squid in my bait bucket and thought, "That must be what he wants!" I threw all my squid in his direction, but he kept coming. No matter how many loud noises I made, short of screaming, I could not scare him away. My heart was pounding. I was standing on the very last rock before the jetty dropped off into the ocean. Jumping into the cold black water crashing over the end of the jetty was not an option.

I don't know why, but he moved over far enough to one side for me to pass. I grabbed my gear and ran down the jetty, not stopping until I got all the way back to my car. When I got home, I was grateful that I smelled no worse than the squid on my hands.

As the years passed and I kept at it, hair-raising experiences became few and far between. Occasionally, the bogeyman shows up at one of my favorite spots. I can *feel* him. Sometimes we share the beach quite comfortably, and on other nights the bogeyman leaves me alone to fish in the night, but then there are times when my hair stands up on the back of my neck and I get the message that it is time for me to leave. That's when I go home.

Coming upon another human being can be even more startling than the bogeyman and skunks, especially when I assume that I am alone and loudly sing silly jingles.

Bob Jacobs, known as Hawkeye, was one of the first guys I asked to take me fishing. He worked in Boston as a computer programmer during the week and came to the Vineyard to fish on the weekends. I tagged along with him a few times, being a passenger in his little maroon '68 Plymouth.

One night we went to Squibnocket, which has the reputation of being one of the best fishing spots on the East Coast. Not far from the parking lot is a shallow ridge that juts out adjacent to the beach, where mussels grow. The mussel bed is a rugged natural structure that not only supplies mussels for striped bass to feed on but also creates a natural barrier to protect the beach from erosion.

Hawkeye went out on the mussel bed, but that night the tide was high, and I felt that it was too dangerous. I had tried fishing standing on the bed* on a high tide, but when the waves from the surf came up close to the top of my waders I knew that I could be in trouble. I had to carefully work my way back to the beach to safety. Night fishing was still new to me and I was not tall enough to wade out into the surf at night. Hawk is probably six feet tall, so he could wade out far enough to reach the deeper water. When most men wade out into the ocean up to their waist, I'm dangerously almost over the top of my chest waders.

Even when you're wearing a belt on the outside of your waders to hold them closed and keep the water out, wading in the surf can be lethal. Tonight, I would stay in front of the parking lot where the beach forms a cove; fishermen call it "the bowl." As Hawk headed out toward the mussel bed, I said, "Flash your light if you get into fish and maybe I'll join you." Then I watched him walk into the dark.

Fishing alone, I was not getting any action in the bowl. I kept

* The mussel bed at Squibnocket is a rocky sandbar that stretches away from the shore. It is covered with mussels, a delicacy to striped bass, which makes it a perfect spot from which to fish.

glancing toward the mussel bed, hoping to see Hawk's light flash. I was still new at this fishing in the dark thing and was trying to focus on fishing and not on the strange noises I heard in the wind.

More time passed, and I squinted my eyes, straining to see any signs of Hawkeye. Finally, I noticed flashing lights coming from his direction.

Since there was no fish activity where I was casting my bait, the thought of hooking some fish gave me a burst of bravery. "Oh, good," I told myself. "Hawkeye must be catching fish. He must be signaling me to join him."

I started down the beach toward the mussel bed, but my flashlight battery was low. I had only walked a few feet when my light faded out. I could barely see my hand in front of my face. Squibnocket Beach is covered with rocks large and small, most of them coated with seaweed and extremely slippery. We call them "ankle busters." Walking on the rocks in the pitch-black darkness, I didn't feel safe enough to make the long walk out to join my friend on the mussel bed. Frustrated, I returned to my spot on the front beach to fish and wait for him to return.

Back at my spot in the darkness, I sat on my tackle box with my line in the water, waiting for a fish. I was looking in Hawkeye's direction and still seeing flashing lights. My thoughts veered from "Hawkeye's catching fish, I should go join him" to "Maybe he's in trouble and he's flashing me an SOS to come and help him." My imagination was running away with me. What if his waders had filled up with water and he was being tossed around by the waves crashing over him?

Although it was probably only a few minutes, it felt like another hour had passed. My imagination was working overtime. Finally, I decided it was better to do something instead of being sorry later if I did nothing. My flashlight was useless, and I figured that my only option was to go to the nearest house to ask to borrow one. I stumbled back to the parking lot and could see a light in a window of a house up the street.

I walked on the tarred road toward the lighted house and knocked on the door. A kind-looking man opened it. I apologized for disturbing him and, as politely as I could, told him my tale about fishing with a friend who might or might not be in trouble. I explained that my flashlight battery had died, and might I borrow a flashlight, so I could go save my friend's life? I can't imagine what he thought. I must have looked pathetic standing in the shadows of his doorway in my baggy waders and most likely smelling of squid.

With a bright flashlight in hand, I started back down the road and onto the beach. *Now* I was going to save Hawkeye's life. I was about halfway to the mussel bed when a man stepped out of the darkness and into my light beam. It was Hawkeye!

He was alive, dry, and, apart from his fishing rod, empty-handed. I told him that I was on my way to join him because I thought he was catching lots of fish. I didn't dare tell him that I was on my way to save his life. I explained to him how my battery had gone dead, and I had walked to a house to borrow a flashlight. He had no idea of all the pain I had endured. He didn't have much of a reaction, and I didn't want him to tell anyone how crazy I had become sitting alone on the beach in the dark. After all, we were just *fishing*!

Once my heart rate returned to normal and I realized that my friend was alive and well, I glanced over toward the mussel bed as I went back to gather up my gear. The same lights that I had thought might be SOS signals were still flashing.

Hawkeye drove me back to the house so I could return the flashlight. Feeling embarrassed, I didn't want to make eye contact with the man, so I quickly handed him his flashlight. I assured him that we were all right and thanked him.

Hawkeye and I headed home, with me trying to hide my embarrassment and pretending that I had had fun.

Now, decades later, as I fish alone at night and I watch all the lights blinking offshore, I know that they are from the buoys and commercial fishing boats. They remind me of the night at Squibnocket that I thought I was saving Hawkeye's life.

5

Learning to Fish the North Shore

TIM WHITE AND I had been friends since 1966, my first summer on the Vineyard. He was an experienced fisherman and I was just beginning my journey of surfcasting. After much persuading on my part, he invited me to fish with him. Neither of us owned a beach buggy, so we did a lot of walking on the rocky north shore.

The north shore ranges from the northwest corner of West Chop facing the Vineyard Sound to the farthest southwest tip of the island, Gay Head Cliffs. This stretch of rocky and sparsely developed shoreline is interrupted only by a few pond openings.

We spent most of our time together fishing from the bridges and the jetties. Through observation, I learned how to catch bait and fish it on the bottom. Tim led me to the water's edge, and after a little demonstration I was left to my own devices. He would take me to unnamed places and, more than teaching me, he let me tag along.

One late night after having some drinks in a local bar, the Ritz café in Oak Bluffs, Duane and I had invited some friends to come back to our two-room apartment on Beach Road. Tim White was with us and he invited me and Duane to go fishing with him. Duane didn't want to go, but I grabbed that two-piece rod I had bought for Duane for his birthday. I was more than happy to join Tim.

We went to the Lagoon Pond drawbridge down the street from our home. It was a dark and spooky night and I felt anxious. The lights from the bridge were shining on the dark water and gave me an eerie feeling.

Tim put his hand in his bait bucket and pulled out a couple of fresh butterfish that he had caught earlier that day. He let me watch how he rigged the butterfish onto his hook, and I did the same. He cast his bait into the channel that runs out of the Lagoon and into Vineyard Haven Harbor. I don't think my line went very far but I imitated what he did and stopped reeling my weighted line in when it sat on the bottom of the ocean. We were there for just a short time before Tim said, "Let's reel these in and go try out front on the jetty." I was willing to do anything he suggested.

I had taken a few cranks of the handle on my reel when it felt like I hit something big. I yelled, "Tim, I think I am stuck on a big rock or a lobster pot!" He started to laugh. "No, you have a fish on."

I was screaming in fear, "No, can't be! It feels like a big rock." He laughed again, told me to just keep cranking that handle and keep my rod tip facing up. I did what he said. Then a huge bluefish was splashing at our feet and he helped me drag it onto the beach. Tim was amazed. He said, "I thought you had a small fish on. This is huge, probably more than fifteen pounds."

We took it back to my apartment and threw it onto my bathroom scale, and it was more than sixteen pounds.

That bluefish was the one that provoked my fishing dreams. Dreams full of excitement but also fear and anxiety. I wanted to go fishing again, but at the same time I was terrified. I had dreams of hooking into a big fish while I was alone, and in that dream, it would try to pull me into the fathomless ocean. I could feel the strength of something huge and mysterious tugging on my line and wanting to carry me out to sea.

The north shore coastline faces north, northeast, or northwest.

With my first big bluefish, sixteen pounds—
the one that hooked me, 1978. On the back
deck of our two-room apartment on Beach
Road in Vineyard Haven.

Since Martha's Vineyard has a prevailing southwest wind, the north
shore of the island usually has flatter water than the south shore. In
calmer water, it can be more difficult to fool the fish.

This shore of the Vineyard was Tim's playground and I was lucky
that this quiet, sneaky fisherman let me tag along with him. He did
me a favor by letting me make my own mistakes, and I made every
mistake one could make. I lost fish in every conceivable way. Such
as on my knot. The improved cinch knot is the best one to use to
connect a leader or a lure to a line, but I didn't know how to tie
fishing knots correctly, so my knot would come apart and the fish
would go free.

Once a fish is hooked, the battle begins, and the drag becomes an
important part of getting it to the beach. On a spinning reel, the drag
is the knob on the top of the spool. When a fish takes a hook and a
drag is too tight, the sudden pull on the line causes it to break. Set
correctly, the drag allows the line to slip instead of breaking under
the pressure. If my drag is set too light, I can't maintain the needed

pressure on the fish. I can't set the hook, or if I do hook it, the fish could "throw" the hook by taking advantage of slack line. I learned which direction to turn the knob by repeating "righty tightie, lefty loosie." I didn't know that I should check my line to see if it had any frayed spots on it. If my line had a weak spot it would break, and another bottom rig or lure was sacrificed to the ocean gods. I would set the hook too soon and pull it out of the fish's mouth. I didn't get the knack of it for a long time. I had to learn that a big fish didn't get to be big by being stupid. It took many lost fish before I could settle back and enjoy the battle.

Many times, while I was struggling in the dark with my line in a bird's nest or my reel fouled, Tim would laugh and tell me that he could help me but the only way I would learn was to work it out myself. At the time, I thought he was being unreasonable, especially when the fish were hitting and he was catching, yet I couldn't get my bait in the water.

One evening we were fishing the boulder-covered north shore beach facing the Vineyard Sound at the Cedar Tree Neck Sanctuary, in West Tisbury. Just as the sun set, a school of bass chased a pod of squid onto the beach. We looked down at our feet and squid were lying everywhere trying to escape the hungry stripers. Tim quickly showed me what to do. We hooked the live squid and tossed them into the feeding school of bass.

I don't remember if I landed any fish that night, but I do remember thinking that the biggest striped bass ever had devoured my live-lined squid. The fish would take a run and then just stop cold behind a boulder. As always, when I had a fish on my line, my glands were pumping adrenaline. My heart was pounding out of my chest and my knees were knocking with anticipation. I had read about striped bass behavior, that they were known to swim behind rocks and purposely rub the hooks out of their mouths. As hard as I tried to outwit this monster, I could not seem to get it to swim out from behind the boulder.

With Tim's advice, I opened the bail on my reel to free-spool my line, so the fish would think it was free and then swim away from its hiding place. I thought this was working until it seemed the fish had swum behind the same rock and wasn't budging. I must have fought this "fish" for half an hour before it became clear to me that I had no fish at all. In the darkness, I was finally able to figure out that my line was laden down with heavy seaweed and I was indeed fighting a rock. Each time I opened the bail, the weed on my line would rush along with the wind and tide, and once I tightened it up again, it was stuck on the same rock. I did have a fish on my hook at some point, but that fish was long gone. By the time I cleaned off the heavy seaweed and retrieved my frayed and tangled line, the school of fish had vanished.

Vineyard Haven Harbor was rich in baitfish back in the 1970s and early 1980s. I caught big bluefish by snagging menhaden with a bunker snagger and live-lining them. Menhaden,* better known on the Vineyard as bunker, can weigh more than a pound each. When the harbor was thick with them, you could hear them splashing around the pilings and the boat moorings trying to escape hungry bluefish. What a thrill it is to feel a nervous bunker on the end of my line trying to swim away from its predator. Then the line begins tearing off the spool of my reel when a larger fish wraps its mouth around it, and the battle is on. Because of all the obstacles in the harbor, I lost more fish than I landed. Unfortunately, because of overfishing the menhaden have become scarce in our waters.†

I had become a pretty good fisherman in the daylight. I had learned enough about fishing and could cast my lure or bait a good distance into the ocean, and after a bit of a struggle, I could often land a fish. I was still dependent on friends to take me night fishing. Since that did not happen often, striped bass still eluded me.

* Menhaden belong to the herring family. They are an oily-fleshed forage fish, a staple for our Atlantic game fish. They have many names, including pogy. On the Vineyard, they are called bunker.
† Bruce Franklin's *The Most Important Fish in the Sea* is the best book to read on the condition of the herring.

Mr. Leroy Goff owned a home at the end of the Mink Meadows Golf Club Road that cuts through the West Chop woods in Vineyard Haven. There are two small jetties protecting a freshwater pond that dumps into the Vineyard Sound on the north side of the island. Fish are attracted by the mix of fresh- and saltwater and come there to feed. It is a productive fishing spot. Although the golf course is private, Mr. Goff allowed people to access his property to fish on the jetties.

I was with Tim White one stormy evening. We were sharing Goff's jetty with a couple of other fishermen. A strong north wind was blowing right in my face. Once again, I watched the other guys casting out into the abyss while my lure seemed to keep landing at my feet. This time I was using a heavier lure, a blue-and-white Atom Junior. Time and again, I cast into the wind and my plug plopped down a few feet from the edge of the jetty. The other fishermen were not getting any fish either, so I just kept trying to imitate their casts and keep my balance on the rocks.

Suddenly, I had a hook-up. My rod bent from the tug of a large fish and my line started to scream off my reel. Adrenaline was surging through my body as my drag was singing. Tim was standing by my side instructing me on what to do so that I would not lose the fish. He talked me all the way down the jetty and onto the beach, where I could finally land the fish. "Keep your tip up, let him run, play him, don't pull too hard or you'll pull the hook out of his mouth . . ." and all the good advice that I pass on to my students today. Finally, after about two years of struggling, I had caught my first striped bass.

I felt proud and triumphant. I unhooked this beautiful creature and laid it on the beach at the base of the jetty. I shined my flashlight on the fish. To me, it looked huge. Dark blue-black lateral stripes ran down the length of its olive-green back. The scales on the belly were shiny silver with subtle iridescent reds and purples. I gave thanks to the heavens, then joined the others back on the jetty.

Miraculously, I hooked up on a second fish shortly after I landed the first. I was shaking with excitement. I was the only one to land any fish that evening. The first striped bass of my life. One was fifteen pounds and the other was sixteen. Both were beautiful "linesiders,"* as they are sometimes called. The guys offered to help me carry them back to the car and my answer was, "No, I got this!" And I wrapped my arms around both fish, held them close to my body, like precious toddlers. I was struggling not to drop them as I headed back down the trail to the car.

I learned later that striped bass will feed close to the rocks on a jetty. I am sure that is why I was the only one who caught any fish that night. It had nothing to do with skill. My inefficient casting landed my lure right on their heads. It was just luck, and my turn to catch a fish.

I sold both fish to my boss Lucia Evans at Helios. I was paid two dollars a pound, "in the round" (not filleted), and I felt proud as I served them to the customers in the restaurant the following evening. Lucia helped me clean them and presented me with a piece of the backbone from one of the fish. I still have it today as a memento of that cold, stormy, joyful night.

---

* One of the many nicknames for a striped bass. In the southern Atlantic states, they call them rockfish. Greenheads, old pajamas, and squid hounds are other popular names.

6

Solitude and Darkness

I stand as the black water of each wave's backwash hug my
*   hip boots*
Making little stars of light as the water fires around my legs
Arching my back, I let out cast after cast, thumbing the reel
*   carefully as it whips that old blue Atom plug past my ear*
*   and out into the fish-filled night.*
Early on, I was hoping for a strike of some huge striped bass
*   to fight,*
But now, to hell with fishing. I would rather stand here
*   casting. I have already caught my prize.*
It is the star filled night.

CONRAD NEUMANN*

"YOU'RE SO BRAVE to fish alone in the dark."

I hear that a lot. People think that it came naturally for me. But I didn't start out feeling comfortable being on the beach, miles from town, in the dark, alone. Living on Martha's Vineyard has given me a unique opportunity to safely roam around the beaches after the sun goes down. If I was not living on an island, I might not have had that same feeling of security.

The shoreline, dark and mysterious, was alien to me. I still have

---

* Conrad Neumann was born in 1933, graduated from Brooklyn College in 1955, and received his MS from Texas A&M in 1957, followed by a PhD from Lehigh. He has worked in oceanography for more than thirty years. He is an amateur poet and a stellar fisherman.

occasional nights when I feel uncomfortable, especially when I am fishing alone around the Gay Head Cliffs, in Aquinnah. These tall colorful cliffs, on the southwest corner of the Vineyard, are part of the property owned by the Wampanoag tribe. They have an atmosphere of ancient mystery. At times, the shadows can play havoc with my imagination. On more than a few nights I've felt my hair stand straight up on end as I cast into the surf with my back toward the cliffs. Rustling noises in the bushes behind me give me chills up and down my spine. My imagination could get the best of me. The problem is that fishing for striped bass can be much more productive in the middle of the night. That is why I kept going back even when I was scared to death.

The fear of being attached to a submerged fighting mysterious weight under the cold, dark ocean was something I craved. Thoughts of fishing filled my mind, night and day. This was the beginning of the end of a normal life for me. The compulsion to fish affects not only the fisherman but also their family, friends, and bosses or employees. Gardening, canning, jelly making, and other hobbies that I once enjoyed are set aside during the fishing season.

My first terrifying experience alone in the night was on Anthier's Bridge, on State Beach in Edgartown. I didn't even have my driver's license at the time. Having lived on the island since I was a teenager, I never felt I had to have a car or drive. We had no public bus system then, so hitchhiking was the typical way to travel around the Vineyard.

One night, I awoke from a dream that a big striped bass was waiting for me at the Big Bridge. I shook Duane awake and begged him to drive me there. "Please, drop me off and come back to get me before you go to work in the morning," I pleaded. "There is a huge bass there, waiting for me. I saw it in my dream." Unfortunately, he agreed. It was not one of my best ideas.

My fishing equipment at the time was primitive. I was still wearing that heavy flashlight tied with a rope around my neck. It was nothing like the small head lanterns that are available today. As I walked in my clunky hip boots, the flashlight swung back and forth with a force that knocked me off balance. I remember I was overflowing with excitement for the first half hour after Duane left me alone. I slung my eel over the railing into the current and settled in with the anticipation of catching a huge fish.

Once the quiet of night set in, the horror began. The silence was interrupted by the loud *quock, quock* of night herons taking to the sky. I had caught quite a few fish from that bridge during daylight hours without ever seeing a rat. Now I heard the pitter-patter of many little feet scampering back and forth over the bridge. I had intruded into their busy late-night world. I became scared. I started to shake with fear. I didn't *want* a fish to take my bait. I just wanted to stay alive.

What if I get a fish on my hook and step on a rat?

What if my flashlight gets hung up on the railing and knocks me over?

What if I hook a huge fish and he pulls me over the railing?

How can I work my way to the jetty to land him? Maybe I will fall in the water and drown.

That was the end for me. I had never caught a big fish off that bridge, and never at night. The worst of it was that I was stranded until daybreak. There were no cell phones in those days.

I reeled my line in and found what I thought was the safest corner on the bridge and curled up into a ball to wait for sunrise. I was so upset by the time morning came. Poor Duane. He was looking forward to eating a fresh striped bass for dinner. Instead, I scolded him and said, "If I ever ask you to drop me off in some dark and desolate place in the middle of the night, don't listen to me!"

Soon after that I got my driver's license.

7

My Mentor

I'M NOT EXACTLY SURE why I was drawn to surf fishing. I learned quickly that walking up to someone who is fishing and asking questions like "How did you catch those fish?" was not the correct approach. I often got snubbed. I don't know if being a woman had anything to do with it, but those were the days when it was rare to see a woman fishing in the surf.

Before I became adequate at casting my line, when I stood too close to the other fishermen, they looked at me with expressions that let me know I was annoying them. It was scary when older, salty men scowled at me. I felt unwanted and understood that I should stay out of their way. I look back now and wonder why I was treated that way. Was it because I was a woman, or did it have something to do with the fact that they were making money bringing their catch to the markets? As I reflect on my past adventures of learning to fish, I wonder why I didn't give up and find a hobby or passion that was not so challenging.

I buried my nose in all the fishing books I could find, and instead of knitting mittens my evening activity was learning to tie knots with monofilament line. My favorite book to this day is *Striper,* by John N. Cole. It interweaves his years in New York during the 1950s as a striped bass surf fisherman with a detailed history of the fish itself. He states this in his foreword:

> And there is the striper's ultimate paradox. Because by the time the striper has taught you what you need to know, you have so come to love this greatest of American game fishes that you can only wish it well. Godspeed! you say as you set free what once you most wanted to possess.

Each February, with the snow falling outside and the stripers long since having left Massachusetts for warmer southern waters, I would lie in my bed under layers of blankets, coal stove stoked, cuddled up with my well-worn copy of *Striper.* Each time I read it, as my obsession deepened, I yearned for spring when I could once again roam the Vineyard shores in search of the elusive striped bass.

In 1978, we sold the forty acres in Milton, New Hampshire, that Butch and I had bought to homestead in the '60s. I used my share of the profit to put a deposit on my home, on Snake Hollow in Vineyard Haven, and I bought a canary-yellow four-cylinder, four-wheel-drive International Scout. It was my first "fishmobile." On my days off from work, during the fishing season from April until November, I could be found at Wasque Point on Chappaquiddick Island.

The first settlers on Chappaquiddick were ancient ancestors of the Wampanoags, the Algonquian people. Chappy, as it is called colloquially, was named "Cheppiaquidne," meaning "separate island." Wasque means "the ending."

The Rip at Wasque Point is a strong, narrow current of water that moves directly away from the shore. Bluefish and striped bass congregate to ferociously dine on trapped baitfish, and the Rip is a perfect place for novice fishermen to practice hooking and bringing to shore their first fish. I spent many days, year after year, catching, losing, and learning the habits of bluefish at this very spot. Typically, the fish come on the last two hours of a changing tide, mostly the west tide when we have a southwest wind. The fish will stay offshore when the tide is moving fast (about six knots), and as soon as it starts to slack, they take advantage of the slower currents and trap the bait on the beach. After all, fish are lazy, especially big bass. The bass, being nocturnal feeders, move in after dark. Sometimes they mix with the bluefish during the day, but more often the large bass feed at night.

Being able to sell fish was a fringe benefit. I sold most of my catch to local restaurants. The chefs knew me from my waitress jobs, so when I returned from the beach, I would knock on the back door of the Black Dog and Helios and sell them fresh bluefish. I would get fifty cents a pound in the round. That was good money and it helped me to fill my gas tank and buy a few more lures. I worked evenings, so after selling my fish, I would run home and take a shower, change into my waitress uniform, and at times serve the same fish that I had caught hours before. I was not blessed with children, so while other women my age were home raising babies, I was learning to fish from the beach. Life was perfect.

I saw other women on the beach, but most were sitting in a beach chair with a book, in the car knitting, or watching the men fish. To this day, I cannot sit and watch people surfcasting without wanting to get in on the action. Early on, my overabundance of determination and lack of fishing experience made me obvious. Before I had mastered my casting skills, if a fisherman was hooked to a fish, I learned to step back and let them land it before taking a cast.

I overheard one man say, "Damn women should stay home washing the dishes or vacuuming!" I just learned to ignore the "damn women" comments.

In the 1970s most of the foul-weather clothing was manufactured with men in mind. Before 1992 all the waders on the market were much too big for me. No one could call me the fashion plate of Wasque Point. I looked more like the Michelin Man with baggy waders over layers of bulky sweaters to keep me warm.

I suppose some people would have quit with all the challenges, but the difficulties I faced made me more determined. Regardless of the obstacles, I was hopelessly "hooked." I had a feeling in my gut that I could become as good a fisherman as any of the guys, and I was willing to embarrass myself to accomplish that.

I didn't need to chase the fishermen around and bother them to take me fishing anymore. I had my own four-wheel-drive Scout and I could drive on the beach by myself. I was now thirty years old, and since Duane and I had no children and he was busy writing music with his three-man band, I had the freedom to fish whenever I had the time.

After years of carrying my gear in a backpack, I was relieved to be able to load everything into my fishmobile. I built rod racks for the roof and loaded the back with a cooler, waders and warm clothes, and, by this time, plenty of tackle and a bucket of plugs. I owned all the necessary gear for catching fish, but I still yearned to be able to find the nocturnal-feeding striped bass.

In the late '70s and early '80s, bluefish blitzes happened almost like clockwork and the fishing was spectacular. After letting the air out of my tires, I could drive my fishmobile three miles over the barrier beach from Katama in Edgartown to Wasque Point on Chappaquiddick. We were almost guaranteed bluefish by casting Ballistic Missiles, Hopkins, Poppers, or Kastmasters into the Rip on the last two hours of a falling tide.

That same year, 1978, I was enjoying the annual Chappaquiddick Labor Day beach party that is held around the corner from the Rip, toward Cape Poge on East Beach. It's a long stretch of beach with tranquil ocean surf. For those who don't have a four-wheel drive, there are parking spaces near the Dike Bridge* and it is a short walk from the bridge to East Beach. It's a perfect spot for a beach party.

Many of the regular Chappaquiddick fishermen with whom I had become friends that summer were there. We were all fishing, eating, drinking, and celebrating the end of another summer. I was happy to be in the presence of some renowned island fishermen.

I had been talking with Arnold Spofford and his wife, Ellen. He was a well-respected surfcaster and the maker of a perfect lure for

* The Dike Bridge is another access to the Chappaquiddick beaches when the beach is closed due to nesting piping plovers or a breach. It became infamous in 1969 when Ted Kennedy drove over the side and Mary Jo Kopechne lost her life.

The Dike Bridge connecting Tom's Neck Point and Cape Poge to Chappaquiddick Island, a wooden structure that at the time was not protected by a guardrail. It was rebuilt after the Kennedy incident.

targeting bluefish, the Ballistic Missile. The lure was designed especially for fishing for bluefish on Chappaquiddick. Its aerodynamic shape cuts through the prevailing southwest wind and carries your line far enough into the ocean to reach the fish when they stay out a long distance from the beach. When it is retrieved, it splashes on the surface of the water, simulating a wounded fish. When a school of bluefish come to feed in the Rip, they can't resist it.

While I chatted with Arnold and Ellen, the sun was getting low and the party was beginning to break up. A fisherman approached me and said that he had noticed earlier in the day that I was casting my ten-foot rod with accuracy and was able to throw my lure a long distance. He said he was impressed with my ability to fish. I was flattered. He introduced himself as Jack Coutinho. I had seen his name many times on the leader board during the Derby.

I said that I had been fishing for a few years and could cast and catch bluefish. I told him that I fished with Tim White and had caught a few stripers but did not know how to find them on my own. I had gone fishing by myself every chance I had. My casting technique was sufficient to get a bait or lure in the water, but I was still challenged by striped bass. He said, "I could teach you how to fish for striped bass. Do you want to fish with me sometime?"

I couldn't believe it. I had stopped following fishermen and asking the guys to take me. Now a well-known champion fisherman was offering to teach me! I figured I better tell him that I had a boyfriend. I expected him to turn away, but he didn't seem to care. I was finally going to learn to fish for the species that had eluded me, *Morone saxatilis,* better known as striped bass. I was ecstatic.

One of the first times we fished together, he picked me up in his Jeep Wagoneer and we drove to the southwesternmost tip of the Vineyard, Aquinnah. He always insisted on taking his Wagoneer instead of my vehicle. Standing at the top of the spectacular Gay Head clay cliffs, you can see all the way to Nomans Land looking east, and facing southwest you see the string of the Elizabeth Islands. The cliffs and the beach below are owned by the Wampanoag tribe.

Fishing in the surf on that beach always gives me the feeling that the Native American souls who fished there long before I came along still linger about the property. Fishing the boulder-strewn water below the Gay Head Cliffs can be treacherous. Standing in the surf on a slippery boulder with the waves crashing up to my chest was unnerving. I had unsuccessfully fished that beach alone a few times, but when the waves filled my waders, I had to leave the beach. Some of the biggest striped bass recorded on the Vineyard have been caught in these waters. Back then, we were permitted to climb up and down the clay cliffs from the parking lot at the top. When the tide was low, we could navigate our four-wheel-drive vehicles over the dunes near Philbin Beach, around the boulders, and down the beach toward the tip of Gay Head, or at times east all the way to Long Beach.

That evening, we parked near the entrance to the beach and walked to the head. Jackie led the way and told me to wade out into the surf and stand on a big boulder. He taught me to wear a tight belt over my waders, so I could stay dry if I was knocked over by the surf.

He stood on another large rock not far from me. The waves were crashing around us and I didn't want to let on that I was terrified. Then, while I was looking over at Jackie, a huge wave hit him square on and knocked him off his rock. I gasped as he went under the water.

A few seconds later he reappeared and stepped back up onto his rock. His trademark baseball hat, which had stayed on his head, was dripping with saltwater and his hand, still on his reel, was retrieving his lure. He never missed a beat! It didn't seem to faze him in the least.

All the fear left me at that moment and I started to chuckle. I knew that fishing with Jackie was going to be an adventure. "This guy is something else," I thought. Jackie and I had an automatic chemistry and I was eager to be his fishing buddy. As frightened as I was at times, when hearing rustling in the bushes behind me or feeling unsure of what I might bump into on a dark beach, I felt safe with him. As a habit, though, I always had a bottle of "courage" in my wader pocket. Some sips of brandy were perfect comfort on a cold dark night.

We fished under the Gay Head Cliffs quite often. He named holes and rocks after some of the other fishermen. There was "Stevie's rock," named after Steve Amaral, and "Whit's hole," a spot that Whit Manter fished regularly. I thought maybe someday there could be a spot named for me.

Another night Jackie pointed to a spot by one of the big boulders and said, "Fish here." He could be bossy, and most of the time I didn't mind because magically he could find fish. It was my job to hook them and land them. It was a dark and foggy night and he went around the corner of the head where I couldn't see him. We must have been fishing for many hours, because I can remember feeling discouraged and thinking there were no fish at Gay Head that night. I didn't want to leave that spot, fearing he would not be able to find me in the dark.

As the sun was rising and I was ready to give up, I felt a tremendous tug. As soon as I landed it, I grabbed it under the gill plate and dragged it around the corner to where Jackie was fishing. I was all pumped up and so proud that I had hooked and landed a beautiful twenty-six-pound striped bass, all by myself. I still remember his smile and knew that he was proud of me too. Once again refusing any help, I dragged it more than a hundred feet straight up the slippery cliffs to the Wagoneer parked at the top. Dragging a heavy bass up the cliffs was treacherous. The cliffs are mostly clay, and they are always wet and slippery. There are occasional bushes to grab on to to help pull you up the steep incline. I needed to prove to him that I was tough and a worthy fishing buddy.

It was fall when I had met Jackie, and winter came quickly. Once the weather turned cold and the fish migrated south, we sat in his bachelor kitchen and he showed me how to make my own bottom rigs and leaders for casting lures. He taught me the basics, including how to care for my rods and reels. We took our reels apart, cleaned and greased them, and put new line on the spools. He taught me to check my line for nicks, so I wouldn't lose so many lures.

I borrowed his fishing how-to books and read them from cover to cover so that I would be prepared for the spring season. For my birthday in January he gave me *The Complete Book of the Striped Bass* by Nicholas Karas. I learned many basics from that book.

Some of the techniques for how to catch big fish, which usually involve fishing bait on the bottom of the ocean, can't be learned in a book but have been passed down through generations of fishermen. It sounds simple but it's not. There are many variables with terminal tackle—this includes hooks, sinkers, snap swivels, and leaders—such as choice of bait and knowing where and when to target different species of fish. The fact that I was not only a newcomer, or "washashore," as we are called on Martha's Vineyard, but a female made gaining any knowledge of surf fishing more difficult. But once Jackie and I became a team, the locals finally took me seriously. A new way of life had opened to me. I was fortunate to have Jack Coutinho in my life as my mentor and friend.

Years later, Hawkeye told me that he felt I was privileged to have Jackie as a mentor. He said since he only lived part time on the island, it was difficult for him to be accepted by the island hard-core. He thought my being a woman was a benefit. He said they would never share information with him, an off-island guy from New York. I told him I didn't think that was so, because no one was sharing information with any other fishermen. Jackie knew that Hawkeye and Tim White were my friends, but he didn't want me to tell them anything, especially our spots. Fifteen years later, when Hawk and I buddied up, although he was an experienced fisherman, I did pass on some of the nuances that Jackie taught me.

Jackie's house was the perfect sportsman bachelor pad. There were not many adornments, but lots of fishing rods hung on the walls. The kitchen counter always held an assortment of lures, hooks, fishing line, reels, and tools to maintain them. The food in the refrigerator and cabinets was limited and simple.

A Wally Brown fiberglass replica of a striped bass that had been mounted on Cape Cod was on his living room wall. At that time, Wally was the only taxidermist in the area. He specialized in fiberglass reproductions and mounted most of the trophy fish caught on the cape and islands.

This trophy was made from a fifty-three-pound fish Jackie had caught during the 1978 Martha's Vineyard Bluefish and Striped Bass Derby. He placed third just below Tim White's fifty-six- and Hathaway's sixty-pounder. When the snow was falling and we turned our attention inside to work on gear, I would recline in the easy chair in his living room and just stare at his trophy fish, dreaming of the day that I might catch such a large, beautiful bass to hang on my own wall. Maybe even a Derby winner.

The passion for fishing that Jackie and I shared brought us close. My relationship with Duane was suffering from my using too much alcohol and drugs. My desire to fish was stronger than my desire to frequent the bars.

Duane was a successful local musician. His three-man band, Mr. Timothy Charles Duane, known as TCD, had many followers on the Vineyard. He was talented, and he had a passion for music. He wrote songs with Kate Taylor for her second album, *Kate Taylor*, in 1977. TCD opened the No Nukes Concert at the Allen Farm in Chilmark in 1978 for Carly Simon, Kate and Alex Taylor, John Hall and Orleans, and the Pousette-Dart Band. They performed regularly at local venues. We had an exciting life, as they say, "sex, drugs, and rock and roll," and I especially loved being around famous musicians, in the recording studios and supporting him onstage when it was not fishing season.

But when the fish were here, we were barely together. I needed to follow my own calling. It was painful because we thought we were soul mates forever, but we parted ways. For a short time, Jackie and I tried a romantic relationship, but it didn't work. When we drank together, we would fight. Jackie would suffer after an evening of drinking. His nerves were frazzled. We might have been too much alike: stubborn, bossy, and feisty. We were a great fishing team and felt comfortable working together on the beach, but as a couple—not so good.

Fishing became my obsession. Jackie taught me how to "read the water." Studying miles of ocean, he showed me how to find deep holes and sandbars where the fish might feed. He took me to his secret spots where he had been successful in catching fish. I followed his lead, and we fished every beach, jetty, creek, pond, and barrier beach opening on the Vineyard and Chappaquiddick.

I learned how the wind direction could affect the fish feeding. One of the most important keys to success was learning the island's complicated tides. We seined* our own sand eels and caught mackerel, squid, and butterfish for bait. We coordinated our days off work, so we could fish together for as many days as possible, from April until November each year. It was a privilege to learn how to fish with eels from the master. I was obsessed with earning my link in the chain.

Jackie passed down to me some techniques that he had learned from his former fishing partner, Stevie Amaral. Nuances that would have taken me years to figure out on my own. Techniques that Steve learned from his father, Gus, who was a participant in all the Derbies from the very first one in 1946 until his later years. Gus weighed in the very first striped bass during the first Derby.

Jackie battled schizophrenia. When he was young Stevie encouraged him to fish with him. Fishing for striped bass brought his mind back to health for many years.

We were a team and shared any money that we earned when we

* A seine is a fishing net that hangs vertically in the water with its bottom edge held down by weights and its top edge buoyed by floats. Seine nets can be deployed from the shore as a beach seine, or from a boat.

With Jack Coutinho waiting for the fish, Chappaquiddick Island, 1989

were fishing together. Jackie was a butcher by trade at one of the local markets, and I was a waitress, so we were happy to make extra income to support our fishing habit.

Public access to the shore was easier than it is today. Having special permission and keys to unlocked gates was, and still is, an advantage. Jackie had a key to a locked gate to what is now called Long Point on the south shore in West Tisbury. We would drive down a long dirt road through the woods, unlock the gate, and then drive onto the beach that led to the east side of Tisbury Great Pond. When the cut was open from the pond to the ocean, we could drive right up to it. When the cut was closed, we could drive all the way to Chilmark Pond in a westerly direction and east all the way to Katama, if Oyster Pond and Edgartown Great Pond were closed. We fished all over the Vineyard and Chappaquiddick, but the Tisbury Great Pond was our home base, especially during the Derby.

We laughed together, and sometimes cried together, and there were times when we screamed obscenities at each other. Those times were usually followed by laughter that brought tears to our eyes. We could spend hours in each other's company, working hard at fishing, and at times not saying a word. During the Derby, everyone knew that we were contenders. We fished together for twelve years.

My use of drugs and alcohol had escalated once Duane and I parted ways. For more than a decade I had been using cocaine, opiates, and pills, and twice that many years of drinking alcohol to excess. When I awoke from a three-day binge, I would make promises to God that I would "never do that again," but I couldn't keep my promises. I felt like a horrible human being.

In 1980, I left Helios and began waitressing at the Home Port Restaurant in Menemsha. A few years after I began working there, I was having difficulty getting to work and my job was in jeopardy. Jackie was getting worried about me, especially when he asked me to fish with him and I couldn't go because I was sick. I started to think that maybe I had a problem when my health was affecting my fishing. Something was wrong when I didn't have the energy to go fishing, but I couldn't figure out exactly what the problem was. When I made excuses because I was not well enough to work, my boss, Will, some-times said, "It's not that 'thing' again, is it?" I would reply, "Oh no, it's not *that* thing." I had no idea what "that thing" was that he was talking about. I was suspicious that he knew something was going on. I began to think that maybe I was just insane, but my denial was so impenetrable, I couldn't put my finger on my substance abuse.

My obsession to chase the elusive striped bass distracted me from my addiction to drugs and alcohol. Since I had no children during those years, other than earning a living, I had time to fish, especially at hours when most humans were tucked into their warm beds. My health was jeopardized by the substances that I ingested. When my ability to fish was hindered, I got a hint that maybe it was time to slow down my daily intake of alcohol. I rarely drove drunk. I knew that if I lost my Scout, I would not be able to drive on the beach to fish. Most of the time, I abandoned my buggy. Sometimes when I did drive impaired, I got stopped for driving "too slow." I should have been thrown in jail, but the Vineyard was tolerant of drunk driving and I was reprimanded and told, "Go home."

By 1984, I was calling in to work "sick" more frequently and my waitressing job at the Home Port in Menemsha was on the line. I was scared. I knew that if I lost this job I would probably lose my home, and I realized I had become unemployable. The year before, I had ended up in the hospital with an infection. After a three-day stay, I went into delirium tremens. With a complication of a bad infection, a blood clot, and then DTs, they almost lost me. They gave me last rites. I spent a month on intravenous antibiotics. When I got out of the hospital, I celebrated with some drinks. Something was wrong with me.

A drug buddy suggested that we should go to detox. He had been there many times. He said if we went, I could not be fired from my job, because the law says they cannot fire you if you are getting help, plus he told me they would give us Librium. That sounded like a plan and the only option that made sense to me.

I didn't have any health insurance; I was having a difficult time making my mortgage. I agreed to go to Fall River Detox for ten days. It is a state-funded program. I was among bikers from New Bedford and Fall River. Tattoos and not many teeth. The first few days there, as I wandered the halls doing the Librium shuffle, I felt like I was a visiting dignitary. After a week when I started to come out of my fog, I realized that detox was exactly where I belonged. Labor Day 1984 was the last time I drank and the beginning of my education in the world of addiction and the long journey into a life of recovery.

It was the thirty-ninth annual Derby and I was clean and sober. Although I felt naked without my substances, I felt full of energy and I could think clearly. Jackie was happy, as he had been worried about me. I had attempted to hide most of my drug use from him, but I could often tell by the concerned look on his face that he knew I was in trouble. I knew by the way he smiled at me that he was relieved to have his fishing buddy back by his side.

It was October 10, 1984, and only five more days until the end of the Derby. It was my first clean-and-sober Derby. We had been fishing hard since the tournament began, but I don't remember if we weighed in a single bass that whole first three weeks. It was discouraging but I was feeling incredible.

On cloudy days and night after night we sat on our bait buckets fishing the bottom or standing in the surf, casting eels or plugs. The last two weeks of the Derby had become our traditional annual vacation from work. We spent most of that time at the Tisbury Great Pond opening.

This night, we fished all night. Instead of fishing with live eels, we were casting lures. We were throwing Danny plugs that float on top of the water and when reeled in slowly swim like a baitfish. They resemble a menhaden or bunker. In the wee hours of the morning, something hit my plug. It felt like a big weed, but to my surprise, when I retrieved my line, there was a menhaden flapping around on my hook. Screaming with excitement, I ran down the beach to find Jackie. "Bunker! Jackie, look, I caught a bunker!" I tried to lob it back out into the surf to use as live bait, but it quickly worked its way off my hook.

These oily menhaden travel in large, slow-moving, and tightly packed schools. They are filter feeders and have no interest in a baited hook. They swim with their mouths open, straining plankton and algae from the ocean. Rather than fishing with a hook and bait for menhaden, we snag them with a large weighted three-pronged hook called a bunker snagger.

This was a good sign that maybe some fish would follow. Our energy level rose, and along with it our hopes.

Normally after fishing for most of the night, we packed our rods up by 7 a.m. and went home to get some sleep. That morning, because of that bunker, we decided to stay longer. The sun came up over the horizon and we saw one other fisherman, George Tucker. He was a little west of us, down the beach toward the opening.

Suddenly, the reflection of the sunlight on the surf was disturbed by the flutter of bunker being chased toward the shore by a school of big bass. The sea was clear and transparent, and as each wave crested, we could see a school of huge fish swimming through the waves. It was a rare sight to be able to see these nocturnal feeders in the light of day just thirty feet from shore. My heart was pounding with excitement. We could see the fish pushing the bunker toward us in a frenzy. We looked at each other, our eyes connected, and we knew exactly what to do. We ran back to Jackie's Wagoneer and opened the tailgate to expose everything we needed, our personal tackle shop.

My hands were shaking as I cut off my lure and tied on a bunker snagger. Jackie did the same. We ran back toward the edge of the water, cast our lines out, reeled in the slack, and started pulling our rods back, jigging and jigging, hoping to hook a bunker.

The bunker being chased through the surf were so thick that it didn't take long. We could see the flash of huge bass bellies as they were chasing the bait, hoping to trap the bunker near the shore. We each hooked a bunker, but Jackie hooked a bass before I did. I could see his rod bend with the weight of a large fish. While he was fighting his fish, a bass grabbed my offering. We were both connected to a fish of a lifetime.

Then I lost my fish. The bass spit out my bunker and my line went slack. Although I wanted to cast again, I didn't want to get in Jackie's way, so I decided not to cast until he landed his fish. I stayed close enough in case he needed my help when the fish hit the beach. He successfully landed it. It was a beauty and we could see that it was close to fifty pounds.

The moment he had his fish on the beach, I cast out again. I reeled up the slack in the line, and with a vigorous backward pull on my rod, it didn't take long before I hooked another bunker. I opened my bail to let the wounded fish swim away from the shore. It was only a few seconds before a striped bass picked up my bait and ran with it. I could feel the weight of the fish and my line was peeling off my spool. My heart was pounding. This time I let it run, and although my knees were shaking I patiently counted out seven seconds to give the bass enough time to swallow the bunker. Then I closed my bail and hauled back on my rod. I set the hook. Luck was with me and I was on again.

My rod bent with the weight of the fish and my drag was screaming. After all my years of searching for the hardest-fighting fish that would challenge my surf fishing skills, that fish was now on my hook. The hunt for a trophy striped bass during so many cold scary nights, and the hours of searching and hoping, was happening now. This was the moment I had been honing my fishing skills for. It was Derby time and I was in battle with a fish that could potentially beat a thousand other fishermen and win the tournament. Jackie stood by, and as my fish hit the beach, he grabbed it under the gill cover and dragged it a safe distance from the water, so the surf could not reclaim it.

I exhaled as I admired our beautiful bass lying side by side on the beach. They looked like twins, but we could see that Jackie's was a bit bigger.

We turned our attention back to the surf and took a few more casts and jigs into the sea. Less than five minutes after we landed our fish, the flutters disappeared, and the ocean surface went still. As quickly as they showed up, they disappeared back into the depths of the ocean. It was eerie how the atmosphere could be so charged with activity and then in a flash, peace and calm surrounded us. It now seemed like this amazing event had happened in the blink of an eye.

George Tucker drove up in his beach buggy to talk to us. He complimented our catch. He was upset because he had had a fish on his line but lost it. He said his reel broke during the battle and he could never snag another bunker. I felt for him, but after all, the Derby was under way.

It was now about 8:30 a.m. Jackie wanted to stay and keep fishing, but I wanted to go to weigh-in before the fish lost weight. If we didn't get back to town by 10 a.m., the next weigh-in was not until 8 p.m. He agreed that we should go to weigh-in while our fish were fresh. We knew these fish were close to fifty pounds and we realized that they could take the leader board.

The weigh-in station was near Jim's Package Store on Oak Bluffs Harbor that year. As we rounded the corner near the Flying Horses, I could hardly breathe with anticipation.

Jackie parked the Wagoneer and we each grabbed our own fish under the gill cover and dragged them into the weigh-in. We threw them onto the table in front of the scale. The weighmaster lifted them one by one onto the scale. Jackie's fish weighed forty-eight and three-quarters pounds and mine was an even forty-five pounds.

Don Mohr had been leading with a forty-two-pound bass. Our fish bumped him down to third place. In his humorous way, he never let me forget it.

With my Derby second-place finish forty-five-pound bass, 1984. Taken by a friend, Howard Weaver, at the old Boston House Restaurant on Circuit Avenue in Oak Bluffs.

We fished every minute that was humanly possible for the final few days of the Derby. If anyone was going to beat us, we wanted it to be ourselves. We never found another big fish after that morning, but lucky for us, no one else did either. Our fish stood as recorded until the final bell rang, ending the Derby. Having fished since he was a young man, Jack Coutinho had finally caught the overall Derby-winning striped bass. I took second place and Don Mohr held third place.

That same morning after we weighed our fish, I stopped to see my friend Howard Weaver, who worked at the Boston House Restaurant on Circuit Avenue. He took a photo of me with my fish in the door-way of the restaurant. Then I drove to my best friend Martha Abbot's house on Pequot Avenue and screamed, "Martha, I caught a fish. I mean I caught a big fish!" She took a couple of snapshots of me and my fish. No one ever got a photo of Jackie with his Derby winner.

Jackie was a butcher at Cronig's Market on main street in Vine-yard Haven, so he was able to keep our fish in their walk-in freezer until the Derby ended. The next week, we took a trip off-island to Falmouth and dropped them off to Wally Brown, the taxidermist. I wanted to have a skin mount done. I couldn't find anyone to do that work. He was the only taxidermist available, and he only did fiberglass reproductions.

A year later when our fish were completed, that mount was my inspiration to go to taxidermy school.

Jackie won a trip to Bermuda, $500 cash, and fishing gear.

In 1985, a moratorium was placed on fishing for striped bass and they were removed from the Derby for the next nine years. The striped bass had become a species of critical concern, so the regulations were tightened for both commercial and recreational fishermen.

Soon after that Derby ended, I picked up opiates again. I craved something, and I just thought I could escape "one more time." My life spiraled downhill fast, and once again I was on the hamster wheel and could not stop. The next six months were the worst period of my life. I was out of control, and this time, I knew what the problem was. Willpower was not working.

Jackie had planned to take me on the trip to Bermuda that was the grand prize for catching the largest striped bass during the Derby of 1984.

I was strung out and the thought of leaving the island to go to a strange country was frightening. I was convinced that a drink was not a solution, but I couldn't be that far away from my drug sources. I decided that I couldn't go with Jackie. I didn't tell him until the last minute. That was a dilemma for him because he had a plane ticket for me and a hotel room reserved. He was upset, but at the last moment, he found another friend to go with him.

On March 28, 1985, I left for Fall River once more. They had started a new drug rehabilitation program called SSTAR, and I was lucky to be accepted. This time it stuck, and I've stayed clean ever since.

Jackie ended up losing his battle with schizophrenia. His pursuit of the striped bass had kept his illness at bay. When it was fishing season, from April until November, his mental health improved and his illness seemed to subside, but winters were difficult on him. He committed suicide in 1990, just before Christmas.

When the moratorium on striped bass went into effect and they were removed from the Derby, Jackie was deeply affected. He didn't want to fish for bonito. He said daytime fishing for bonito was not "fishing." I loved catching bonito. He would get angry with me and say I was going to burn out chasing bonito during the day and I wouldn't have the energy to bass fish with him at night. I assured him that wouldn't happen. I was young and compulsive. I could fish in the day for bonito, fish the nights for bass, and still have the energy to work as a waitress.

We fished a few more years together, but I started to separate from him and fished more on my own. His mental illness was coming to the forefront and I was feeling frightened. I didn't know how to handle his paranoia. He told me "they" were talking about him on the radio. He was obsessed with his Wagoneer and felt that people were following him. I couldn't convince him that he was delusional.

I was in therapy myself at the time, and my therapist told me that Jackie was in the advanced stages of schizophrenia. She told me to encourage him to get help. I did. He had seen a doctor many years before, but they had treated him with Thorazine and it whacked him out. He didn't like feeling that way.

I was becoming fearful of his unpredictable behavior. Since there was a moratorium on striped bass, we fished together for bluefish, but he was more cranky and negative. He was frustrated and would cuss and yell. The serious but fun-loving fishing buddy I knew was gone. I know he loved me and would never hurt me, but the more time I spent with him in the dark, the more uncomfortable I felt.

During the winter, we kept in contact. We talked at least once a week, and if I did not hear from him, I called him or went to his house to see him. I was worried that he might take his life but didn't know what to do about it. He should have been hospitalized. By 1988, we were getting ever more distant. I believe that when he decided to take his life, he could not find any other alternative to relieve his tortured mind.

I have partnered up with other fishermen over the years, but no one can replace Jackie. I will always be indebted to him not only for teaching me how to fish for striped bass, but for showing me how to learn the signs in nature to become a better fisherman. I miss Jackie Coutinho—he was a true fishing buddy.

8

History and Controversy

IN 1946, SOME ISLAND BUSINESSMEN looking for a way to bring tourism to the Vineyard during the off-season started the Martha's Vineyard Bass Derby. For the first two years, only striped bass qualified for prizes, but in 1948 bluefish were added, and in 1954 it officially became the Martha's Vineyard Striped Bass and Bluefish Derby, which it remains today. I am sure they had no idea that this event would become one of the most esteemed, all-inclusive fishing competitions in the country.

The first couple of years I fished the Derby, I hadn't caught a fish big enough to bring to weigh-in.* Striped bass were the target fish and bluefish were not held in high esteem. Men dominated the tournament. I was not the committed fisherman that I am today.

In 1978, the year of the thirty-third annual Martha's Vineyard

---

* The building where Derby officials weigh in each fish is open twice each day throughout the Derby, from 8 a.m. to 10 a.m. and from 8 p.m. to 10 p.m. For many decades, for the month of the Derby, the old Junior Yacht Club building at the lower end of Main Street in Edgartown is transformed into the weigh-in station, in a tiny wooden shack on the harbor. The Derby Committee is a nonprofit and does not own any real estate.

Original Derby Committee, members of the Chamber of Commerce

Striped Bass and Bluefish Derby, I was witness to a Derby-winning striped bass being caught.

I had been off-island that day but got back in the late afternoon. I was fishing with Tim White at that time. I knew Tim was fishing from the Big Bridge between Oak Bluffs and Edgartown, and I wanted to go see how he was doing. For some reason, I didn't bring my rod with me. There was quite a crowd fishing there when I arrived. I found Tim fishing with Mark Sauer. Not long after I joined them on the bridge, we saw a huge pod of menhaden. We could see the bunker fluttering on the surface of the water, desperate to avoid being eaten by a pod of large hungry fish. They were splashing frantically in the channel toward the bridge.

Some of the fishermen were snagging the bunker and putting them in their buckets to use for bait later. Tim and Mark seemed to be the only ones who knew the best way to use a bunker for bait. After snagging one, they opened the bails on their reels to let the wounded baitfish swim, free spool. It's natural that a predator is attracted to a baitfish that is wounded and vulnerable. Once a bunker is snagged with a bunker snagger, it fights to stay with the school, but because it has been injured by the weighted hook, it sinks toward the bottom of the school. This makes it an easier target for a hungry striped bass.

Mark said his bunker was grabbed by a fish, but it was a large toothy bluefish. It cut his bait in half and he could not get the hook in it. He never got another bunker.

A large fish grabbed Tim's bait. He opened his bail to let it run, and when he was sure the fish swallowed the bunker, he set the hook.

I will never forget the fight that ensued. As he fought the fish from the bridge, his rod was bent with its weight. Tim's body tensed as he held his rod tight and close to his body. The fish began to swim down the channel toward open water, so Tim cautiously climbed from the bridge to the jetty. He balanced on the rocks, walking slowly, keeping his line taut so the fish could not throw the hook. He slowly, cautiously walked with the fish all the way to the end of the longer jetty on the Oak Bluffs side of the channel. A crowd gathered. After a long battle that seemed to last more than half an hour, the fish was still fighting to be free. I watched in amazement as this huge fish breached out of the water. It was an unusual sight to see a fifty-pound striper break the surface and jump through the air. Finally, the battle won, Tim dragged the fish from the surf and onto the beach. He had landed the most magnificent striped bass I had ever seen. Everyone guessed that it was over fifty pounds.

It was late in the afternoon and the weigh-in would not open until eight o'clock that evening.

Tim covered the fish with seaweed to keep it from drying out so that it wouldn't lose any weight. He didn't have a cooler, so he hid it in the rocks near the bridge at the base of the jetty. He waited for the crowd to disperse because he didn't want to draw any more attention to his fish.

I drove home to get my fishing rod and returned to fish with Tim and Mark until it was time for weigh-in. All was quiet, and we never saw another fish caught.

The sun went down, and it was getting close to the time when the evening weigh-in would begin. When Tim uncovered his fish, he discovered that rats had taken a few bites out of it. A few rat bites didn't take much away from the massive body of this monster.

We arrived in Edgartown at the weigh-in with smiles that could not be concealed. We knew that this bass was a contender and Mark and I were excited for Tim.

I will never forget the look on Tim's face when the weight on the scale was read out: "Fifty-six pounds, five ounces!" This was the biggest fish weighed in so far during this Derby, and it put Tim in first place. When the Derby staff asked him where he caught it, he told the truth and said, "The Big Bridge." No one believed him. In those days, no one ever told the truth about where they caught their fish, and the Big Bridge was not a likely spot to catch such a huge bass.

Someone took a photo of Tim with the fish standing in front of the chalkboard with the results. After many backslaps and cheers, the three of us went to celebrate with a couple of drinks at the Harborside Inn Restaurant. Tim is a quiet, private person, but that evening he was bursting with pure excitement and jubilation. In all the years that I had known him, I had never seen him show that much emotion.

Before long, a notorious fisherman, Dick Hathaway, weighed in a larger fish.

Dick was a grand prize Derby winner for striped bass. In 1956, he won the Derby with a fifty-two-pound, nine-ounce bass. He'd also been the grand winner in 1965 with a fifteen-pound, two-ounce bluefish, and in 1966 with a sixteen-pound, ten-ounce bluefish. A legend. Unfortunately, he had a reputation for being a scoundrel. Dick Hathaway walked through the doors that morning in 1978 with a large striped bass.

At that time, there were no computers. Everything was written and recorded by hand. The weigh-in staff of two or three volunteers worked in the building each morning and evening and weighed and recorded each fish brought in by a Derby participant. Helen Scarborough was the weighmaster, and for many years, with pen and notepad, she carefully recorded every fish that was brought into the weigh-in building. It's been said that Helen was the only official in the building that morning when Dick came to weigh in.

Unlike today, the scale was not digital. It had a round clock-type face with numbers from 1 to 20. A metal tray hanging from the bottom was large enough to hold the fish. The weighmaster had to count how many times the hand circled the dial: twenty, forty, sixty pounds.

Since Helen was the only staff person, Dick placed the fish on the scale himself and relayed to Helen that it registered sixty pounds, two ounces. Helen recorded the fish's weight. Dick signed the weigh slip that every fisherman must sign, stating that they have been truthful.

The story goes that Dick quickly left the building but stopped long enough for a photo to be snapped by a tourist. Soon after, a few more staff came to the weigh-in and decided that they had some doubts about the weight of the fish. About twenty minutes after the fact, Dick was asked to bring the fish back for a second look and to answer some questions. He said the fish was gone; he had sold it to a guy from New Jersey and it was already cut into fillets and he couldn't bring it back.

The Derby had accepted the fish, and so it had to stand as recorded. That's one version of the many stories told about the incident.

This is another version still told in the shadows. No one has ever come forward with any proof.

Once Dick was outside the weigh-in he passed the fish to one of his buddies and it was weighed in again, but this time it weighed forty pounds. This "passing of fish" was rumored to happen frequently with large bass, and it prompted the Derby Committee to require the weighmaster to clip the tail of every fish weighed, a practice still followed today.

Dick's fish had broken the record for the heaviest striped bass *ever* brought to weigh-in during the history of the thirty-three years of the Martha's Vineyard Striped Bass and Bluefish Derby.

The story and photo of Dick's fish were printed in the local newspaper, the *Vineyard Gazette,* on October 20, 1978.* The fish looked smaller than Tim's fifty-six-pound bass. Tim took his grievance with the photographs to the committee, but he told me nothing could

---

* https://vineyardgazette.com/news/1978/10/20/dick-hathaways-striper-caps-another-successful-derby.

1979. My early weigh slips, handwritten by Helen Scarborough. Note the line that reads, "I attest that the statements hereon are true."

1984

be done to change the weighmaster's decision. They had accepted Dick's fish.

Tim is a private and guarded man. His reaction at weigh-in that evening was fitting compared to the stories told about Dick's nonchalant attitude to catching the largest fish ever in the history of the Derby. I can only imagine what it would feel like to catch the largest striped bass *ever* caught in more than three decades of the Derby competition.

Tim, naturally, felt betrayed and never fished another Derby. I tried to reason with him, but his resentment ran deep. I think that more than the loss of valuable prizes, it was the loss of the prestige that comes with winning the Derby with a striped bass that got to him. As reported by the *Vineyard Gazette* archive article about that 1978 Derby, Dick won an all-expenses-paid trip to Duck Key, Florida. He was also to compete in the Natural Light Beer/Motorboat Magazine Master Angler Tournament for a week in November. In addition, he won $500 cash and $300 in Derby fins,* and a Penn International conventional reel worth more than $200.

For Tim to have had to give all that up to a dubious fish was salt in the wound. Dick won the Derby again the following year, 1979, with a fifty-five-pound, three-ounce bass.

I first noticed Dick Hathaway in 1977 at Wasque Point on Chappaquiddick when I watched as he slashed the line of another fisherman that crossed his line

Bob Post, fisherman and author of *Reading the Water,* published in 1988 by Pequot Press, was a close friend of mine. Bob passed away in 1994. His wife, Pia, allowed me to view his transcripts of the interviews that he did in 1986 for his book. They were transcribed directly from taped interviews he had with each fisherman, me included. Jackie Coutinho was upset with me for granting Bob an interview. He feared that I was telling closely guarded secrets that he had passed on to me, but I assured him that I didn't talk specifics.

Dick's interview never made it into *Reading the Water.* According

---

* Derby fins were given out instead of cash. They looked like play money and were accepted in all the local stores just like cash. The Derby Committee wanted to keep the award money on the island.

to his interview, Dick fished in the 1940s when he was fourteen years old. He was working with the Grant brothers, who ran a gravel pit and construction company in Edgartown, and Dick talked of his first fishing trip with the brothers, who took him out to Chappaquiddick and lent him a rod and reel.

After a few casts, Dick hooked a big fish. His drag was loose, so he could not gain any line while he was cranking the handle of the reel. He said the guys ran over to him and told him, "Tighten the drag, tighten the drag." He said he had no idea what they were talking about and after ten minutes of turning the handle on his reel and not making any gain, he thought the reel was broken. He threw the rod and reel in the sand and hand-lined the fish into the surf. When he could finally see the fish, he jumped on it in the water. Ralph Grant had to pull him out of the waves with his arms around the fish as if it were a baby. It was about a thirty-five-pound bass.

Dick said, "They chewed me out for throwing the rod and reel in the sand."

Reading through Bob's interview with Dick, I can see that his beginning was not much different from mine. Neither of us had a clue when we first fished, and neither of us had a driver's license, so we had to depend on the kindness of other fishermen to bring us to the far ends of the island. Once he got his license he began spending time alone through the night in search of fish just as I had.

Dick went into the service for six years, and when he returned at age twenty-nine, he became obsessed with fishing. He told Bob Post, "I brought enough sandwiches to work and as soon as I got done with work at four-thirty, I'd jump in the car and go right to Gay Head. Every single night, every night, Saturdays and Sundays."

He added, "I used to do some foolish things. I'd walk twenty miles maybe, and there were a lot of people who would not do that. I'd stay out all night and then go to work the next morning. Not just during the Derby but every day they were running. I would sleep for a couple of hours in the front seat of the car. I had a blanket and an alarm clock. I used to sit on the dunes up there, like at Squibnocket. If you went with me, you'd think I was nuts! But I'd wait to see where the pods of bait were coming from, the east end or the west end. You know sooner or later when the tide gets right, the baits coming in, so it's a good spot.

"Sometimes I'd have to go all along Dogfish Bar and over by Pilot's Landing and then plenty of times I fished all the way to Long Beach."

Bob wanted him to clarify: "Would you walk on the beach, all the way from Dogfish Bar in Lobsterville to Pilot's Landing in Gay Head to Long Beach at Squibnocket?"

"Yes, Dogfish to Long Beach. I would catch three or four bass and drag them back too. Sometimes I've gone a little further. I've walked Long Beach to Squibnocket."

Bob asked, "Like along Moshup Trail?"

Dick replied, "That's about five miles, clocked. But it's rocks, nothing but rocks. They followed me. I was catching fish there for years."

"Wait a minute, Dick, would you walk from Squibnocket, starting at the parking lot, up to Long Beach, and then you'd walk back again? That's a ten-mile walk, five miles each way."

Dick said, "Yeah, a lot of guys have done it with me, but they only do it once. Tommy Teller did it a few times. I was in the hospital having my appendix out. I got out of the hospital that day, and of course I had to go fishing. So, I get Tommy and we walked up around the point of Squibnocket, and I caught three big bass in the thirties. He got nothing. He had to carry my fish back. The next night Tommy said, 'The heck with that,' so I got Tony Lima to go."

Imagine carrying more than ninety pounds of fish for more than five miles, over slippery, ankle-busting rocks down a beach, probably in the dark. One early spring evening, I fished Squibnocket. I caught a twenty-four-pound bass. It was my first bass of the season, so I decided to keep it. Big mistake. By the time I lugged it back to the parking lot, it felt like it weighed about a hundred pounds. I learned a lesson that night. Never keep a Squibnocket fish unless it is a Derby winner. The thought of carrying three huge bass five or more miles on the beach, although not impossible, makes me wonder about the credibility of Dick's stories. I supposed Bob had some doubts also and so did not print his interview in *Reading the Water*.

The Derby had a resident and nonresident category until the mid-1980s. Dick would take a group of off-island fishermen to his secret spots. Jackie said they had a pecking order. They would hand fish to be weighed in to whoever would have the most benefit in prizes.

Dick said, "Most of the guys I went with during the Derby were from off-island. They've all won the Derby, first, second, or third, at least once, the ones that fish with me. Clyde Omar was with me. We would go down the beach and I'd stop and say, 'Well, this is it, this area right here.' That's when we were getting them all to bottom fish. Those guys would all put out their sand spikes and set out their bait. I would wait until they were all set up and then there would be no place for me. So I had to go down the beach another hundred yards, park, and put my bait out. I had the spot!"

When I first started to fish with Jackie Coutinho, he pointed Dick out to me on Long Beach in Gay Head. I could see a long line of four-wheel-drive vehicles and many fishermen lined up on the beach. Each person had at least two rods set in sand spikes, bottom fishing. They called it the "picket fence." No one could or would fish that area for a good quarter mile.

Bob asked Dick about his 1978 winning bass. He only talked about beating a guy from Maine who landed one near him on the beach that looked to be over fifty pounds. It was an unremarkable story.

Bob asked him, "Sixty pounds, two ounces?"

Dick replied, "Something like that."

End of interview.

In an interview with David Kinney, author of *The Big One,* Helen Scarborough acknowledged that there is a controversy about Dick's fish. "Only he and God knows [*sic*]," she said.

Many of my fishing friends who have been in pursuit of a winning striped bass would love to break that record. It would be wonderful to have the bass record held by a fish that no one has doubts about. I dream of that sixty-one-pound striped bass waiting to be crowned the new champ.

In 1999, Dick Hathaway once again was in the spotlight. The local newspapers reported that Mark Plante and Alley Moore witnessed Dick and his fishing partner, Peter Jackson, breaking the Massachusetts state regulation of one fish per day per angler. That is also a Derby rule. They said they saw them catching many striped bass and burying them under their truck. The *Martha's Vineyard Times* and the *Vineyard Gazette* reported that after that they were banned from joining the tournament for the next ten years.

Though the ban has now ended, Dick has not registered in the Derby and has not been seen fishing on the beach.

In 2017, eighteen years later, I talked to Peter Jackson while on an offshore trip with him, fishing for haddock with Captain Donny Benefit. He told me he was down the beach from Dick that night and he did not see him bury any fish. He told me that he did nothing wrong that night. Now that the ban has been lifted, Peter is once again a Derby participant, and in 2017 he won the senior boat blue-fish division with a 16.15-pound bluefish.

Dick Hathaway died on June 25, 2017, the undefeated Derby record holder. I wanted to have a conversation with him, but because I'm a Derby Committee member, he grumbled cuss words at me each time I passed near him. His message was, "Stay away from me."

I know today that these unusually large striped bass, sometimes referred to as lunkers, are few and far between. It makes me sad that Tim never participates in the Derby, because he is a great fisherman. By tagging along I learned a lot from him. I learned how to fish the bottom with bait, how to catch butterfish, and more of the basics of surf fishing. Occasionally, I see him fishing. He has traded his surf-casting gear for his new passion of fly fishing.

The challenge of breaking the all-time biggest bass record during the Derby is on many fishermen's minds. The sad thing is that Dick Hathaway was one hell of a hard-core fisherman. He certainly did not need to do anything underhanded to win.

Tim with his
fifty-six-pound,
five-ounce striped
bass, 1978

Dick Hathaway
with his sixty-
pound, two-
ounce striped bass

9

Fishing Logs

I HAVE BEEN RECORDING my fishing trips for many years. Jack Coutinho suggested I keep a fishing log, and I am grateful that I took his advice. This firsthand account has become a useful learning tool. It shows the many ways that surf fishing has changed over the decades—changes in the availability of baitfish, the decline of some species, and the complete disappearance of others from our waters. It shows weather changes and even the decrease of my own energy. My logs show how my attitude has changed over the years and how I have become much more conservation-minded. This record of where and how we caught different species, and in some cases what we didn't catch, has helped me become a better fisherman. This chapter has excerpts from some of my early logs.

The list below was recorded on an old piece of cardboard. On October 16, 1979, the day after the Derby ended, Jackie and I ran into an amazing pod of big fish. We fished this unrevealed spot for a week.

October 16th, 1979
12 Bass, 300 lbs. Average fish 25 pounds.
37 pounds of Squeteague* 24 pounds of Bluefish Fillets.

Oct. 17th
5 Bass, 136 pounds, Average fish 27.2 lbs.
1 seven-pound weakfish to eat.

Oct. 18th
5 Bass, 140 lbs. average fish 28 lbs.
2 weakfish, 2 bluefish.†

Oct. 20th
17 Bass, 422 pounds, Average 24.8 lbs.
2 small bluefish.

Oct. 22nd
11 Bass, 311 pounds, Average fish 28.3 lbs.
2 small bluefish.

Oct. 23rd
14 Bass, 377 lbs., Average fish 26.92
16 lbs. of bluefish, 1 weakfish

Oct. 24th
3 Bass, 89 lbs., Average fish 29.6
28 lbs. of bluefish and Squeteague fillet. End of Blitz.

Between the two of us, we ended up catching 1,789 pounds of
striped bass, 90 pounds of filleted weakfish, and about 100 pounds
of filleted bluefish.

I don't remember who was first to find this school of fish, but five
of us fished side by side most of that week: Steve Amaral, Whit Man-

---

* Also known as weakfish.
† I wonder what happened on the nineteenth and the twenty-first. Work must have gotten in
the way.

ter, Bernie Arruda, Jackie Coutinho, and I. Each evening we drove the beach to find the exact spot and then hid in the dunes until the sun started to set, keeping low so other fishermen wouldn't figure out where we were. We were making money and we did not want to share the bounty.

We fished from sunset until sunrise, and then, as fast as we could, we loaded our catch into our beach buggies and headed off the beach. We dropped the striped bass off at Boggess's fish dock in Vineyard Haven. From there the fish were shipped to Fulton Fish Market in New York City. We returned to the dock the next day to pick up a check. We sold the bluefish and the squeteague (weakfish) locally but also kept some fillets to eat. Some of the others caught as much, if not more, than Jackie and me combined.

We didn't know that the striped bass was on the brink of extinction and would become a species of critical concern. We certainly didn't know that by 1986 the weakfish would have disappeared totally from the Vineyard.

Telling tales in the coffee shops was taboo, and during those days, if I had ever divulged any of our secrets I would have been in big trouble. I felt that it was a privilege that these hard-core bass fish-

1,789 pounds of striped bass

ermen accepted me into their group, and I was not about to jeopardize my spot in the pecking order.

At left is a scrap of paper on which I kept a record of the most incredible week of bass fishing. Why I didn't write it in my notebook is a mystery to me.

Another excerpt from my log shows our frustration and bewilderment as it became more and more difficult to find fish. We had no idea that toxic chemicals had penetrated the northeastern spawning grounds. We didn't know that the striped bass were targeted heavily up and down the Atlantic coast by thousands of other fishermen. There was no internet or Google on which to research information. The only publication I remember was *Salt Water Sportsman* magazine, and I don't recall reading about the striped bass issues that were facing us. Since we were focused on supplementing our income, we purposely kept ourselves isolated from other island fishermen and visitors from off-island.

April 28, 1980

It's been quite a month! Fishing stories float through the diners, bar rooms, and on every main street in each town. Billy Unatowski said he saw a bass in some guy's car yesterday but that has never been confirmed. Jackie and I thought we would give it a try Saturday night, the 26th. We drove out to Wasque Point. What a gorgeous night. Hardly any wind and a nice big moon. We plugged to no avail. It felt so good to be fishing again. It gave me the opportunity to work the kinks out of my new twenty-pound test Ande line. We didn't stay long. We then rode to the creek at the head of the Lagoon. They planted herring there two years ago, but we didn't see any.

Each spring Alfred Vanderhoop, chief of the Wampanoag tribe, would let us come to the Gay Head run and take herring* as long as we didn't sell the roe, which would have interfered with the commercial fishermen's livelihood. This became an annual tradition. It was the first time each season that we pulled on our waders and ventured out into the night.

* River herring, or alewives, are anadromous (sea-run) fish that spend the majority of their life at sea but return to freshwater to spawn. A moratorium was put into effect in 2006 because they had become a species of concern. Fishermen were no longer allowed to take any alewives. The moratorium remains in effect as of this writing.

April 29, 1980

We decided to go to the creek in Gay Head to get some herring to cut the roe. We called tribal chief Alfred Vanderhoop.

The herring arrived from their long journey down south, and the run was alive. We lowered our net into the creek and it filled within a few minutes. It took both of us to lift them into our containers. We filled two forty-gallon plastic garbage cans in no time at all. They were so heavy that it took at least another hour to get the herring to the car. They must have weighed more than one hundred pounds each. We laughed and laughed as we were slipping and sliding in the muck at two o'clock in the morning. Being on tribal land somehow made this event spiritual, even thru our foolish behavior.

We stopped at John Gates and Caroline's and got them out of bed to give them some herring. We ended up with about twenty-five pounds of roe to eat and share. We also gave some of the cut herring to my friend Pam Clark to pickle and smoke. She has a catering business. All that was left over I buried in my garden. Nothing wasted. I love that.

Soon we'll be fishing almost every day and I will remember what my purpose in life is. Winter is difficult.

April 30, 1980

We packed up the Wagoneer and headed for Wasque. What a perfect rip! We threw out Stan Gibbs Swimmers, Dannys, Crocodiles, and Pencil Poppers. We beat the water for a couple of hours and nothing. Oh well, it's still just a little early in the season.

May 3

We loaded up the car and headed for the Edgartown Great Pond, down at the waterworks road, and went white perching.* I had six in the bucket before Jackie caught one. We had some good laughs as I teased him about being able to catch more than him. He usually always caught more fish than I did. We ended up with fifteen fish altogether. We scaled and cleaned them, and I had two perch and spaghetti for dinner.

In those days, unlike today, we were permitted to drive down the long, bumpy Quansoo Road, and when the pond was open to the ocean, at low tide, we could drive over the creek and all the way to the West Tisbury Great Pond opening. When the barrier beaches are opened, whether by nature or bulldozer or shoveled by hand, the fish come in to feed on the baitfish and crabs that dump out of the pond. Historically most of the large striped bass landed on the Vineyard have been caught at one of the openings.

May 6th, 1980, a day I won't forget.

It was about 6:30 in the evening and I was retrieving my plug slowly through the surf. I saw a big pink belly flash in the wave as it hit a plug. Although it grabbed *my* swimmer, for just a split second, I was not sure that the lure that it had in its mouth was attached to my line.

Suddenly, *"Whack"*—it was indeed my fish. My new eleven-foot graphite rod was bent with the tension and once again my body was shaking with adrenaline. This fish took an amazing run trying to free itself from my hook. As my line screamed off my reel and my rod felt like it was attached to a Volkswagen bug going sixty miles an hour through the surf, I hung on with all my strength. I am not sure how long it took me to land that fish, but I knew this was the biggest fish I had ever had on the end of my line. Jackie was at my side and ready to help me as soon as the fish hit the beach. He grabbed it under the gill cover and pulled it up above the tide

* White perch live in brackish water. They spawn in the early spring. Their delicate white meat is excellent table fare.

line, so the ocean could not reclaim it. We had his Wagoneer close by, so we didn't need to carry it very far. My years of pursuing a trophy bass finally paid off. I caught a magnificent 45-pound striped bass. Too bad it was not Derby time.

The word spread fast through the fishing community that I had caught a lunker. It was unusually early in the spring season for such a large fish. Before that day, I had heard that the guys were saying that Jackie was landing all the fish that we were catching. Now I had eyewitnesses that I hooked, fought, and landed that fish on my own.

After struggling for three years, I had finally earned some respect from the men. Now, maybe I'll be considered a fisherman. Duane was with Timothy and Charlie doing music at Timothy's house. I stopped by with my fish and they took a couple of photos before I sold it to the Black Dog. They paid two dollars a pound. Imagine ninety dollars for one fish.

My first forty-five-pound bass. May 6, 1980, in front of my 1979 International Scout fishmobile.

We have been back to the opening quite a few more times but I haven't had any luck. Jackie lost one about thirty pounds one night.

I've haven't been feeling well for a while now so last night I stayed home. Jackie and Stevie Amaral went to Wasque. Stevie got a forty-pounder and Jackie got a thirty-nine-pounder. I'm lying here resting because we're going to Wasque tonight at 10 p.m. We're almost certain to get one. The Edgartown Pond is open but it's not producing yet.

May 12, 1980

Well, well. It has begun, and I surely started on the right foot. We fished last Tuesday night and once again no fish. We went home to sleep for a couple of hours and headed out again on Wednesday morning. It was a grey and lousy day but still no fish. We beat the water to death. Then after resting for a few more hours, we went to Tisbury Great Pond opening on Wednesday evening. It was a windy, stormy afternoon.*

There were about a dozen guys fishing the opening. Jackie and I were among them, and as usual I was the only woman. The wind was ferocious, and the surf was high. I was using a 3-ounce Stan Gibbs blue and white swimmer. I could cast it into the wind. It sailed far enough into the water that I knew it was in the zone for a fish to find it.

May 17, 1980

We've been fishing quite a bit. I got a twenty-nine-pounder on Tuesday and Jackie got a thirty-three-pounder on Wednesday afternoon. The bluefish came into Wasque on May 14th. We may go today since the bass fishing is slow. People have been getting hundreds of pounds of bluefish.

---

* Striped bass are known as nocturnal feeders, but on a cloudy dark day, especially in the spring, targeting migrating fish can be very productive.

There are probably a hundred people fishing there, but it will be good to have a nice fresh piece of bluefish.

Later: We went to Wasque, Jack, Jim Noble, and me. It *was* a zoo, but I had fun. We got nine bluefish between us, all around seven pounds. We each kept one to eat and gave the rest away. I saw my first Oyster Catcher. Jim called them Oyster Crackers.*

The following year:

May 6, 1981

We went to Gay Head last night hoping to get some herring. The tide may not have been low enough or maybe the northeast wind kept stopping them, but we didn't get any. The tide at Wasque is good, high to low, till about 7:30 tonight. It's Wednesday and I'm going there.

May 16, 1981

I finally got my first striper for the season. May 14th at Wasque on a white, medium Stan Gibbs. The tide had been falling about three hours. A twenty-six-pounder, sold it to the restaurant for two dollars and fifty cents a pound. Sixty-five bucks. More than a night of waitressing. The wind was southwest, a nice night. I went by myself; Jackie was there and he got three bass after I left. I went back last night and worked hard but—nothing.

May 28, 1981

The bluefish have been here since the 20th. No more bass at Wasque. The bluefish seem to push them away. I've been fishing Squibby, sunsets and sunrises. I've had hits but not hooked a fish there. I haven't heard of any fish except blues at Wasque. Rumors of fish on the north shore.

* Oyster catcher: A shorebird that eats shellfish. It is black and white with a long orange bill. At that time, they were rare. I never saw another oyster catcher after that day in 1980, until 2008 when I began to see a few on Norton Point Beach.

Five months later:

Columbus Day, October 12

There was an incredible blitz on the south shore yesterday. I was working at the Home Port and because of the holiday I couldn't get the day off work to fish. Jackie called me and told me about it. I was sick thinking about what I had missed. He said he caught about a dozen striped bass all over forty pounds but not one was a fifty-pounder. I'm going with him tomorrow and I can hardly breathe with anticipation.

October 13

Jackie and I drove from Hadley's toward Chilmark looking for the schools of bunker. It was a beautiful sunny day. We finally found them up near the Chilmark Pond. We were able to snag some but it was not easy. They were staying out from the shore and we were having trouble reaching them. We caught about eight bass between us but they were only about thirty to thirty-five pounds. Eddie Medeiros is leading the Derby with a fifty-five-pounder. Bernie was there today and told us that he had a couple of fifties yesterday but could not even make a daily. I'm so pissed that I had to work yesterday. Missed a day that will be remembered for a long time.

Spring two years later:

May 6, 1983

Today is an important day for me, I got my forty-five-pounder three years ago on this day. Today I was too busy to fish and I'm not feeling very good. Something is wrong with my life, but I can't quite figure out what's wrong. I'm very unhappy about this. I need to rearrange my life so this won't happen again.

May 10, 1983

I'm going fishing at midnight so I'm in bed trying to get some rest so I can get up to fish.

4 a.m. Just got home from Wasque. No fish yet, sure was a beautiful night.

May 11, 1983

The days are very hectic now. I started a job cooking lunch for ninety-year-old Mrs. Cook in West Tisbury, five afternoons a week. I'm waitressing at the Home Port in the evening and rushing to catch a midnight tide at Wasque. The wind has been blowing wicked northwest. I heard two bass were caught last night just before dark on the end of the east tide. I've been fishing the west tide.

May 12, 1983

I went out to Wasque and was fishing by 6:30. Tim White and Roger Andrews were there. I fished until almost 9:30 . . . NOTHING! I found out that only one fish was caught so far on the Vineyard this year, a thirty-five-pounder on May 10th. So everything else has been rumors.

Work, fish, sleep has been my pattern lately, I'm getting tired.

May 14, 1983

Got home from work at midnight and went out to fish at 2 a.m. I went with Jackie and we had fun, but still no fish, no bass, no blues. There were five of us there all night. The sunrise was just beautiful but everyone was very discouraged because it's so late in the season and nobody has had even a hit. Jackie and I took a ride to Edgartown Great Pond opening. Tim was there sleeping in his new truck. No fish anywhere. Have been up for twenty-four hours. Feels good to crawl into a nice warm bed.

May 19, 1983

Went fishing with Jackie until 9:30 p.m. . . . . Still no fish. He's pretty disgusted because he took the week off work to fish to no avail.

May 20, 1983
    Last night I fished until 10 p.m. . . . . Still no fish. No Bass,
No Blues! This is getting ridiculous!

We could take as many bluefish as we could catch until 1989, when
the Atlantic States Marine Fisheries Commission put a ten-bag limit
on them. That year they also ruled that in order to sell fish, anglers
needed to have commercial permits. This is an excerpt from the new
regulations:

> Any person selling a bluefish is identified as a commer-
> cial fisherman and must have a commercial fishing permit
> that allows the sale of bluefish. This commercial definition
> includes, among others, all hook and line fishermen who
> sell bluefish, regardless of fishing mode (that is, fishing from
> shore, manmade structures, private boats, or charter boats).
> For states without a permit, a federal permit is required to
> sell bluefish.

The regulations for striped bass also changed at that time.

10

So Many Changes

WHEN THE MARTHA'S VINEYARD Bass Derby was started in 1946, striped bass were the only species included in the prize structure. In 1948 bluefish were added, but in New England striped bass are still one of the most coveted saltwater game fish. Their delicious fillets rank high as table fare, and because they have complex feeding and spawning habits, they are a challenge to catch, especially with rod and reel.

What makes the Vineyard unique is that five weeks each fall we have the Derby. The competition attracts more than three thousand participants, and close to half of them are from off-island. Each fall, the island is invaded by four-wheel-drive vehicles loaded with fishing gear. Derby madness fills the air.

The Derby originally began on September 15 and ended on October 15. I understand that those dates were chosen in order to miss the migration of large female striped bass. The organizers did not want to encourage the fishermen to take fish after October, when the egg-bearing females are most vulnerable as they are feeding heavily, getting ready for their long journey south to warmer water. In the last decade, the dates have varied, and another week has been added. The tournament now runs for almost five weeks. It sometimes feels that it is too long, and because I fish like a crazy person, it might be the life of me.

Striped bass and bluefish have a history of alternating periods of abundance with years of scarcity. In the 1930s, bluefish were recorded as being plentiful, then they declined in population until the late 1940s, when they made a comeback. In 1948, they were added to the Derby prize structure because they became abundant in Vineyard waters.

That first year a four-pound, six-ounce fish won the bluefish division, and the following year the first-place blue was a five-pound, six-ounce fish. At that time there were approximately sixteen hundred participants. These statistics suggest that the population of bluefish was just starting to increase. Then it declined again in 1952 and 1953: not one bluefish was weighed in during those two years. By 1956 the bluefish were back and more substantial fish weighing ten pounds or more were brought to the weigh-in.

Even with the addition of bluefish, the overall winner of the Derby was the person who caught the largest striped bass. Most fishermen did not give much attention to the bluefish winner. As a matter of fact, some still feel that bluefish are a nuisance.

The first fish that I learned to catch were bluefish, simply because they were more abundant and easier to catch. Nuisance or not, I enjoy catching them.

Bluefish are the cause of the loss of massive amounts of fishing gear. The tackle shops benefit when the bluefish migration hits the Vineyard. They are essentially eating machines. They are created to bite. They have large razor-sharp teeth that are set into strong, unyielding jaws that will chomp and continue chomping on anything that slightly resembles food, including vulnerable members of their own tribe. Steel leaders that won't easily yield to their sharp teeth are highly recommended when fishing for blues. Even fifty-pound-test fluorocarbon leaders are not much of a deterrent against their sharp choppers.

Some fishermen feel that wire leaders discourage striped bass from taking their bait. I'm not convinced that it makes much of a difference, especially when fishing in big water. I've caught many striped bass with eighty-pound steel leaders. When fishing in what we call skinny water, where the ocean is calm and shallow, it's possible that heavy terminal tackle should be avoided.

One late October in the mid-1980s, an immense school of huge bluefish came into Lobsterville. The air was thick with a fishy odor and you could see the oil slicks all over the surface of the water. Hawkeye and I were fishing together one of those nights. It was after the Derby and since we were no longer allowed to sell them at that time, we were releasing all of them. We decided to keep one to share for dinner, a small one. We brought it home, and before we filleted it, we weighed it. We were shocked as it tipped the scale at eighteen pounds. That confirmed the fact that we were throwing back twenty-pound bluefish. I went back up-island to Lobsterville Beach night after night repeating the same insanity. My arms and back were aching. I decided to stop fishing for these enormous bluefish for the rest of that week. The fun had become work. I realized that there was not much sport in catching these monsters, and I was also damaging the muscles in my arms. It was an amazing once-in-a-lifetime big-fish blitz.

Fishing for bluefish with eels can be quite tricky. Unlike the striper that attacks the head of the eel, a bluefish will instinctively grab the tail.

There have been many times when I've felt the strike, set the hook, and played a big bluefish right into the wash, a few feet from the beach, only to have it let go and leave me with a useless two inches of eel dangling from my hook. We call it a cigar butt. Using lures is a better technique for targeting bluefish. When I'm paying two dollars for each eel, it can be an expensive fishing trip.

When fishing for striped bass, because they are more selective than bluefish and because the inside of their mouth is lined with small barbed toothy areas, an invisible fluorocarbon leader is more effective.

In 1981 three other species of fish were added to the Derby prize structure: weakfish, bonito, and false albacore. Now there were five different fish to target. The striped bass was still held in the highest esteem.

Weakfish are known as sea trout but also called squeteague by Native Americans. The name is based on the weakness of the muscles around the mouth. I have lost many squeteague because the lips have torn away from the fish and allowed them to escape from my hook. I know it was a weakfish when I reel my line in and find a lip on my hook. They are delicious to eat. I always thought they taste somewhere in between bluefish and bass: a little milder flavor than a bluefish, and white and lean like a striped bass.

Jackie and I were fishing somewhere up-island on the south shore. We were catching stripers. Lots of them. Suddenly, I thought I had landed a small bass, but when I shined my light on it, I was overwhelmed with the beautiful iridescent pinks and purples on the flanks of this shimmering fish. I fell to my knees and said, "Oh, Jackie, look how beautiful! Look at all the beautiful colors." It was the first squeteague I had ever caught.

"Get up," Jackie replied. "The bass are here, get to work." That's just the way he was. We were selling our catch, and when the fish were biting, there was no time to fool around and admire their beauty.

I caught many more squeteague after that night, and when I was not fishing with Jackie, I had a chance to stop and note all their beautiful iridescent colors. Until the mid-1980s there were many weakfish around the Vineyard. Frequently while I was fishing for striped bass, a school of weakfish would be mixed in or they preceded the bass bite just as the sun was getting low. When I fished Lobsterville in the late fall armed with a Boone's Needlefish, squeteague up to ten pounds were plentiful. The addition of the weakfish in the Derby was short-lived, though, and like the striped bass before them, they became almost nonexistent. In 1987, only six years after being included in the Derby, weakfish were removed from the prize structure.

Weakfish are still plentiful in some of the coastal states from the Carolinas to Rhode Island. When weakfish stocks first started declining more than thirty years ago, many blamed it on overfishing. Recreational fishermen blamed it on gill-net fishermen. Others blamed commercial operations in the southern states where the fish spend the winter. But when harvesting declined, stocks did not increase. In New England waters, we still find very few weakfish to this day.

The Atlantic bonito were abundant in Vineyard waters. I have my old weigh slips from 1978 that show I was weighing bonito into the tournament, but they didn't become part of the Derby prize structure until 1981. They are delicious to eat, and I would also sell them to the same restaurants that bought my bass and bluefish. Since Jackie did not want anything to do with them, I learned to catch them from the guys who fished the Oak Bluffs steamship pier back in the 1970s.

Jackie was a striped bass fisherman and felt that including bonito in the prize structure was ridiculous. "Daytime fishermen are not fishermen," he would grunt.

The pier was posted with "No Fishing" signs, but we would ignore them and climb over the fence. The ferry dock watchman would come to the end of the pier and tell us to leave when the first boat was about to arrive each morning.

Harold Hill, Arthur Winters, David Duarte, and a man named Howard Weaver who worked at the Boston House on Circuit Avenue were some of the regulars. Since I was the only woman, as usual, it felt like they adopted me. They kindly guided me and taught me how to fish for these "funny fish," as we sometimes called bonito and false albacore.

Bonito are challenging to catch because they swim like torpedoes. They have sharp teeth and keen eyesight. We use a small rod usually not longer than eight feet and light line with no leader because they shy away from terminal tackle. The ferry pier was probably at least twelve feet above the surface of the water. We had to lie flat on our bellies with a long-handled gaff to help each other land fish. In those days, the Derby scale was not so accurate, so it didn't matter as much as it does today with the current digital scale if your fish lost some blood from the gaff injury. Today's scale is precise to the hundredth of an ounce, so any loss of weight can make a difference.

During the fortieth Derby in 1985, I was bottom fishing at Lobsterville for bluefish, using fresh butterfish for bait. I had a heavy eighty-pound steel leader and thirty-pound monofilament line that was rigged with a four-ounce pyramid lead weight and a large 7/0 hook. I had a fish on my line.

As I was trying to land it, I kept thinking, "This doesn't feel like a bluefish." That year I had already weighed in a 14.35-pound bluefish the first day of the Derby and a 15.35-pound bluefish the second day, both from that same spot. To my surprise, it was an 8.55-pound bonito! I had broken all the rules I had learned about using light line and no terminal tackle for targeting bonito. Could that ever happen again? I don't think so. That fish took second place overall in the Vineyard resident category that year. I would call that lucky.

I remember when the Needlefish first came on the market. I thought, "That won't work, it has no action and it looks like a stick." The first time I tossed one into the water, a bonito grabbed it. That changed my view on that "stick." Now I always have a Needlefish in my tackle bag.

I caught the first false albacore of my life off the Oak Bluffs ferry pier in 1985. I was fishing for bonito, using a white Needlefish lure. Suddenly a fish hit my lure like a freight train. The fish took an incredible run and I watched my spool of line get smaller and smaller. If this were a bonito, it would be the biggest bonito I had ever caught. As usual, I was using eight-pound-test monofilament, so I did not want to put too much pressure on the fish for fear that my line would part. My hands were trembling and I thought for sure it would strip every yard of line from my reel. Finally it slowed enough that I was able to wind some of my line back on the spool. It soon took

My first-ever false albacore. It won first place in the
resident category, 1985.

another run that made me think again that it was going to strip all
my line from my spool, but once again it slowed down enough that I
could gain some line back. Finally, after another few minutes, which
seemed like an hour, I was able to bring the fish close enough to the
pier. One of the other fishermen gaffed it for me and we realized it
was not a bonito but a large false albacore—an albie, as they're called
on the Vineyard. It was before 10 a.m. and the weigh-in was still
open in Edgartown, so I grabbed the fish and headed for the scale.
Even after losing blood from the gaff, the fish weighed 11.70 pounds.
I took the lead for the largest resident albie and held it through the
entire Derby of 1985.

I fished religiously from the Oak Bluffs ferry pier, live-lining fresh
mackerel or menhaden, until the Steamship Authority banned us
around 1985, they said because of insurance liability. After getting
thrown off the pier, many of us moved over to Memorial Wharf in
Edgartown. I still fish there today.

The schools of false albacore became more and more abundant after that. By the early '90s we were catching false albacore up to twelve pounds every day. We would be lined up on Memorial Wharf, eight rods bent at once with huge albies on our lines. The Derby at that time awarded first through fourth for daily prizes for them. It was difficult to win a daily with a twelve-pounder. As the false albacore became more and more abundant, their inclusion in the Derby became controversial since they are a nonedible fish. Their meat is bloody and greasy and they have a strong fishy flavor. A few people swear that they can be eaten, but even if one finds them palatable, I can't imagine them being very healthy. The Derby now has a limit of three fish per angler, for the entire Derby. They don't award any daily pins for albies, only weekly and grand overall prizes.

The bonito usually arrive in Vineyard waters in late July or early August. At that time it is possible to catch bonito from the shore, but when the false albacore arrive soon after, they drive the bonito out into deeper water. They are larger and faster than bonito, and they compete for the same food source. The only way the bonito can survive is to go offshore to feed. For the last twenty years the albies have arrived in dense schools, and fish over ten pounds have become scarcer. Most of them weigh six to eight pounds. The boat fishermen are very successful in catching bonito, but from the shore it is a challenge, to say the least. The days of catching four to six bonito a day for me have ended. The last bonito I caught from shore was in 2001. In 1998 I took second-place shore grand slam. To get a grand slam, you need one of each species, and to win, they must add up to the most pounds. In 1995 I had a striped bass that was over 41 pounds, a decent bluefish, and a 10.24-pound false albacore. One 4-pound bonito would have put me in first place for the grand slam, but without a bonito, no slam.

Weakfish, bonito, and false albacore were added to the Derby prize structure in 1981, but the striped bass was still the most prestigious of fish. Fishermen who caught the largest striped bass were awarded trips to Costa Rica or Bermuda, and the largest bass was mounted by Wally Brown, the taxidermist from Falmouth. Grand prize winners for the other species received plaques, money, and fishing gear.

Then, in 1984, Derby participants were notified that the decline in the striped bass population was a cause of grave concern. The Derby Committee made a rule change: now each angler could weigh in only one striped bass per day, and it had to be at least thirty inches long. The state minimum at the time was twenty-four inches.

In 1985, striped bass were removed entirely from the prize structure. Now the fisherman who caught the largest bluefish would win the Derby. This was the first year that a seventeen-foot Boston Whaler was awarded as the grand prize.

These decisions were not made lightly. In 1979, Congress had passed the Emergency Striped Bass Act to study the alarming decline of the species. What scientists from the U.S. Fish and Wildlife Service learned about striped bass would assist them in helping the fish recover. This study showed that because of overfishing the striped bass population was much more susceptible to natural stresses and pollution. It also showed that fluctuation of water temperature at spawning grounds is the most significant natural stress on this fish. The scientists concluded that reducing pressure on the fish would have a positive effect by enabling females with eggs to spawn.

The Chesapeake Bay is the primary spawning and nursery area for between 70 and 90 percent of the Atlantic stocks of striped bass. Research conducted in the Chesapeake's Nanticoke and Choptank Rivers indicated that highly acidic rain reacts with aluminum in the soil, causing it to dissolve in the water. The combination of high acidity and aluminum is lethal to newly hatched stripers. Larval striped bass are also very susceptible to toxic pollutants like arsenic, copper, cadmium, aluminum, and malathion, a commonly used pesticide.

An Atlantic States Marine Fisheries Commission management plan, based partly on recommendations of this study, set size and pound limits to reduce the catch. In 1985, Maryland imposed a total moratorium on striped bass. The Martha's Vineyard Striped Bass Derby followed suit that same year and removed striped bass from the prize structure. Thus the competition became a striped bass derby with no bass. The Triple Crown category was created for those who fished for bluefish, bonito, and false albacore. The Triple Crown was awarded to the person who weighed in all three species and had the heaviest aggregate weight.

Jackie was the last first-place grand winner before the moratorium. When he weighed in his 48.75-pound striped bass during the 1984 Derby, he felt that there was not much hoopla. No one ever offered to take photos and the newspapers never reported much about his winning the Derby. Since I came in second that year, I agreed with him. Neither of us got any attention from the newspapers. We believed that because the harvesting of striped bass had become a sore subject up and down the East Coast, the committee and the newspapers downplayed our winning bass that final year.

Jackie had finally won the Derby with the largest striped bass, but the prestige that had once come with it was no longer there. He had a difficult time with the changes. His anger was obvious and it fanned the fire of his schizophrenia.

As time passed the striped bass became scarcer. It was obvious that they were in trouble. Here on the Vineyard, there were rising concerns about the mortality of the striper. My small group of fishing friends did not have a clear picture of why they were disappearing. We now know that it was not happening only because of overfishing but also because of pollution, loss and alteration of habitat, and inadequate fishery conservation practices.

In 1989, both Virginia and Maryland lifted their moratoriums on striped bass. Limited commercial and recreational striped bass fishing resumed. The Derby moratorium continued until 1993. By that time, I was a member of the Derby Committee. The committee was cautious about reinstating the striper back into the prize structure. The harvesting of the species was still, and remains today, a sensitive issue. The committee did not want to offer a monetary prize that would tempt the more than two thousand Derby participants to aggressively target stripers once again.

I had become a marine taxidermist by that time. I had a thirteen-inch fiberglass reproduction of a striped bass that I had hand-painted that I had bought from a supply company. I offered to make a special

Grand leader trophy created by my studio, Island Taxidermy Studio

trophy with it and donate it to the Derby. I mounted it on a wood panel and attached a brass engraved nameplate. The Derby awarded it to the single largest striped bass caught during the 1993 Derby, boat and shore division combined. Buck Martin was the recipient of that award. He caught a 54.74-pound striped bass on South Beach as he slept in a beach chair with his bait in the water. I might add that it was the first striped bass he ever caught in his life. Charlie Blair gave him the squid and baited his hook for him. Now that's a lucky catch.

In 1985, to commemorate the fortieth annual Derby, a separate fly rod division was added to the tournament categories. Fly fishermen no longer had to compete with the all-tackle fishermen. If they wanted to purchase a separate all-tackle registration, they could compete in both divisions. The registration fee was fifteen dollars and that first year they were awarded daily pins but no monetary prizes. Since that time, there are many more participating fly fishermen and they are awarded donated prizes of rods, reels, and line that are quite valuable.

In 1987, the prize structure changed once again. Since 1985, when the striped bass was removed from the prize structure, the major prizes were awarded to the largest bluefish. Now the Derby Committee decided to have a draw between the four largest fish in each category. Top winners from the bluefish, bonito, false albacore, and weakfish categories drew out of a hat for the grand prize. That year, it was the seventeen-foot Boston Whaler and a Yamaha motor. The resident and nonresident categories were also eliminated.

The following year, 1988, the award structure was changed again. It was the first year that boat and shore divisions were separated. The shore and boat anglers didn't need to compete with each other, but with only one registration a fisherman could weigh in their catch from the beach or a boat. Now there were eight fishermen eligible for the grand prize. It remains the same today, but we now have a major prize for each division.

The Martha's Vineyard Striped Bass and Bluefish Derby had changed from a nighttime, hard-core striped bass contest to an all-inclusive tournament, including women, junior, mini-junior, and senior categories.

The first forty years after the Derby was established it was run by the Rod and Gun Club and the Chamber of Commerce. In 1986 the organization became a nonprofit and is now run by a board of directors and a committee of approximately thirty-five nominated volunteers. Ed Jerome was voted the president, and he remains in that position today. Since the nonprofit status was established, the committee has awarded annual scholarships to the Martha's Vineyard Regional High School and the Vineyard's Public Charter School. Since 1986, it has donated more than $600,000.

When the striped bass was removed from the Derby prize structure in 1985, more and more fishermen turned their attention to the daytime feeders, bonito and false albacore.

My dear friend Bob Post, although he was skilled at fishing for striped bass, felt intimidated about fishing Memorial Wharf for bonito. Bob described himself as "a fisherman trapped in the body of a dentist." Each year, for one or two days during the Derby, he asked me if he could fish Edgartown harbor with me. I jumped at the chance to spend time with my humorous friend. He always made me laugh, and after spending so much time seriously fishing the tournament, I was ready for a little comedic relief. Bob was a novice at this technique and relied on my experience to guide him to hook and land a bonito.

Memorial Wharf is a difficult place to target these little green torpedoes, bonito and especially false albacore. When you get a hook-up it is a challenge to land a fish. It becomes a dance, lifting your rod over each spile without catching your line on any of the splintered pilings as your fish zigzags in front of the dock trying to get free from your hook. At times they swim under the Chappy ferry, not just once but sometimes twice, as the three-car ferry, *On Time,* crosses from Edgartown to Chappaquiddick. It can also be difficult to concentrate as tourists gather around you asking questions and watching in awe. If you bring a fish too close to the dock before its energy subsides, it will shoot right under the dock and cut your line on the barnacles that cover the spiles. It's typical to lose half of the fish that you hook. Every decade the cast of characters changes, but there is always an eclectic lineup of fishermen, from school-age kids to senior citizens.

Bob and I were fishing with live butterfish. We snagged the bait and free-spooled it in the current. This particular day, the tide was running very hard and we needed to put a small weight called a split

With a butterfish

shot in front of our bait to weigh it down, so it would not float on the water's surface. A split shot is a small ball of lead, about the size of a pea. It has a little slot in the top that your line fits into and then you pinch the lead around your line. A couple of split shots can weigh your bait down under the water and into the target range of a fish swimming past the dock.

Bob was putting a split shot on his line and asked, "Can I use your pliers?" I was looking down, putting a bait onto my own line, when I said, "You don't need pliers, Bob—just bite it." Then I looked up and saw the look on his face and realized I was talking to my *dentist*. I corrected myself, saying, "Of course, here are my pliers. Never, ever, ever use your teeth to bite a lead split shot." He smiled.

Since I was not targeting stripers during the moratorium, I spent most of that Derby not far from my home in Vineyard Haven, on the west side of Tashmoo channel. After throwing my bait out, with a weight to hold it on the bottom of the ocean, I used my bait bucket for a seat. I spent hours keeping busy, checking to make sure my bait stayed on the hook, and patiently sitting on my bucket as I waited for a bite. Most of the time I was alone, but sometimes I was with Jackie. Occasionally another fisherman would come by. Bob Post had stopped to chat a few times.

It was one of the last nights of the 1986 Derby, the wind was howling, and the rain was coming down in buckets. I decided to take a night off.

The next morning the phone rang. It was Bob Post. He said, "Where were you last night?" I told him I decided to get a good night's sleep. He said, "I caught a nice bluefish." I was happy for him because he had put a lot of time in and he earned it. But then he told me that he had caught it in the same hole I had been fishing almost every night for a month. I said, "You bugger."

He ended up winning the shore division for the largest bluefish. It was 18.95 pounds. I was genuinely happy for the little sneak, but only because we had a special friendship and I loved him.

In 1987 I had just opened the doors of my taxidermy business and he wanted me to do a skin mount of his Derby winner that he had frozen over the winter. I didn't feel that I had enough experience to tackle his huge bluefish.

He said, "Please, I trust you."

So I did the job. I love the fact that he trusted me before I trusted myself. Bob Post, unfortunately, passed away from leukemia in 1994. His family still has his bluefish hanging on their wall.

11

Fishing for Keeps

EACH APRIL, THE COUNTDOWN BEGINS until we are revisited by our most precious migrating fish, the striped bass. I am in a state of impatience as I wait for the shadbush to bloom, knowing the spring blossoms signal that the return of the alewives,* and the fish that feed on them, are not far behind.

Spring is also the time when our minds whirl with questions, wondering what the state of Massachusetts, and all the eastern coastal states, will decide to do with the size and bag limit† for the year. Many of us have spent the winter months sitting around tables at club meetings, hashing out our opinions about state and coastal regulations, saltwater licenses, and the keeping or releasing of fish.

In the '70s when I caught fish, there was not a question of keeping an edible fish. Striped bass and bluefish were plentiful, and I kept

---

* Alewife are a diadromous species. Diadromous fish migrate between fresh- and saltwater. They live in saltwater, returning to freshwater to spawn. Spawning occurs in early spring.
† Bag limit: the maximum number of fish permitted by law to be taken by one person in a given period.

The Blitz taxidermy sculpture by Island Taxidermy Studio

most of the fish that I could land. I could sell fish without a commercial license at that time, and there was a willing market.

When we were into catching valuable money fish, if I stayed on my knees admiring my catch for more than a minute, my fishing partner, Jackie, would shout at me, "What are you doing! Get fishing!" When the fishing was hot, it was not a time to pay respect to the beauty of the fish. We had fun, we fished hard, we kept our gear in shape with our earnings, and we brought fresh fish to the tables of family and friends. When we fished for striped bass, dollar signs danced in our heads. Along with being a fun activity, it was also a job. We never thought we could be doing something that was anything but positive.

So, what happened? By the early '80s, bass were becoming harder to find. I experienced this decline firsthand. The number and size of fish that we caught had noticeably decreased compared to five years earlier.

Surf fishermen had a difficult time believing that we could do that much damage with rod and reel, one fish at a time. Was it the commercial gill netters from all the coastal states that were taking too many fish?

I found the chatter among the fishing community disturbing. I realized everyone was pointing a finger away from themselves. The

recreational fishermen focused the blame on the commercial fishermen and the overfishing of the draggers. Pollution was blamed when
we discovered the damage from dumping chemicals and sewage into
the ocean and estuaries. There were no regulations to building on
the wetlands, and the loss of marshlands was a factor. The food chain
was disrupted and the sacred striped bass were obviously in decline.
The fear of totally losing the striped bass was frightening. We had no
internet back then, so information about what fishermen experienced
all over the country traveled slowly.

Once the dust settled from all this finger pointing, we realized we
all had a role in our environment and no matter whether we fished
with rod and reel, with nets and seines, or if we built structures on
the wetlands, or we littered the beaches, we were part of the problem. Although there was much disagreement on the reasons for this
decline, we concluded that if we truly cared about the mortality of
striped bass, it was every fisherman's duty to do their best to become
part of the solution and stop being part of the problem.

Up and down the Atlantic coast, fishing communities started to
take a stand. In 1984, Representative Gerry Studds of Massachusetts
introduced a bill that granted the Atlantic States Marine Fisheries
Commission the authority to ban and regulate striped bass fishing.
In October of that year, President Reagan signed the bill.

From Maine to Virginia, attitudes were changing on the local,
state, and federal levels. Protective measures were being put in place.

In 1985, the Martha's Vineyard Striped Bass and Bluefish Derby
omitted striped bass from the prize structure. I was not on the committee at that time, but I can imagine it was a difficult decision. Some
of my fishermen friends were not happy. Striped bass, the species that
had made the Derby successful, the most prestigious fish to bring to
weigh-in, were now eliminated from the prize structure.

Some called it a daytime fisherman's derby, with disgust in their
voice. All the mystique of fishing in darkness for the nocturnal-
feeding bass was a thing of the past. Some felt that chasing bluefish,
bonito, and false albacore was for the retired or nonworking crowd
who could fish in the daylight hours. Some of the hard-core bass

fishermen who worked all day and fished only at night did not join the tournament.

The striped bass may have been the forerunner in opening our eyes to the fact that no natural resource is inexhaustible. Since those times, attitudes on keeping fish or releasing them have changed drastically. It has not been an easy transformation but a slow and personal process, different for each individual fisherman. Instead of pride for landing the fish that has challenged respected fishermen over a lifetime of fishing, keeping a trophy striped bass was now looked upon as shameful.

My theory is that if you take a fish from the ocean, and let it die because you don't have any use for it, or time to fillet it and cook it, that's called "killing." Taking a fish to eat is called "taking" or "harvesting." Killing is a waste of a resource. When I decide to keep a fish to eat, I pause to honor it. I thank it for giving its life and providing food for me and my family.

As I look back in Derby history between the years of 1948 and 1951, four- to six-pound bluefish were the grand overall winners. I've heard tales of people landing bluefish and not being able to identify them because they were so scarce in the 1950s. Through the '70s and '80s it was hard to imagine that the bluefish would ever be hard to find. The abundance of bluefish is cyclical.

I sometimes think of the bluefish as a "scourge" while I'm fishing for stripers. Bass don't have sharp teeth, so I can use monofilament or fluorocarbon leader between the line and the hook. Their jaws are lined with rows of tiny barbs used for gripping their forage, and they open their large mouths to inhale an eel or bait. They swallow their catch whole. Bass also have tiny barbs on the tops of their mouths and down their esophagi. They clamp down on their catch. When I attempt to hook a bass but miss it, my bait comes back whole with obvious scrape marks on it.

A bluefish has tremendously sharp teeth and a strong jaw. I've heard them referred to as "the mouth that swims." They are eating machines.

You do not want to put your fingers anywhere near a bluefish's mouth. When they clamp down, it's a death grip. A large bluefish could do major damage to a finger. When they grab your eel, on the opposite end from where the hook is attached, they will hold on until they are close to shore, then let go. You end up with that useless cigar-butt-looking piece of eel. When the price of eel is two dollars each, one fishing adventure can get quite costly. I usually bring some lures or other bait with me so if I get into a school of bluefish, I can switch over.

My mentor, Jackie Coutinho, would pull his bait out of the water and take a nap in the car when schools of bluefish would start to destroy our eels.

Jackie was a striped bass fisherman, period. Bluefish didn't excite him the way striped bass did. Since bluefish were so abundant, more experienced fishermen didn't feel there was much of a challenge to catching them. Jackie would start cussing up a storm when the bluefish started chopping up our eels. Because I was not as experienced as he was at that time, I wasn't annoyed when the bluefish showed up. I just wanted to feel any tug on the end of my line. When I first started to fish, hooking a huge seaweed would get me excited.

I always kept some fresh-caught butterfish with me. Bluefish can take the entire six-inch bait in one bite, so it's easier to hook them. When the blues started biting, I baited up with a butterfish and fished until they were gone. Then I would wake up Jackie when the coast was clear, and we could target bass without having our eels bit off. It didn't even faze Jackie if I would end up with a huge bluefish to bring to weigh-in. He would cock his head back, press his lips together, and nod and smile at me. When I caught big fish, especially when I was by myself, I knew that he was never envious and his smile showed that he was proud of me. He usually caught more and bigger bass than I did. He was a striped bass magnet. I could usually outfish him with bluefish, most likely because he didn't put as much energy into catching them.

Snapper blues are immature bluefish and, like the adults, their populations become abundant and then decline. They are about five to ten inches long, have sharp teeth, and feed like the adults, tearing up everything they can get their jaws around. Bonito and false albacore fishing can become frustrating when the snappers are so thick you can't keep a live bait swimming for more than a minute before the snappers tear it up. For the first twenty years that I fished, snapper blues were abundant. Then for many years there was not a snapper to be found. After a ten-year natural fluctuation, in 2013, I noticed a larger population of these little rascals returning. They can be a nuisance, but plenty of snappers means plenty of adult bluefish for our children in our future.

Unfortunately, respect for all creatures does not come naturally to some people. The sea robin has a prehistoric-looking bony head with many spikes. The spikes are nonpoisonous, but you need to be cautious when taking sea robins off the hook as the spikes can pierce your skin and draw blood. It was a common sight to see not only young kids but also adults smashing sea robins on the jetty rocks or on the dock to get them off their hooks. This was a typical and unfortunate method of getting any undesirable fish off your line.

Some fishermen need to be taught to have compassion for these strange-looking fish, and most don't know that although a sea robin is not easy to fillet, they are delicious. I think they are beautiful creatures, but most fishermen see them as an ugly nuisance. When I've observed someone smashing a sea robin or other unwanted fish, I've given many lectures, saying, "If you are not going to keep it to eat, then let it go free." I tell them that every fish has its role in the ecosystem and when we kill something just because we don't like the way it looks, we upset nature's larger plan. It's not the right thing to do to any creature.

Making the decision to let any fish have its freedom has changed. The subject of keeping striped bass is a sensitive one, a difficult subject for me since I'm from the days of yore, when we kept almost everything.

Mike Cassidy was chairperson for the Derby when the minimum size to keep a striped bass was thirty-six inches. On one occasion, it was his responsibility to take some Slovakian visitors fishing to promote the tournament.

He took them out to fish on South Beach, Katama, in Edgartown. They were having a wonderful time, drinking vodka, enjoying the ocean, and communicating to Mike through hand signals like they were playing charades. Mike spoke no Slovakian and his party was not proficient in the English language.

One of the men hooked a fish. With Mike's guidance, they dragged it from the surf onto the beach. Mike put a tape measure on the fish. It was a big one, but not quite thirty-six inches. Mike took a quick photo of the men with the fish and said, "It's too small," and proceeded to release it into the surf.

The Slovakian grabbed the fish from him, yelling, "No, too big."

Mike said they played tug-of-war with the striped bass, with Mike attempting to let the fish swim free with a firm reply of "No, too small," the Slovakian man holding on to the other end of the fish, yelling, "No, too big." Mike finally won the battle when he pretended to put handcuffs on his wrists so they could understand that keeping this fish was against the law. The visitor finally gave up and the fish swam free.

I'm sure these fishermen from another culture must have been thinking that we Americans are an awfully arrogant bunch. How could a fish almost as long as a yardstick be called too small? A perfectly delicious fish that could have fed many people, thrown back into the sea. Mike told me that the visitors were treated to a dinner of striped bass before they left the island.

I know fishermen who have large families to support, or they are elderly and live on a fixed income, and if they catch a fish of legal size, without hesitation it is brought to the table.

The price of wild, local striped bass can be as high as twenty-two dollars a pound in the markets. You can purchase farm-raised striped bass year-round, but you can only buy local, wild striped bass when it is in season.

In Massachusetts, the commercial season for striped bass is approximately two months long. It opens sometime in June and closes by August. The catch is regulated by the Marine Fisheries Commission each year. Commercial fishermen must stop fishing for striped bass when they reach the determined quota. That quota changes from year to year, according to what the Marine Fisheries board sets. They hope the quota for the commercial fishermen will give consumers fish to eat but will sustain a healthy stock of striped bass. Recreational fishermen can fish for them year-round after obtaining a saltwater permit, but can only take one fish per calendar day, and that fish must measure a minimum of twenty-eight inches long.

There are novice fishermen who have put a lot of time and energy into trying to catch their first keeper. When a fisherman is lucky enough to catch a fish over forty or fifty pounds, naturally they want to bring it for a ride around town to show it to family and friends and maybe drop it off at their local taxidermist.

When I decided to become a taxidermist, I elected to learn the method of doing skin mounts instead of fiberglass reproductions. Since I use the actual skin to mount a fish, I can return the meat to the client so it can be eaten. When a fish is molded to make a fiberglass replica, the chemicals used for this process permeate the meat and make it inedible.

The pendulum has been swinging since the early '80s, and each fisherman has a point of view on the subject of keeping fish. We all started somewhere on our fishing journey, and sooner or later have been fortunate to experience many adrenaline surges of that tug on the end of our line.

There are those who have taken so many fish over the years that they feel that releasing fish is a way to make amends and do their part to help conserve a declining species. Some fishermen feel that they could not think of any reason to keep any fish, large or small. I know for a fact that some of the fishermen who declare the loudest "No one should ever keep a striped bass" are the ones who already have a taxidermy trophy fish hanging on their wall.

I follow the adage of live and let live. I think it's a personal decision. The bottom line is that we should all obey state regulations and federal laws. When we stay within the law, our decision should be no one else's concern. It's up to each individual angler to decide whether to keep fish or to release them. I talk to many local fishermen, I try to stay current reading articles in fishing magazines and newspapers, and I'm plugged into most of the hubbub on the internet. I understand that my perspective is limited to my experience. I choose to release about 98 percent of my legal catch each year, keeping just a few for food.

When a fish is released, if it's not handled carefully and the hook is not detached with care, the fish might not survive. Most anglers have switched from the traditional J-shaped hooks to circle hooks. The J-hooks are often swallowed by a fish, causing damage to the gills or vital organs. The circle hook is designed to hook the fish on the corner of the mouth, so it decreases the mortality rate of released fish.

When a fish takes a bait and swallows it and the fisherman begins to reel it in, the circle hook is safely pulled away from the fish's throat until it reaches the corner of the mouth. This results in fewer gut-hooked fish. Mike Laptew, underwater photographer and a fishing friend, educated me about using circle hooks in 1996. It sounds crazy, but they work. I am happy to know that the fish I set free are in a healthy condition and are most likely going to live on.

I'm in awe of every creature that swims in the ocean. When I pull a fish from the surf, I look closely at it, and no matter what species, it looks like a work of art to me. Closely observed, each scale that protects its fragile skin shines with a spectrum of iridescent colors. I'm in awe of fishes' eyes of yellow, gold, green, or blue. I love a close look at the thin, transparent fins that they use to propel themselves through the ocean, and their strong tails.

The caudal fin is the tail fin and is used for propulsion. The striped bass has a strong caudal fin that is not attached to the spine but is supported only by muscle. It controls swimming speed and movement.

Mike Laptew told me the following story about one of his underwater adventures.

He was filming with his underwater camera on a dive in the channel between Lobsterville and Menemsha, swimming around the Menemsha jetty. He told me that for a few consecutive years he saw a huge striped bass swimming around the rocks at the base of the jetty. He recognized this fish because it was missing one eye and it must have weighed at least forty pounds. He could swim close to it, on its blind side, to film its large, strong body.

When the fish would sense that he was there he told me, "It would disappear right before my eyes. I didn't even see it leave! I would hear a loud bang, as if someone hit a big drum." The caudal fin is so strong that when the striper realized Mike was near her, she swung her big tail with such strength, so she could get away quickly, that it created a deafening "bang" under the water.

Fishing gets me away from my everyday mundane life. I can take a walk on a beach, enjoy the wonders of nature, and maybe catch a fish. I especially enjoy sharing fresh delicious fillets from my catch with my friends and neighbors. Fishing gives me a feeling of union with nature. My passion to fish has brought me not only sustenance but also insurmountable pleasure. I've found deep friendships with other fishermen whom socially I would have not had the opportunity to get to know. Surf fishing helps to transcend all social, spiritual, and political differences. Through this love of fish and the ocean my life has been enriched. I've found careers in taxidermy, creating workshops that teach the techniques of fishing, shore guiding, and writing for sportsman magazines and local publications.

I recently reached a long and deeply thought-about verdict. I decided that if I ever get the fifty- or fifty-plus-pound bass that I have been searching for for the last forty years, I will take a photo and probably kiss it, as I give thanks to the fish and to my higher power, release it, and watch it swim on to live another day.

12

Derby Dames

MY PERSONAL HISTORY with the Derby started in 1976, thirty years after the tournament was established. At that time, most of the participants were hard-core fishermen and it was the men who dominated the leader board. Through its history very few women fished the Derby, and seeing any woman's name on the leader board was even more rare.

When I became a Derby Committee member in 1990, I realized no one had ever organized the history of the tournament. It took me about three years to collect old photos and memorabilia from the public. I collected photos, some one at a time, and others from a few plastic garbage bags that had been stored, some with water damage.

Along with two other committee members, Lori VanDerlaske and Chris Scott, I spent many hours sorting through these precious photos. We salvaged what we could and tried to keep them from getting damaged any further. I kept them in my office closet for a few years and we later paid the Martha's Vineyard Historical Society to sort and keep them for future generations. The museum held public showings

Left to right: Dick Hathaway, Buddy Oliver, Derby Queen participants, 1962. In the fore-ground: Buddy Oliver's son, Jessie Oliver III.

and asked people to come and see if they could identify people in the photos. They archived them so that the public could go to the museum and look for photos of old friends or family members.

Among those photos were ones of the historical Derby Queen events. In 1949, a social event was held at the close of the Derby. A local seventeen-year-old high school girl, Jeanne Brown, was crowned Derby Queen. I suppose they thought that this was one way to get women to participate in the tournament. Not many went fishing. In 1960 a dance was held and once more a contest for a Derby Queen.

Since the late twentieth-century, women have finally been able to walk into a tackle shop or go online to buy a pair of waders that fit. That door

A Derby dance at the Tisbury School auditorium, 1949. Jeanne Brown, a seventeen-year-old senior, was chosen as the Derby Queen.

Woman Angler Reels in a Fifty Pound Bass

Mrs. Albion A. Alley Jr. reeled in a fifty pound bass Monday night, fishing at Squibnocket, and this fish may well be a record for women's shore striper fishing. The best last year's derby could produce in this department was a twenty-one pound plus bass. In fact the resident grand prize winner, Wallace Pinkham's fifty-five pound plus fish, was the only one in the whole derby bigger than Mrs. Alley's. The fish, weighed on the Heathland Farm scales, actually tipped the beam at forty-nine and three quarters pounds, but anyone who wants to quibble about the four ounces can lay it to evaporation, or something. Mrs. Alley plans to enter the fish in the Schaefer contest.

It took twenty minutes to bring the fish to gaff, and Mrs. Alley did it all by herself, though her only previous catches had been much smaller fish. Albion Alley, her husband, said, "She did real well, too." And he ought to know, since he has been flailing south shore waters since before he could quite handle the rod.

From the *Vineyard Gazette,* 1955

has finally swung wide open. It only took about four hundred years after the days of Dame Juliana Berners for women to be respected as anglers.

The Derby archives hold the history of a few accomplished women surfcasters and boat anglers. According to the *Vineyard Gazette,* in 1955 Mrs. Albion Alley Jr. weighed in a fifty-pound striped bass. At the time, it was thought to be a women's shore striper record. I find it funny that she is called by her husband's name, "*Mrs.* Albion Alley," and the newspaper commented that "she did it all by herself"!

When my son, Chris, was four years old, he prided himself on landing an eight-inch scup "all by himself."

In 1955, Louise de Somov, from Long Island, New York, won first place in the nonresident category with a forty-five-pound, nine-ounce striped bass caught from the shore. One of her prizes was a California Sportsman Lodge to be erected on a piece of land in Gay Head that was donated by Cronig's Real Estate. According to a friend of theirs, she and her husband did not use the cabin very often and ended up selling it. Louise's husband was Serge de Somov, better known as "the Mad Russian." He won the Derby three consecutive years, in 1963, '64, and '65, and again in 1969. The couple's success at catching large striped bass was credited to the lobster tails that they were said to use as bait.

The late Jean Hancock from Chilmark still holds the Derby record for the twenty-three-pound, four-and-a-half-ounce bluefish she caught from her husband Herbie's boat in 1972.

Bernadette Metcalf is fondly remembered fishing with her husband, Ray, on a section of the Norton Point Beach connecting Martha's Vineyard to Chappaquiddick Island. While Ray fished near their Jeep, Bernie, as she was called, enjoyed taking long walks on a stretch of beach west of Wasque Point. After the breach caused by the hurricane of 1938 closed in 1951,* she noticed a sandbar that had formed beyond a deep hole near the shoreline. Ray and Bernie made this spot their own. They were known to haul many lunker striped bass and bluefish from this hole. Butterfish was the bait that they loved. Ray caught a fifty-one-pound, fourteen-ounce striped bass Derby winner in 1974.

I met Ray and Bernadette Metcalf when they were well into their senior years. I would sit next to Ray, snagging butterfish from Memorial Wharf in Edgartown. Bernadette was usually close by. He told me that his fishermen friends teased him when he caught big fish. They always said, "Your wife caught that!" The year after Ray passed away, the butterfish became very scarce. They seemed to have disappeared for a couple of years. Today Metcalf's Hole is still a productive spot for big fish; although it is not an obvious hole, it is named on some maps.

The Vanderhoop, Widdiss, Flanders, and Smith women naturally fished their backyard in Gay Head and Menemsha. Gladys Flanders and her daughter, Jean Smith, were up-island women who spent time at Lobsterville Beach. They were better-known Derby participants than any down-island gals because they weighed in many Derby fish. I would see them in the evening sitting in their beach chairs near the jetty, getting ready for an evening of bottom fishing. They were much older than I was, and I felt like it would have been awkward to go up and talk to them. Watching them from a distance, I imagined that I would be just like them someday.

Lorraine "Tootie" Johnson fished the Vineyard waters for about sixty-five years. For most of her life she slung bait and plugs from the shoreline and was also a familiar silhouette at Lobsterville Beach. In her senior years she fell in love with the fly rod and could be seen

---

* The barrier beach opened again with Hurricanes Edna and Carol in 1953 and '54. It closed in 1969 and stayed closed until 2007. It closed again in 2015 and remains a connection between the two islands today.

walking the beaches in search of a keeper bass. She told me that she had to have a piece of purple wampum or beach glass in her stripping basket before she felt confident enough to target a big fish. Tootie had no problem admitting that her favorite thing to do was to beat the men. "Some people don't realize how their voices can travel over the water," she told me one day. "I love it when I hear some guy say, 'Hey, the old lady got *another* one!'"

Irene Henley, the woman I met driving out to Cape Poge alone back in 1979, is still mentioned when the subject of women surf fishermen comes up in conversation.

In 1995 Lori VanDerlaske not only won the Derby shore division but also set a women's fly rod world record with a beautiful eighteen-pound, fourteen-ounce bluefish.

On Cape Cod in 1960, Rosa Webb caught a world-record 61.5-pound striped bass. She fished from a tin boat with her husband, David. They were known to catch many sixty-pound striped bass flipping dead mackerel from their tiny tin boat in North Truro. It is reported that less than half an hour later her close friend Kay Townsend landed a 63.5-pound striped bass on a beach nearby. Both these fish bested the women's all-tackle record of 57 pounds. They still hold a women's all-tackle record.

Kay Townsend and Rosa Webb with Women's all-tackle leader striped bass, 1960

One afternoon not long ago, I stopped at a convenience store to get some coffee. It was Derby time and my four-by-four was loaded to the hilt with my fishing gear. As I ran toward the store, I heard a man's voice say, "Hey, is your husband finding any fish?"

I never looked up and didn't miss a step as I yelled back, "My husband doesn't fish!" as the door to the store closed behind me. Some people's notions about women being able to fish take a long, long time to change.

Times are changing and it's uplifting to see a few more women fishing the shores around the Vineyard. When I took second place in 1984 with a forty-five-pound striped bass, I won $300, a rod and reel, and some other fishing gear. I did not win any acreage in Gay Head like Louise de Somov did, but with that fish, combined with the non-Derby forty-five-pound fish that I got on May 6, 1980, I did achieve a lot of respect from the local fishermen, and respect is all I really wanted.

I share some of my journey of being a woman surfcaster in hopes of drawing more female anglers out of the shadows. It was a hidden blessing for me that the fishermen who took me under their wings let me make all my own mistakes. I lost fish in every conceivable way: drag too tight, drag too loose, frayed line, setting the hook too soon or too late, and even losing my footing and falling down on my face. It's a good thing that I'm stubborn, or maybe just determined, because after many years of struggling, I have finally found my place in the fishing community.

I was never able to carry a biological child. God knows how hard I tried and that having children and a family was important to me. Every spare minute was spent chasing fish while most of my women friends were raising kids. I suppose fishing helped to fill that void for me.

I met my present husband, Tristan Israel, in 1985. I had just returned from my second bout in a rehabilitation center in Fall River. I was stark raving sober!

When we met, Tristan told me that he loved to fish. It was exciting to find a musically talented, handsome, sober guy who loved to fish! He didn't have any fishing gear, so I supplied him with my extra rods, reels, lure, hooks, and leaders. He even bought waders. We attempted to fish together. He resisted when I tried to teach him a few new techniques.

I soon realized that what he really meant was that he loved to catch fish. There is a big difference between loving to catch fish and loving to go fishing. Of course it's fun to catch fish, but then it is another story when the fish are not feeding in front of you and the hunt is on.

Tristan really didn't have any interest in maintaining his gear, getting up at sunrise, standing in the cold or pouring rain, trudging miles down a beach, and waiting and waiting and waiting some more for a fish to come. He does enjoy fishing by sitting in a chair or sleeping on a blanket on a beach with his radio on, listening to the Red Sox game, coffee in hand, and only when the weather is mild. Regardless, we were married on September 10, 1988. We planned that date because it was before the start of the Derby.

Jackie said, "I don't care who you marry as long as they don't mind if you fish with me." Tristan was just starting a landscaping business that kept him busy. He is also an accomplished guitar player and writes his own songs. When he has time, he performs locally. Right after we were married, he became involved in local politics. After serving on the Conservation Commission and the Planning Board he was elected to the Board of Selectmen of Tisbury. He was a selectman for twenty-five years, he's a county commissioner and serves on several nonprofit boards. Perfect: he found his niche, and that left me lots of time to pursue my passion, fishing.

In 1991, Christopher, a two-and-a-half-year-old child, came into our lives through the foster care system. Motherhood became a priority and my time to fish was limited.

Each fall when the Derby began, I could no longer fish sunrises or the crazy hours that I did before becoming a mom. Chris woke up every morning at 5:30, so after fishing through the night, I needed to be home by 5 a.m. That was also prime time to catch my bait so that I could live-line butterfish to target bonito in Edgartown harbor. Once the sun comes up, the bait can become scarce. It is one of the most productive spots to catch bonito and false albacore. After being up most of the night, I can sit on the dock and fish a live bait. That uses a lot less energy and I can keep a bait in the water for hours.

Memorial Wharf is the public boat dock in Edgartown. A passenger ferry boat, the *Pied Piper* from Falmouth, docks there a few times a day, loading and unloading tourists. When the ferry docks, everyone must take their baits out of the water. It gets complicated when you have a fish on the line. Sometimes they hold the boat so you can land a fish, but most of the time the fishermen need to get out of the way. There are charter boats, kayaks, and sailboats coming and going by the dock. The three-car Chappy ferry going back and forth across the harbor is another obstacle. The bonito and false albacore are small tuna and they can swim up to forty miles per hour. When hooked, they speed away from the dock across the harbor. It's not easy to land one with all the boat activity. I have lost many fish that got cut off because they swam under the ferryboat.

One late morning, after getting Chris off to daycare, as I was sitting on the dock struggling to snag a couple of butterfish, a woman visiting from California came by asking questions. Many tourists come by that dock wondering what everyone is doing. I answered all the typical tourist questions.

I told her that I was catching butterfish to use for bait to catch bonito or false albacore. I explained that the butterfish are tasty table fare but they are more precious used as bait during the Derby. She left and the next morning showed up again. She told me she came to the Vineyard from California for her vacation, that she had lived on the island for many years but had moved to Los Angeles.

The next morning, I dropped Chris off at daycare and returned to Memorial Wharf. It being late morning, I was once again struggling to find some bait. The woman was back again. She then told me she woke up before five o'clock every morning. Finally, I asked her if she wanted to learn to snag butterfish. She was delighted and said, "Yes." I felt like I was reliving the Huck Finn fence-painting story from *Tom Sawyer*.

I gave her my keeper and my little rod ready for snagging butters. It is rigged with a big treble hook on the bottom of the line and a small single hook about six inches above it, to hold a small piece of squid for the bait. Butterfish have a tiny mouth, so we wait for them to go toward the bait and then we jerk the rod up to hook them on the bottom treble.

The following morning when I showed up, she had caught a couple of butterfish and put them in my keeper bucket. I was back in the game, using live bait and catching bonito. When she came from Los Angeles, she enjoyed sitting in the sun snagging baitfish. For the next few years, she continued to get bait for me and some of the other regular dock fishermen. I was so grateful to her that I gave her all my women's weekly prizes to show her my gratitude.

Once Chris started kindergarten, I asked Tristan if he could get him ready for school during the Derby, so I could fish the sunrise and catch my own bait for live-lining for bonito. He agreed and became Mr. Mom for a month each year. I always made sure that he and Chris had food and clean clothes, but I neglected many of my household duties so that I could give my all to the monthlong tournament. If I was not fishing, I was getting a couple of hours of much-needed sleep. They enjoyed their time together without me.

We were finally able to adopt Chris six years after he came to live with us, when he turned eight. Since he is a member of the Wampanoag tribe, it was a complicated situation. The tribe told us there was no word in the Native American language for "adoption." The state has two options, foster care or adoption. While Chris was held in the foster care system, the goal was to reunite him with his family of origin. For the six years that he was in the system, our responsibility was to get him to all his therapy appointments and visitations with his biological mom, dad, brother, and other relatives. There was not much time left to let him be a little boy. All his activities revolved around pleasing the adults in his life. Unfortunately, the parents proved time and time again that they could not parent Christopher and his brother. After years of conferences with the Wampanoag tribe and the state of Massachusetts, they finally agreed to let us adopt him. Later, through a DNA test, his father of record proved not to be his biological father and his brother became a half brother. Not to mention that aunts and grandparents now became non–blood related. He wanted so badly to be adopted that he used our last name for years before it legally became his own. Once he was released from the system, we had time to get him involved with age-appropriate activities and our life as parents became more manageable.

Chris had a complicated childhood, and because he was a child of abuse and neglect, he came to us with emotional problems. He was developmentally and language delayed, diagnosed with reactive detachment disorder and ADHD, and besides was suffering from anxiety and depression. He was also found to be bipolar and was diagnosed with Asperger's syndrome. We made a commitment to him. Our work was cut out for us. He loved fishing and we enjoyed our time fishing together. We spent most late afternoons in the summer, after I finished my day in my taxidermy shop and he was not in school, fishing for scup at the Vineyard Haven drawbridge, the exact spot where I had begun fishing. He especially enjoyed riding in the four-wheel drive on the south shore beaches. He called it the "big beach." By the time he was four, although his speech was still limited, and he could not get the concept of a knock-knock joke, he was casting as well as any of my experienced fishing friends.

It was a struggle to keep Chris integrated into the public grammar school. At age eleven we ran out of options to help him get an education and resources to help him with his behavioral problems. He was sent to a residential school off-island for the next couple of years. The special education director said that Christopher used up every resource that was offered on the island and helped to create a few new ones.

It was not a respite for us as we were back and forth weekly, visiting and attending meetings with the professionals. After two years, Chris was returned home to us and integrated back into the school system on the island. He graduated from the public high school, and when he turned nineteen we got him enrolled in Project Forward at Cape Cod Community College. He lived with a family in a program called Toward Greater Independence on Cape Cod. After the first three months, they could no longer keep him under the same roof with the other kids, but we got him his own apartment and the program continued to oversee his schooling and appointments. After that year, he was on his own, and when he turned twenty-one he stopped going to school and would not keep any of his doctor appointments. We no longer had input over his decisions.

While he lived with us, it was too stressful to take vacations with him, so we did not do much traveling. Once he was safe and living off-island we took our first major vacation, to Sicily.

I researched surf fishing in Sicily and found a Sicilian surfcaster on the internet, Nicola Pizzino. Once I proved to him that my grandparents came from Sicily—I sent him the Ellis Island document proving my heritage—he opened communication and accepted us into his family. Nicola and I remain friends today.

Sunset on Eastville Beach, Vineyard Haven, 2000. Left to right: Lorraine "Tootie" Johnson, the author, Lori VanDerlaske.

Tristan and I rented a small apartment on a beach just a short distance from Catania where Nicola lived with his family. The first few days we were there, I wandered down to the beach in the evening when I saw the fishermen show up before sunset. They would not talk to me. They turned their backs to me. A woman on the beach in Sicily was still taboo. I felt like I was back in 1976 on the Vineyard.

I walked into a couple of tackle shops to share some lures and information from lure-building friends here in the States. The same cold reception. Nicola was the only fisherman I could find who would accept me as a fisherman.

Tristan tells people, "Most women love jewelry stores where they are surrounded by diamonds and gold. My wife is her happiest in a tackle shop or sportsman show amongst hooks, sinkers, and shiny lures." I appreciate having his support while I pursue my passion. He does think I'm a bit odd because I love being out in the bad weather and the darkest nights, but he never acts like it's anything but normal to have a wife who loves to fish.

I know my situation of living on the Vineyard is unique. When no one would take me fishing, I had the freedom to wander around on beaches in the dark of night alone and feel relatively safe. Women who live in the real world are not always so privileged to feel safe while pursuing a dream, especially when it involves an outdoor, male-dominated activity.

Other than a couple of days fishing in Cabo San Lucas in Mexico, Costa Rica, Nantucket Island, and the Cape Cod Canal with Charlie Cinto, my fishing experience has been limited to Martha's Vineyard. In 2017, I fished a few days on Cuttyhunk with some members of the Martha's Vineyard Surfcasters Association. That was a dream for many years.

Recently, I have been asked to speak at fishing shows and clubs around New England. I created a PowerPoint presentation that includes the history of women fishing. I suppose I have finally earned respect, not as a woman fisherman but as a fisherman.

13

Respect, Secrecy, and Fishing Ethics

THERE ARE UNSPOKEN FISHING ETHICS. Fishermen have secret spots, techniques, lures, and baits. I found a quote in *The Log of a Sea Angler,* published by Charles Frederick Holder in 1906. He is talking to a fisherman on a dock in Provincetown, who tells him, "You know most folks that fish for fishes keeps their business to themselves; They hikes off to some secret places and if they get a string they keep mighty mum." The secrecy behind fishing has been practiced from the beginning of recorded history.

I always thought that one reason why fishing information was kept secret was because money was involved. When I started my quest to become a surfcaster in the mid-1970s, most of the shore fishermen I knew held regular jobs but supplemented their incomes by selling fish. The catching season is fairly short. In early spring, when the water temperature rises and hungry striped bass and bluefish migrate up from the south, each fisherman hoped to be the first to sell to the Vineyard fish markets and local restaurants. The price paid for fresh fish drops as the fish become more plentiful.

After I teamed up with Jackie Coutinho, I became aware of small and secretive groups of hard-core island fishermen. Another reason for secrecy could be the lack of access to fishing spots. At that time we all knew that certain territory was claimed by certain groups, and I learned quickly enough to respect that. On the north shore from the west side of Tashmoo toward Menemsha, the parking spots are scarce. It was not unusual to hear that a fisherman's tires had been sliced if they intruded in another angler's spot. Cedar Tree Neck in West Tisbury was one of the areas where slashed tires were reported. Cedar Tree Neck Sanctuary is down a long dirt road. They don't want fishermen to park at the sanctuary or fish on the beach during the day when it is open. They lock a gate at night, but there is a small parking area on the side of the woods, just large enough for a couple of vehicles. I know a few fishermen who after an evening of fishing returned to their car to find their tires flat. One person came back after fishing to find his car had been towed. It's a long, dark, and scary walk back to the main tarred road. When I heard that, whether they were rumors or not, I decided to stop fishing there for many years.

The windows in Jackie's Wagoneer were smashed and all his gear stolen one night while he parked in an isolated spot in Gay Head. After that event, and even today, I usually empty my vehicle when I'm fishing desolate areas and only bring the gear I can carry. It's a shame that we need to keep our gear under lock and key and can't trust some of the other fishermen.

We never wanted to trespass on someone else's spot, and we expected others to have the same respect for places that we were known to fish. Jackie and I would purposely fish a few different beaches the first week of the Derby during the daylight hours. We *wanted* to be seen. When we found a spot on the beach where a nice deep hole had formed and we knew we wanted to spend time fishing it, we set up our bottom-fishing gear and sat with our bait in the water. It was a message to other beach fishermen that this was our hole. We made sure that we were seen on the north shore, the south shore, and maybe one place on Chappaquiddick. Once we established our territory, as far as we knew, the other fishermen stayed away.

Jackie could be a tyrant when he found someone fishing in his territory. He was only about five foot seven, but he was strong. He was a butcher at Cronig's Market when it was on Main Street in Vineyard Haven and wielded a big cleaver, cutting large pieces of meat all day.

One night he confronted the "Too-Tall Bergeron" twins on the west jetty at Tashmoo where we spent a lot of time fishing. He growled at them, "What are you doing here? You don't fish here." Both men, being well over six feet tall, towered over Jackie. We had never seen them fish there before. When I heard the story, I was glad that I had not been there that night. They told me later that they could have squashed him like a little bug, but decided not to get into it with him and left. I never saw them fishing there again. At that time, very few people fished that beach.

We had a pretty good idea where other anglers were fishing, and if we found out they had caught a big fish, we would never set up close to their territory. Not only could a fight break out, but we would be embarrassed to show up there the next day. Naturally, if the word got out about a major blitz, all ethics went out the window and at times battles ensued.

To earn respect as a fisherman, it's necessary to have not only the skill of hooking and landing a big fish but also the knowledge to be able to find them. It's about the hunt. Hunting is probably more worthy of respect than actually catching them. Although the days of selling our catch have ended, most fishermen remain secretive. I've learned from the old-timers to keep tight lips.

Since Stevie Amaral had been Jackie's fishing buddy for years, we usually ended up fishing near or with him until he partnered up with Mike Alwardt. I am not clear how Stevie felt that Jackie and I became a team. While fishing with Stevie, Mike won the Derby in 1995 with a 57.82-pound bass—the second-largest bass in the history of the Derby.

Jackie and Stevie had a terrible disagreement years after Jackie and I had become tight fishing buddies. One night while Stevie was fishing the opening at Tisbury Great Pond, he lost his favorite Danny plug on a cast. Jackie found it the next day but for some stubborn reason would not give it back. They both knew it belonged to Stevie. They didn't talk to each other for years because of that Danny. Stevie might have had an emotional attachment to that lure. Just before Jackie took his life, he made amends to Steve, and I am pretty sure they talked about that Danny plug.

A lure, especially if it catches lots of big fish, can become a personal favorite, and I know firsthand how someone can become emotionally attached to certain pieces of tackle. I had three rods stolen from my home just before the start of the Derby in 1981. Among them was my very first one-piece rod, a ten-foot Peterson that I bought at Brickman's, a store on Main Street in Vineyard Haven. The other rods were secondhand custom rods made by well-known local fishermen Buddy Oliver and Clayton Hoyle. They did not have much monetary value but they were like my right arm in the dark and they caught hundreds of pounds of fish. I was devastated, and still get upset when I think about how they were taken from my front porch where I stored them.

Bernie Arruda, a loner whom we bumped into often, especially at the Tisbury Great Pond opening, was a hard-core and respected fisherman. He had landed many bass over fifty pounds. I never saw him buddy up with any other fisherman. He has now stopped nighttime bass fishing during the Derby. As he got older, he spent most of his time at Memorial Wharf in Edgartown or on the tip of Menemsha jetty fishing for bonito and false albacore. In the spring, I would see him fishing in the freshwater ponds for trout. This last year, I did not see him fishing at all. Bernie was in on the Columbus Day blitz of 1981, and although he caught a couple of bass over fifty pounds, they were not large enough to get a daily prize.

Whit Manter and his dad, George, who was the West Tisbury chief of police, were always fishing at Quansoo on the west side of West Tisbury Great Pond opening. We could hear them across the pond as they banged their eels up against their metal hubcaps to stun them. The loud metallic clang could sometimes be heard above the whistling wind and crashing surf. It was common practice to stun our eels at times when they got unruly and tangled our lines even before we could get them into the water. Jackie would say that we needed to "knock some sense into 'em."

We would often see Jamie Gasper, with a couple of other fishermen, in a small motored skiff coming from the lower end of the West

Tisbury Great Pond to fish the Quansoo opening. They would also stay the night, and after they left, when the sun came up, we could see evidence that they used squid for bait. Like many other fishermen at that time, they would leave dead skates and dogfish scattered all over the beach. We could see that by using squid weighted on the bottom for bait, you need to "clean the fishing hole" of all the junk fish before you can target a bass. It seems that some fishermen think they will catch the same dogfish or skate again and again. It's a habit of some that instead of releasing them, they leave them to die above the tide line. This always disturbs me. I feel that every fish we catch is a gift and if you have no use for it, throw it back and let it live. When fishing for striped bass on the beach, next to a person fishing with squid, I've noticed that I might catch a few less fish on eels, but I usually rarely catch anything other than a striped bass.

Most of the resident island fishermen take a vacation from work during the last two weeks of the Derby and fish from sunset until sunrise, no matter what the weather brings our way.

It was also common knowledge that if you were fishing the Wasque Rip on Chappaquiddick during a blitz and you crossed one of the hard-cores' lines, they thought nothing of cutting your line with a knife or burning it through with a cigarette. Dick Hathaway was notorious for doing this. I saw it done many times. I learned quickly to keep track of my lure in the surf and stay out of the way of the more experienced fishermen as much as I could.

Clyde Omar, one of Dick Hathaway's fishing buddies, drove a big cherry-red Chevy Suburban. He was the first surfcaster to take clients on the beach. The Chappaquiddick fishermen were not very happy with him. The frenzy caused by a blitz of large feeding bluefish was difficult enough without adding six or more inexperienced fishermen to the mix. We could see him coming down the beach loaded with rods on the top of his Suburban and the interior packed full of novice fishermen. Aside from Forster Sylva, Bobby Fountain was the only visible caretaker on the beach for the Trustees of Reservations at the time. He would yell as Clyde was arriving, "Here comes Clyde with his Pilgrims." The fishermen lined up shoulder to shoulder casting into the Rip would groan. The term "pilgrims" is still used today for inexperienced surfcasters.

Cheryl Hope and her husband, Roy, fished many of the down-island spots, including the west side of Tashmoo channel. Cheryl and I spent more than a few nights on that north shore beach, sitting side by side on our bait buckets, chatting while we waited for a fish to take our baits.

Cheryl landed a fifty-pound striped bass right in that spot a few years before I began fishing. She gave me hope that maybe I could catch a trophy fish. She had a taxidermist perform a skin mount of her trophy fish. It was the first fish I saw that was not a fiberglass reproduction. I was in awe seeing this fish on her wall, looking into its open mouth and seeing the real gills and scale detail on its side. Her fish inspired me to become a taxidermist and to want to learn to use the actual skin of the fish.

I used to see Donnie Mitchell walk down the path and set up on the bottom on that same stretch of beach. He was about eighty years old and had been a dory man on a swordfishing boat when he was younger. He told me he once hooked a very large bass right there. To date I never hooked anything over thirty-eight pounds on that entire stretch of beach, but these stories keep me going back.

Some more of the seasoned hard-core island fishermen at that time were Francis Bernard, Al Doyle, Buddy Oliver, Porky Francis, Percy West, Ralph Grant, Cooper Gilkes, Eddie Gentle, Ray Metcalf, Danny Bryant, and many members of the Alwardt family. I can't pretend to have known every island bass fisherman personally, but we knew of each other and we knew where each group spent time. When the fish were plentiful, I shared the beach with many of them.

We didn't open up to many of the off-island fishermen, but Hank Schauer, a friend of Jackie's from New Jersey, earned the respect of many of the locals. He came each spring and fall to stalk striped bass. Hank would walk alone for miles around all the up-island beaches while casting a lure. Jackie and I fished with him many times over the years. He passed away in 2014 at the age of eighty-five and had come here to fish just two years before.

Kib Bramhall is another respected island surf fisherman and artist. I met him when I worked with his daughters at Helios restaurant back in the mid-1970s. He was on the staff of *Salt Water Sportsman* magazine, which I read from cover to cover while attempting to learn to fish. I talked fishing with him anytime I could get his attention. I had an old Penn 700 reel that a fishing friend from New Hampshire, Bob Gomache, had given me. Kib had one just like it, but it was broken at the reel seat. He gave it to me to use for parts. That Penn 700 was a prized possession for many years until it was stolen with all my other gear. Kib still holds the Derby record he set in 1981 for the largest striped bass caught on a fly rod. It was a forty-two-pound, fourteen-ounce fish. That is quite an amazing feat in the ocean, from the shore, on a fly rod. Kib Bramhall has the reputation of being a top-notch fisherman. There are many stories from island old salts who have fished with him. Kib always seemed to lie low, though, and has always been quite elusive on the beach. I never heard a negative word about him. I've had the pleasure of fishing near Kib at the Gut for albacore in the early morning and on the beach for bass, usually around sunset.

Bob Post, David Finkelstein, and Sherman Goldstein were a group of young professional businessmen—Bob a dentist, David an optometrist, and Sherman an entrepreneur. They fished Makonikey shore regularly. We all knew where they were fishing most of the time. If one of them weighed a fish in during the Derby, we were pretty sure we knew where they caught it. Jackie and I would never go to Makonikey to fish the following day. We received the same respect from them.

Bob Post interviewed some of the island locals and a few visiting shore fishermen for his book *Reading the Water,* which was published in 1988. One of its sixteen chapters includes an interview he did with me. Jackie was upset with me for granting him an interview. Although I assured him that I didn't talk about any undisclosed details or secret spots he took me to, I was severely scolded.

His book has become a classic. I couldn't believe it when, a few years later, as I was standing at my car, filling my gas tank, I was asked for an autograph. A man who later became a dear friend of mine,

With Bob Post fishing Wasque Point on Chappaquiddick Island. I'm wearing the new-style Gralite waders, the best you could buy at the time. They were made from PVC. They would stiffen up in the cold and you would freeze, and in the heat you would sweat. This was the smallest size they offered. Note that neither of us is wearing a belt. We both should have had belts on our baggy waders.

Ed Lapore from Connecticut, was the first one to ask me to sign his copy. At the time I was perplexed about why a book about some local fishermen could become so popular. I think now I understand why.

Bob Post was a gentle soul, and I think that because of his unobtrusive and nonaggressive presence he was the only person who could pry any information out of most of the bass fishermen. It was during the days when fish were being brought to market and everything was secret and fishermen were not talking, at times not even to best friends. Now fishermen are paying more than $200 for a first edition of his book and I am still signing my name to my chapter.

I feel privileged that I was fishing during these times and was lucky enough to be trusted with fishing information that was cloaked in secrecy. I'm thankful that I didn't give up, despite all the rejection I felt, and that I persevered through all the fear and frustrations.

Many attitudes have changed. Now, if word gets around where a fish was caught, some fishermen think nothing of showing up there the following day. It seems that today's generation of fishermen think that hooking and landing a fish is the entire game. I believe that I have gained more respect by knowing how to find fish on my own. I work hard at locating them and not following the crowd. Novice fishermen will sometimes ask me, "Where are the fish?" One reply I use is, "In the ocean." Or if someone sees me with a nice fish and asks, "Where'd you catch 'em?" my answer, as I pinch my lip, might be, "Right in the corner of the mouth." I was taught never to ask a fisherman where they caught a fish. I usually tell people, "Don't ask me where, because you'll make me tell a lie."

It's a matter of respect.

I don't want to hear all the chatter during the Derby. If I hear that so-and-so is catching fish in a certain spot and I don't find fish where I've chosen to go, I start to second-guess myself and then I am unhappy about where I'm fishing. Standing on a beautiful beach, enjoying a vermilion sky as the sun gets low, or standing under a star-lit sky, feeling upset with myself for not listening to other fishermen, is not a place in my mind that I want to be. I want to be happy, at least content, right where my feet are, catching fish or not.

Today there are many more fishermen living on the island and visiting from off-island. When I first started driving the beach, there were not many four-wheel-drive vehicles around. It seemed like only the serious fishermen or the very affluent owned four-wheel drives. Jackie told me stories about how when he was a kid they drove the beach in old pickup trucks with big overblown tires.

I had a conversation with Ruth Meyer. Her dad was the original owner of Larry's Tackle Shop in Edgartown and she was the proprietor for many years. Her entire family fished in the 1950s and early 1960s. Her dad drove her mom, her brother, and herself on the beach from Katama in Edgartown along the three-mile barrier beach to the Rip at Wasque Point on Chappaquiddick in a homemade beach buggy.

For Ruth and her family, fishing from the beach was a fun family event. She told me that her dad was always kind to her mom, who,

Jim Cornwell's beach buggy, a 1930 Model A Ford

no matter how many times she tried, could not seem to handle a rod and reel. Her dad, out of respect to the regular fishermen, would not let the family cast between them at the Wasque Rip until they could learn to cast directly in front of where they stood. Those were the days when fishermen would get angry and sometimes cut your line if you crossed them.

Jim Cornwell, now in his eighties, has been chasing striped bass since the days of the homemade beach buggy. He modified his 1930 Model A Ford with two Model A truck transmissions that gave it several speeds, forward and reverse. He said it could beat any SUV on the beach.

Even during the summer months, up until the late 1980s I could drive the beach from Katama to Cape Poge on Chappaquiddick on some evenings without ever seeing another fisherman or vehicle. Unlike today, there were no ropes, fences, or signs marking trails. There were no posted rules, so everyone was expected to use common sense when four-wheel driving.

The SUV has replaced the station wagon as the family car. The only beaches that we are allowed to drive on, with special permit stickers, are Norton Point, which is accessed from Katama in Edgartown, and sections of Chappaquiddick—unless the piping plovers are nesting. That happens anytime after June until September and the beaches are closed to vehicle traffic. Many, many miles of beach become inaccessible.

The days of driving on the beach at Gay Head and Long Beach are over. No more driving to the Tisbury or Edgartown Great Pond openings. No north shore access for beach driving, and unless one has permission to park, most of the access from the public town beach side of Lake Tashmoo all the way to Menemsha channel is limited.

Compared to forty years ago, especially during the summer months, the beaches can get crowded not only with fishermen but also with families enjoying a day by the ocean. On the south shore in Edgartown, the access to the beach at Norton Point has become so congested during the summer months that the Trustees of Reservations, who manage the beach, have started to limit the number of vehicles allowed to enter. I don't enjoy being on a crowded beach, so I rarely go during peak hours. I head out after six in the evening when most of the beachgoers are leaving.

I know this is not exclusive to the Vineyard. The entire world has become overpopulated, and no matter what your leisure activity is, we all have needed to learn to share space. The beach grass and dunes are fragile and we all have had to become more conservation-minded in order to cause less damage to the wildlife as we enjoy the wonders of nature.

The days of fishermen cutting your line because they are annoyed that you are fishing too close to them has ended. Helping a novice angler is more effective than intimidating them out of your way. When I'm fishing on a popular beach, like Wasque Point, and someone crowds me or casts their line over mine, I stop fishing and inform them of the etiquette of fishing. When I see people taking undersize fish, I give them information. I point out the state law and bag limits for whatever species they are taking. I explain that the reason for these restrictions is so that we will have fish for future generations. Since the Vineyard is short of environmental police, the responsibility is on the shoulders of the more experienced anglers. We need to police ourselves. Integrity is doing the right thing when no one else is looking.

In the summer of 2017, a thirty-minute ride north of Woods Hole, toward Boston, the Cape Cod Canal blew up with schools of large striped bass that were feeding on mackerel. The canal is an artificial waterway that connects Buzzards Bay in the south to Cape Cod Bay in the north. It's seven miles long, six hundred feet wide, and is part of the Atlantic Intracoastal Waterway. Known as the Big Ditch, it is one of the most famous fishing spots in New England. For a month, the striped bass continued to trap schools of thousands of mackerel on the rocky edges of the canal. Anglers came from as far as New Jersey, New Hampshire, and Maine to be part of this epic blitz of bass up to fifty pounds.

Charlie Cinto, striped bass record holder, has fished the Ditch for more than sixty years. He lives in Plymouth, Massachusetts, a twenty-minute ride away. He knows all the subtleties of the tides and variables of the long rushing currents that run back and forth from the east to the west end.

When I heard that fishermen were landing fish from twenty to fifty pounds daily, I was tempted to ask Charlie if I could come over and fish the canal with him. A few years before, I'd had a great time fishing the Ditch with him. It was my first time fishing the canal and I wouldn't have wanted to be with any fisherman other than Charlie. The current runs strong, so hooking a fish while standing on slippery boulders is a challenge, and it was a new experience for me. We caught bass up to seventeen pounds that morning

Charlie is now ninety, but he is still active and he's quite strong. When he's not busy in his "man cave" making lures, he's out fishing. One typical morning, he left his home in Plymouth at 3 a.m. to go fishing on the canal before the crowds showed up at sunrise. He has fished there for so long that he knows how to determine the tides and exactly what rock he wants to stand on to target fish. This particular morning, after he had been fishing for a couple of hours alone, a few fishermen showed up and started to fish so close to him that he could barely swing his rod to cast. Seven miles of running current and a guy stands so close to him that he can't fish.

He politely said to the guy next to him, "Hey buddy, I have a bad shoulder, could you please just move down a little?"

The stranger replied, "Why don't you just go home, old man." Horrifying. No human being should talk to anyone like that, and even worse, he was in the presence of a legend. Although Charlie wanted to punch him, he decided to leave, and now has second thoughts about fishing the Big Ditch.

This blitz of 2017 became a horrific scene of greed by some of the striped bass fishermen. Charlie did not partake in the slaughter. He told me the mentality of the fishermen has changed over the years and the days of fishing etiquette have ended. Some fishermen ignored the Massachusetts striped bass limit of one fish per day and were carrying two fish at a time up to their vehicles. Some stashed them in the rocks or bushes, letting them die, to sneak them out later. Some days there were a thousand fishermen lined up shoulder to shoulder. After getting reports from some of the fishermen who play by the rules, the Massachusetts Environmental Police (MEP) finally made some arrests. Five individuals were issued criminal summons along with several civil citations. In one swoop, the police seized 332 pounds of illegally caught striped bass, as well as many more pounds of illegally filleted fish and fishing gear. Sixteen pounds of fillets were seized from one fisherman, but they had started to spoil and had to be destroyed. Most of the remaining fish was donated to the New Bedford–area Salvation Army. I can't imagine how many fish were taken illegally. It's called poaching. Unfortunately, the MEP are shorthanded, and although these fish were slaughtered day after day, the authorities could not police the many miles of fishermen during the weeks of the blitz. I only hope this discouraged a few more from breaking the law.

14

Superstitions, Quirks, and Omens

FOR THE LARGEST FISH weighed in each day during the Martha's Vineyard Striped Bass and Bluefish Derby, participants receive awards of daily pins and a monetary prize of five to twenty dollars—enough money to help add gas to the tank or purchase more fishing gear. Many of the participants covet the daily pins and wear them proudly on their hats for all to see. There are also weekly prizes for all four species with merchandise and gift certificates. At the end of the tournament, eight grand leaders win valuable prizes donated by sponsors, plus they become eligible for a chance to win a truck or a boat worth near $50,000.

Each Derby participant receives a new hat with the Derby logo embroidered on the front and a Derby logo pin with a number on it. They tell the weighmaster their number that corresponds to their registration in the computer. Some fishermen pick a random number, but I have always wanted one that had some significance in my life. A fishing hat can be the most important fishing accessory. Not only does it keep your head warm and dry and the sun out of your eyes, but it also can bring good mojo.

Squibnocket mussel bed, 2014

I chose my first few Derby buttons at random, but I now have the same number each year after having had some good luck. Many Derby participants wear their buttons upside down on their hats until they catch a fish. That's not one of my quirks.

It was the second day of the monthlong tournament and just before the sun peeked over the horizon, I hooked and landed a forty-two-inch, twenty-four-pound striped bass. I was thrilled that it was early in the tournament, and although it was not an overall grand leader, it was a fish that could possibly win a daily pin or maybe a weekly prize. I catch and release many fish throughout the fishing season, but there was no doubt in my mind that I would keep this one and bring it to the weigh-in.

It was a bit of a walk to get back to my fishmobile and I wanted to get the fish into the cooler, on ice, as soon as possible. When I catch a large fish that I want to keep, I string a rope under its gills and out through its mouth. I take hold of the rope and immediately start running back to my car. After many years of fishing, I've figured out that while adrenaline is still racing through my body, I have the strength to carry a heavy fish. Once the excitement wears off, I'm not so strong. That morning, arriving back at my vehicle, I lifted the fish into my cooler full of ice. I then put my backpack loaded with fishing necessities away and stepped up onto the running board near my back door so that I could reach the rod holder that holds my rods on the roof. With the back door open, I began stripping off my coat, sweaters, and waders and piling them onto the seat. Once I took my waders off, I noticed I had forgotten to put my left boot sock on. I always wear heavy socks under my waders to protect my ankles from abrasion and to keep my feet warm.

The following morning, I awoke to my alarm at 3 a.m. and drove to the same spot and pulled into a small parking lot near a path that leads to the beach. Some mornings, especially coming home after fishing a late tide and after only three hours of sleep, I leave home wearing my pajamas. I don't imagine anyone will see what I'm wearing under all my fishing attire and I am more comfortable wearing jammies underneath. I was going through my daily ritual of getting dressed for battle, standing in the doorway of my car. I pulled on my lucky sweater and reached for my boot socks. I pulled one of the green wool socks onto my right leg and then I hesitated. I couldn't make myself put that other sock on my left foot.

"So, this is it!" I thought to myself. "I found the key to having good luck. Omit my left sock and the fish will come to me."

A week went by. My ankle was uncomfortable, the toes on my left foot were getting cold, and I had had no unusually spectacular fishing events. I gave in and began to wear both socks once again. I want to deny it, but it is obvious that I am superstitious.

Looking back over the years, I realize I have always worn a lucky fishing sweater. Most are not very attractive, but I am convinced they have helped me catch some magnificent fish. I sometimes wear a purple wool sweater that is so full of holes it should have been discarded at least ten years ago. I'm not ready to part with it yet because I've had some productive fishing trips while wearing it.

In the early '80s I lost my luckiest sweater. It belonged to my boyfriend Duane, and I caught the biggest and the most fish in my life while wearing it. It was a brown acrylic turtleneck with two deer on the front. Duane told people that his parents had asked him what he wanted for Christmas and he said, "Oh, just give me a couple of bucks." So they sent him this sweater with two big buck deer on the front. I think it brought me lots of luck, but then again I wore it in the late 1970s when large striped bass were abundant. When the fishing is difficult I wonder whether if I still possessed that "two bucks" sweater it might change the outcome.

I have a few articles of clothing that I keep in reserve, and when the fishing is slow for me, I pull them out of storage. I call them the big guns. Most of them are hand-me-downs from fishermen whom I admire. I have a green plaid wool shirt with a big rip in the elbow that belonged to Jackie. I save this for times when I really need some luck. Sometimes it works, and sometimes it just brings me memories of my mentor.

When I can't think of any practical reason why the fishing is so slow, I think of the idiom my friend Philip Willoughby would say. Philip gave me the nickname "Minnow." When we were fishing for bonito and sat together for hours swinging our legs over the edge of Memorial Wharf, patiently waiting for a bite, and I would complain about not catching a fish, Philip would say, "Well, Minnow, maybe you're not holding your mouth right." I've spent hours by myself on a beach in the dark shifting my lips and wiggling my nose, attempting to change the position of my mouth. Just in case I'm holding my mouth wrong.

Philip fished the Derby from the time he was a young boy, and finally in 1996 he won the shore division for the largest false albacore, 11.68 pounds. He drew the key for the grand prize, and I'll never forget his message as he jumped with joy on the stage at the closing ceremony. He screamed, "All you kids, don't drink and drug, just go fishing and this could happen to you." Unfortunately, after getting clean and sober, he lost a battle with cancer a few years later and died.

Folklore tales and myths have been passed down for generations. I've heard about many fishermen's superstitions and bad-luck omens, and some, although ancient history, one might want to avoid.

Never bring a banana fishing. Every boat fisherman knows that it is bad luck to bring a banana on board. I've heard stories dating back to the 1700s claiming that bananas caused boats to sink. Many times, the only visible sign of a shipwreck was the cases of floating bananas. This led to the superstition that the bananas themselves were to blame for the ship sinking and the lives that were lost at sea.

Some stories suggested that cargo ships carrying crates of bananas brought venomous spiders aboard and many of the crew died from spider bites. Once again, bananas were blamed for bad luck on a ship.

When I was mate on Ed Jerome's charter boat, the *Wayfarer*, for a couple of summers, bananas were taboo. I never heard of a boat captain who would allow a banana on board. It's an unspoken rule.

Many stories attribute a lack of fish to bananas. I don't take any chances and never bring a banana fishing with me.

One evening I had a teenage boy and his parents with me while I was working as a shore guide. The previous days I had had successful trips finding striped bass on Chappaquiddick Island. This evening, the fish mysteriously disappeared. The tides and weather conditions had stayed the same all week and we fished all the same spots that had produced striped bass. We were fishing hard but could not find anything after trying for five hours. I'm always disappointed when this happens even though my clients love four-wheel driving on the beach, witnessing a sunset, and seeing shorebirds and all the natural beauty of our islands.

As we headed home, the young boy was in the front seat next to me and his parents were in the backseat. I looked in my rearview and could see that the mother was eating a banana.

I said, "Oh no, I see you are eating a banana!" I didn't want to make it obvious that it was her fault that we got skunked, but I couldn't help myself and mentioned that a banana is often an omen of bad luck and it's a known fact that bananas keep the fish away.

Many boat captains thought that bringing a woman on board was bad luck. Sportfishing charter boats take women aboard all the time, and currently there are quite a few women who own and are captain of their own boats. Cynthia Riggs, author and proprietor of Cleveland House, a bed-and-breakfast in West Tisbury, is a most extraordinary woman. She is an author, poet, and sailor, and in 1948 she qualified for a place on the U.S. Olympic fencing team. She holds a U.S. Coast Guard Masters License for hundred-ton vessels. That's a captain. She has no tolerance for the boundaries that our society can put on anyone, male or female.

Linda Greenlaw, another author, was the first female captain of a commercial swordfishing boat on the New England coast.

For years I've watched commercial fishermen leave the docks from every harbor on the island as they head out for conch, fluke, lobster, haddock, and sea scallops. I never noticed any woman on board. I was surprised in the spring of 2017 when the commercial fisherman Donny Benefit invited me on board the *Payback* to go haddock fishing on Stellwagon Bank.

I joined him and his crew on that cold morning in April 2017. Peter Jackson was his first mate and Cooper Gilkes and Eddie Cottle were crew. We had an incredible two days. Using rods and reels, we caught the legal bag limit of haddock. The fish didn't go to market. Each of us got a share and the captain doled out the remaining fish to people in need in the community. We witnessed an epic pod of whales feeding and had a safe journey. As far as I know, my presence didn't cause any bad luck, and I didn't bring any bananas.

The fisherman and underwater photographer Mike Laptew not only has some of his own quirks but has adopted some omens from other fishermen. He had the opportunity to fish with Lou Tabory, a well-known fly fisherman and author of *Inshore Fly Fishing*. Lou told Mike that the butterfly is an omen for him. Mike was on the Vineyard doing some filming and he learned exactly how powerful the presence of a butterfly can be. While he was talking on the phone to his wife, Donna, who had stayed behind at home in Rhode Island, Mike spotted a butterfly!

He was excited and told Donna, "Honey, a butterfly, I see a butterfly." At that very moment a bird swooped down and grabbed the fluttering little creature in its beak and right in front of Mike's view quickly swallowed this good-luck omen!

Well, doesn't it make perfect sense that within the next twenty-four hours Donna called Mike with the news that both their water heater and furnace had broken down and needed to be replaced? Then the alternator on Mike's car broke, and when he got it fixed and found time to go fishing, no fish could be found! Was that poor butterfly that ended up on the bird's menu an omen of bad luck?

When I spend many hours at a time in the dark on the beach, my imagination can run away with me. It doesn't surprise me that sailors and seafarers who spend the majority of their lives at sea can be prone to many superstitions.

Many professions have superstitions, but it seems that fishermen have more than their fair share. Folklore dating back for centuries records such stories. Seeing a shark is a bad omen, but dolphins are known to be a good one. I've heard that it's bad luck to change the name of a vessel.

They say, "Don't whistle while you fish." I've heard it said that by whistling you can cause the wind to turn into a gale. I'm guilty of whistling. I don't have a very vibrant whistle, but I find myself attempting to whistle a tune to entertain myself. Maybe this year I'll stop that practice if the wind begins to blow too hard.

Charlie Cinto gave me a lucky rabbit's foot. I forget it at home most of the time, but I bet if I caught a huge fish with the rabbit's foot in my bag, I would never leave it at home again.

A few years ago, near the end of the Derby, the fishing was slow. When fishermen talk about being skunked, they mean they have not caught anything. During one of these dry spells, I was losing faith that I would ever catch another fish. I did everything I could to change the energy and get the skunk off my trail. I have never changed my clothes so many times in one fishing season, wished on so many stars, kissed eels, walked clockwise around my bait bucket, pretended to ignore my baited rod, switched hats, and tried to hold my mouth correctly. The daily Derby weigh-in boards indicated that not many fish were being weighed in, and that made me want to try harder to find a fish. I sometimes wish when the fishing is slow that I could just leave my fishing spot, go home, and hop in a warm bed and give up. The problem is, I don't know how to give up. I often say to myself, "Don't give up a minute before the miracle."

My love of fishing and my patience can become challenged. I have struggled with my mood as I spent too much time alone in the dark. I get angry with myself when I get unhappy while doing what I love to do, whether I am catching or not. I remind myself that at least I'm on a beach fishing. A bad day of fishing is better than a good day at work. Usually, after spending endless hours by myself in the dark during the first week of the tournament, I start talking to myself. As time passes, especially when the fishing is slow, I start answering myself. By the third week of the monthlong Derby, I feel like I am in group therapy with me, me, and me.

I get more serious when the fish don't want to cooperate, so I study my tides and the wind direction and do my best to find feeding fish. I change my bait often so that it is fresh. I fish spots that have historically produced striped bass and occasionally big bluefish. I keep my gear in good working order and know that I have done the footwork. Now it's time to wait. I keep my line in the water for many hours each day and night. It's the only way I know how to catch a fish.

Shooting stars are an omen for me. I believe that if before the falling star burns out I can get a crystal-clear picture in my mind of exactly what it is that I wish for, then my wish will come true. I watch the falling star and say aloud, "I wish for a big fish." Of course, I always try to picture a big trophy bass on the end of my line. It hasn't worked yet, but each time I see a shooting star, I wish my wish.

Rocks, shells, and trinkets that I find on the beach find their way into my pockets. I always think that a perfect purple piece of worn quahog shell or heart-shaped rock should surely bring good luck. I suspect that it is not what I am wearing or the trinkets I have in my pockets that affect the fishing, but I'm not sure. There are times when the fish are scarce or just not feeding. Yet somewhere in the back of my mind, I do believe that if I find the right combination of clothing and omens I will hold the key that unlocks the door to finding a Derby-winning fish.

I've had this discussion with numerous fishermen about their habits or the special rituals they perform when they prepare to go fishing. When I asked Walter Lison, he growled in his usual manner, "I don't have that problem." He made me think twice about my habits and superstitions. He could be right that those of us who must have all these details in place can be plagued by the loss of an article of clothing or not being able to find the perfect shell on the beach. Hard to

comprehend, but there are some anglers, without an omen or superstition, who just go fishing. No special hat or sweater and no spitting
on a favorite lure. But many fishermen are like me: they have certain
rituals that must be done before, during, and after fishing. Some of
these fishermen have shared their peculiar behaviors with me in a
most matter-of-fact manner.

Bob Merritt, whose tall silhouette is familiar to me when I see him
on the end of a jetty in the middle of the night, told me his good-luck
charm was his buddy Jerry Jacobs. Jerry is not always able to join
him, but Bob told me he is always excited when Jerry comes along
because it's almost a sure thing that he will catch fish. Unfortunately,
Jerry's luck isn't affected by Bob's company, because he is the one who
usually goes home empty-handed.

Chip Bergeron, a fly fisherman who is seldom caught in the act,
wears the same hat that helped him win the nonresident category in
the 1984 Derby with a forty-eight-pound striped bass. The morning
of his big catch he saw a deer. That has become his omen. I can
imagine how excited he must get when a big buck crosses his path.

You can spot some of these superstitious beach fishermen by their
raggedy attire. Maybe a hat that's been worn for much longer than it
was intended, a sweater whose aroma could attract critters, or strange
pins and bangles hanging from a jacket worn by one of the most
well-respected businessmen in town.

When my son, Chris, was young we would discuss subjects like
God, Santa Claus, and the Tooth Fairy. I always told him that I
believe in magic, because if you believe, anything is possible.

15

Tangling with the Fly Rod

IT TOOK A LOT OF PRACTICE casting my spin fishing gear before
I could cast a lure a great distance into the ocean. In the beginning
I had many missed casts and my lure would get caught in the wind
and land behind me or down the beach to the left or to the right—
anywhere but in the water. Reading fishing books helped, but there
was no book that could teach me the subtle techniques of fishing and
casting. Secret fishing techniques were mostly passed down through
families and close fishing friends. Until I found my mentor, Jackie,
I was struggling.

I learned to cast mostly by observing experienced fishermen. I
have been told that I cast like a man. I don't know what that looks
like, but since all the fishermen on the beach at the time were men,
that makes sense. I believe that the distance and accuracy of a cast is
achieved by technique rather than strength.

I had been surfcasting for more than twenty years before I became
interested in fly fishing. I had seen a few local fishermen use a fly rod,
like Roberto Germani, Cooper Gilkes, and Kib Bramhall, but the
more widely used method to fish in saltwater was surfcasting with a

Fly fishing in the Lagoon, Oak Bluffs

ten- to twelve-foot surf rod. With a surf rod, the lure that you throw carries the line off the spool. With a fly rod the heavy line carries the fly. The casting techniques are almost opposite from each other.

Roberto Germani moved to the Vineyard from Providence, Rhode Island, in 1982. We became fast friends fishing on Chappaquiddick beaches with our surfcasting gear. While driving by the Big Bridge between Oak Bluffs and Edgartown one day in February, I spotted him casting a fly into Sengekontacket Pond. I stopped to see what he was up to. He said that he knew the fish were not here yet, but he just wanted to practice his cast. He became a legendary island fly fisherman in a short time. He could be seen fly fishing out of his green canoe with his dog Banjo by his side.

Ken VanDerlaske and his wife, Lori, moved to the Vineyard from New York to teach fly fishing for the Orvis company. Ken convinced me that I should buy a fly rod. He knew how challenging it had become to find and hook a bonito, especially with the schools of albacore getting thicker each year. He showed me that when a school of bonito ran the beach, I could only get one shot at the school with spinning gear and my surf rod. I could cast my lure into breaking fish, and by the time I reeled my line back onto the spool and readied myself for a second cast, the school was long gone. If I didn't get a fish on the hook on the first cast, my chance to hit that school of fish again was slim. Traveling forty miles per hour, these speedsters can be very picky when feeding and don't allow room for errors in casting.

Ken demonstrated how he could cast his fly into a school of fish, gracefully pick up his fly on a roll cast, and in a split second cast again, landing his fly in the spot he predicted the fish would move to—and then repeat that a third time! Three chances to hook a fish within a few seconds. I was sold. My husband, Tristan, gave me my first fly rod for Christmas in 1994.

When I first attempted to use it, I truly believed that its design was defective. It felt too long and flimsy, and the butt behind the reel was much too short. Compared to my spinning reel, the handle on the fly reel is ridiculously small, and it cracked my knuckles as it spun around each time I hooked a fish and it took a run. After years of fishing with a ten- or eleven-foot heavy surf rod, the fly rod felt awkward. I kept stripping my leader into the tip of the rod and would put my reel in the sand, attempting to free it, because my arms were not long enough to free it from the rod tip. I found working with a fly rod difficult. Nevertheless, I kept at it and tried to overcome these frustrations.

Ken and Lori let me tag along with them from time to time. It was a privilege. Just as with surfcasting skills, I learn best by imitation.

When standing between Ken and Lori, I could cast quite well, but when I fished on my own, I would struggle with tangled line and hook the back of my hat or even my back end, especially after the sun went down. I had been flailing my flimsy fly rod to the point where I was hurting my neck and back. I got so frustrated that I would put it away and go back to my spinning gear. The years were passing, but when I add up all the sporadic times I fished with my fly rod, it was only a few weeks' worth of effort.

To this day, I am still struggling to *enjoy* the fly rod. I think most of us "old-timers" (I hate to include myself in that group!) have the technique of surfcasting so ingrained in our minds and bodies that mastering the fly rod can feel more like work than pleasure. Having an arthritic shoulder doesn't help either. After decades of performing the same motion with my body, each time I cast I don't give it much conscious thought.

In 2009, I decided to become a surf fishing guide and also to teach the basics of fishing with a surfcasting rod. I created a website, Vineyard Surfcaster (www.vineyardsurfcaster.com), and offered fishing workshops. I found there was a demand for taking off-island anglers fishing, but also for teaching the island folk who didn't have anyone to help them get started. It was also a fun way of making extra money. When I first started to teach surfcasting, I had to stop and think about what I was doing. I broke it down step-by-step so that I could explain my technique to first-time anglers.

The surfcasting rod and spinning gear is heavier and less flexible than a fly rod. After just one backward motion followed by a forward cast, I follow through with a downward motion until my rod tip is pointing toward the horizon. This allows the weight of the lure to pull the light line off the reel spool through the guides on the rod and a great distance into the ocean.

Casting a fly rod involves almost an opposite body movement. In order to cast the lightweight fly, the fly angler uses a fairly heavy line that can be "swung" in the air and carry the fly. The casting is done with a series of pendulum-like motions where the rod is tipped back and forth between two o'clock and ten o'clock, while the fly line follows its tip. By repeating this motion, the fly angler can give the line enough forward speed and length to deliver the tiny fly into the water. The most difficult action for me is stopping when the rod tip is pointing to ten o'clock. This is where my body rebels and wants to punch the rod forward, only to have my fly line drop from its graceful loops to a pile of tangles.

I was told that once I started to fly fish, I would hang up my surfcasting rod and never look back. I have had some enjoyable times with the fly rod and have even tied some of my own flies, with the help of Cooper Gilkes in his fly tying class. But I am not ready to put my surf rod away. When a twenty-knot wind blows in my face and a raging surf pounds at my feet, my heart beats with anticipation of a lunker striped bass grabbing my lure. That's when I want to be armed with my surf rod. When the surface of the ocean is just barely ruffled and a gentle wind is blowing, I am more inclined to grab my fly rod. I usually only bring the fly rod with me in early spring when the schoolies arrive, and then in late July and August when the water temperature rises and the big fish move offshore into deeper water.

I have seen experienced fly fishermen who can fish adverse conditions, but I'm not that proficient. I learned to fish from the generation that kept every legal fish to bring to market and the fifty-pound-plus striped bass was always the target. I am not proud of all the fish we harvested, but that was just how the attitude was at that time. Currently, because of the awareness of the depletion of so many fish and the fragility of the ecosystem, I don't keep many fish each season, but I am still challenged to try to break my own personal best records—and a fresh fish dinner is always met with gratitude. I don't want a fly rod in my hand when, after all the years of surfcasting, a big female finally finds me, maybe a sixty-pound striper. Once that happens, I might be satisfied and ready to accept more challenges of a fly rod! Here on the Vineyard, more and more fishermen fly fish in the ocean, especially when the false albacore arrive during the late summer months. Because the false albacore has a torpedo-shaped body and powerful tail, pound for pound it is one of the most powerful game fish a fly fisher can hook from the beach. False albacore's main diet consists of small baitfish. A fly is the closest imitation to a tiny silverside or sand eel.

One evening Lori VanDerlaske and I were determined to get me hooked up to my first fly rod striped bass. It was a dark night and we were up to our waists in murky water at the back of the pond at Tashmoo. It was a calm, spooky evening. It's not easy to throw a fly when you are standing up to your elbows in the water, but I had become skilled enough with the fly rod to want to give it a try. Some time went by, and as we cast our lines we stayed close enough to each other that we could hear our whispers in the dark. I finally felt the tug, set the hook, and very cautiously stripped in my line until I brought a fish to an arm's length away, where I could grab it.

"I got one, I finally got one!" I screamed. "I caught my first fly rod striper."

It must have measured all of twelve inches! We laughed so hard that we cried as I held up my tiny trophy fish. I removed the hook and released the little critter, after giving it a farewell kiss. This may seem to be a minor victory after being a hard-core surfcaster with quite a few decent fish under my belt, but I will never forget that evening and especially sharing that moment with a special friend.

To date it is still a challenge for me to hook and land a striped bass with a fly rod, especially when a school of toothy bluefish swim by me and steal my flies in the process.

Bluefish were another challenge for me, but after sacrificing many flies I finally landed my first one in 1999. The thrill of landing a fourteen-inch bluefish was overwhelming. I danced in the surf under the stars.

On May 16, 2000, I was once again driving the beach on Chappy heading out to target striped bass. During that entire week there had been a spring run of big, hungry bluefish. The tendinitis in my forearm was aching from catching bluefish in the Rip the preceding Saturday with my eleven-foot graphite rod and I did not want to hook into any more bluefish.

I was waiting for the sun to set so that, as usual, most of the day-time fishermen would go home. I had hopes that the bluefish would disappear after dark, as they often do, and the bass would come in close to shore. Under cover of darkness, big lazy stripers come in to feed on all the bits of bait that the gluttonous bluefish leave in their wake.

I took the three-car Chappy ferry and drove over the Dike Bridge to East Beach. I take this route when Norton Point is closed to vehicles because of birds nesting or beach erosion.

After driving past dozens of fishermen, I stopped to talk to my friend Chip Bergeron, fly fisherman extraordinaire. The fish were feeding quite a distance from the shore and Chip was having difficulty casting his fly far enough to hook one. Although he is a skillful fly caster, his cast was not long enough to reach the fish. With the hook removed from a three-ounce red-and-white Robert's Ranger lure, I started teasing the fish toward the beach to bring them within Chip's target zone. I was having fun *not* hooking a fish but watching them chase my plug close to the shore. Chip landed a few beautiful bluefish. Then he coaxed me into trying my hand with his fly rod. At first I was reluctant, but he was persistent and convinced me to give it a whirl. We traded rods. He took my eleven-foot graphite surf rod, which I call my machine gun, and I took his intimidating skinny, flimsy, whippy fly rod. I strapped his stripping basket around my waist and was ready.

After a few failed attempts to strip the fly through huge charging bluefish, I hooked up. With little grace and absolutely no technique, with my expert guru coaching at my elbow, the fish led us on a long walk down the beach. It was a challenge, but I landed my catch. It was not huge, but I was sure it was my personal best and I was thrilled. I carefully packed the fish in ice in my cooler to be weighed later that evening. Chip and I parted and I continued on my journey to the Wasque Rip. I managed to catch and release three nice keeper striped bass, the largest being thirty-four inches. I had an entertaining and triumphant evening unwinding from a day of work in my taxidermy shop. After I left the beach I brought my bluefish to be weighed in at Coop's Bait and Tackle so that I could enter it in the Martha's Vineyard Surfcasters Association in-house derby before I filleted it and served it for dinner. It weighed 5.94 pounds—my largest fly rod bluefish to date.

Since then I have upgraded my fly rod. I bought a rod that has better action and a reel with a stronger drag system. The rod is an Orvis Clearwater II, nine-foot, nine weight, and the reel is a Redington AL 9/10. I have always prided myself on the fact that I am versatile in my fishing techniques. I catch my own bait, from sneaking up on night crawlers to jigging my own squid. I fish for many species and use many techniques, from bottom fishing to slinging eels and plugs. Now I just need to conquer that silly, flimsy fly rod without ending up at the chiropractor with a neckache and sore shoulder.

16

Delusions of Grandeur

WHEN I'M FISHING, especially when I'm alone at night, I do a lot of wondering. Such as why is it that whenever I set out to fish, I'm bursting with high hopes and feelings that the fish will be there? More times than not, I return home after hours of fishing and never have a bite.

People say to me, "You catch lots of fish!" However, what they may not be aware of is how many hours I put into fishing and all the times I come home empty-handed and bewildered because I didn't even get a little tug on the end of my line. Yes, I have caught lots of fish in my life, but compared to the hours I've put in, I would say the fish are the victors.

I also wonder why is it that after all my years of fishing I haven't yet been able to break my own personal record of forty-five pounds for a striped bass. I've known fishermen who have only fished a few times and caught fifty-plus-pound fish. Can a fisherman become overskilled and underlucked? I wonder.

I figure there are two categories of fishermen: recreational fisher-

Pilot's Landing, Aquinnah, 2014

men and "hard-core" fishermen. The first group might set out for an afternoon fishing excursion. They have a great time, whether they catch fish or not, and after a few hours they call it a day. Then they return the following week or month to have some more fun.

The hard-core fishermen might go out to fish on a rainy evening, stay until the sun rises, and catch nothing, only to return the next day or night and repeat this insanity.

I've had many conversations with fellow fishermen, trying to find the word that best describes this driven behavior. "Compulsive" comes pretty near, and "insanity" is a close second.

The Martha's Vineyard Striped Bass and Bluefish Derby runs from the middle of September to the middle of October. During this competition, fishing can become hard work. Because it's a five-week Derby there are times when I struggle and ask myself if I'm really having fun.

The 1996 fall fishing season was very slow, to say the least, and some of my theories of why I enjoy fishing flew out of my head and washed away in the surf. My buddy Hawkeye used to say, "Fun has nothing to do with it!" I don't want to think like Hawkeye, because I know that I used to be able to maintain some sort of balance between competition and having a good time. The Persuaders hit the nail on the head when they sang, "It's a thin line between love and hate."

Recently, a couple of people approached me and said they were out to beat me in the Derby. That made me feel uncomfortable. I seem to have a reputation, but I hadn't won any major prizes in years, so I wasn't quite sure what they were talking about. I'm having a hard time competing with my own fishing history and there are lots of personal records and goals I would like to accomplish.

I'd like to think of myself as a recreational fisherman, and I think that most of the time, I am just that. However, since I don't fish all winter, when the spring season begins I spend a lot of time replenishing my fishing deficiency. Then again from September through November I have an insatiable appetite to stand on the water's edge under a starry sky, looking for that trophy migrating bass. I know that the fish will soon begin their journey south, winter will be upon us, and I will be back to my day-to-day responsibilities. Another saying that keeps running through my head: "Once you've become a pickle, you can never go back to being a cucumber!" I suppose I've become a pickle, and my cucumber days are over. I have known many people who have fished all their lives and are able to stay in the cucumber category. So what exactly is it that separates recreational fishermen from the hard-core?

Recently I became aware that I have delusions of grandeur each time I set out, rod in hand. What causes this state of mind? I know many fishermen who have had the experience of the last cast, the one that finally attracts the fish they are in search of. After fishing for hours on end, I've said to myself, "Just one more cast," and finally a big fish takes my bait. This could be the reason why I keep fishing while more reasonable fishermen have given up for the day and gone home.

Maybe it's called faith, or perhaps it is called optimism? What about hope? I do know that I always start out excited with images of landing a world-record fish. Here's what I'd been dreaming day and night in the weeks before the 1996 Derby opened:

First I'd pop off a forty-inch striped bass during the first couple of hours. Then I would switch to targeting a bluefish. After I caught a twelve-pound bluefish, I could relax until the sun started to rise. Once it got light I could see myself hooking up to a bonito and a false albacore before the weigh-in opened. That would be the perfect start for the Derby: a grand slam on the very first day.

Here's what actually happened:

The first night of the 1996 Derby I was fishing with my photographer friend Mike Laptew. He had come from his home in Rhode Island to fish with me and to video the first couple of days of the Derby. Mike's love of fishing had led him to a career as a free diver and a spearfisherman. Having reached all his goals by becoming a national champion in that field, he decided to trade his spear for a camera. His underwater videos of striped bass are phenomenal. I have become a better fisherman from watching his videos that show the behavior of fish in their natural habitat.*

Our plan was to be on the beach and have our line in the water the minute after midnight when the monthlong Derby began. My adrenaline level was so high I could barely breathe. I had done some searching the previous week and found some decent bass. The tide was perfect, the northwest wind was in our favor. I brought Mike to one of my favorite secret north shore spots where I've hammered big stripers under these same conditions. We fished for bass from a minute after midnight until about 6 a.m., catching and releasing five or six bass each. Unfortunately, not one fish was over thirty-one inches. It was a beautiful and productive night but a little disappointing after all my anxiety and my delusions of grandeur.

Mike left me on the beach to go film opening day at the weigh-in at 8 a.m. It was predawn, so I stayed behind, hoping to catch a decent bluefish. Finally, aha! I got one. I thought it might possibly weigh the required minimum, four pounds. I kept it and got it on ice as quickly as I could.

It was just daybreak, so I put away my eleven-foot heavy rod and grabbed my lightweight eight-foot rod. I focused on catching a false albacore or maybe a bonito. I was not about to give up yet.

No bonito and no albie.

* For more about Mike and his videos, visit his website: www.laptewproductions.com/videos.

I looked at my watch: it was 7:45 a.m. My curiosity got the best of me and I knew I'd better get to weigh-in to find Mike and see if any of the other contestants had found fish that night. At least I got a little bluefish for the first day.

That year the weigh-in was in Oak Bluffs near Jim's Package Store at the bottom of Circuit Avenue. I arrived at approximately five minutes past 8 a.m. My God! Fishermen were lined up at the door with lunker bass! Mark Plante had a forty-seven-pound bass, Steve Amaral had a decent fish, and Gordon Ditchfield had a bluefish that weighed almost twelve pounds! There were probably more than twenty fishermen who had twenty- to forty-pound bass.

"Well," I thought, "we all have to eat humble pie at some point," so when the long line subsided I finally swallowed my pride and snuck my bluefish out of the cooler and handed it to the weighmaster. Only 3.69 pounds! Oops. It was under the four-pound minimum for that year's Derby regulation. I was crushed, but nevertheless it did make for a delicious dinner.

Later that morning the weather turned. The wind picked up and it started to pour rain. The previous night, Mike and I had been all alone in my secret hot spot, so I knew where the fish were not.

I should have gone to bed after being up all night, but then came another delusion of grandeur! Once again my mind was consumed with the hope of catching a big striped bass. I told myself, "I know where they got those fish: my second-favorite spot! It's a nice cloudy, rainy day, the wind has come around southwest, and stripers love feeding in these conditions even in the daylight hours. I can catch the other end of the tide." The passion of the chase had taken over once again.

By then it was noon and the Derby was only twelve hours old. Mike went to bed. I'm sitting on my bait bucket in the pouring rain on the south shore, wind in my face, blowing about twenty knots. The beach is deserted because all the fishermen who slammed big fish between midnight and six in the morning are tucked into their warm beds, catching up on some sleep.

My self-talk has begun.

I'm having a good time.

This is fun.

I'm doing the right thing.

The fish were here last night; they're bound to return this afternoon.

Boy, I'm having so much fun.

I'm sure I'll be able to catch a beauty for tonight's weigh-in.

I've been waiting all year and it's Derby time once again!

Then the hours passed. I saw no signs of fish. My thoughts took a turn for the worse.

This is ridiculous.

This isn't fun!

I'm supposed to be having fun!

The Derby is only fourteen hours old and I'm already obsessed.

I'm soaked and exhausted, and if I sit here all day I'll be too tired for tonight's fishing.

I'm not *having fun!*

I'm going home!

I packed up my gear and drove my fishmobile off the beach and headed home. I got into my warm bed to catch a couple of hours of sleep before I picked up Chris from his after-school program. I made dinner, weather band radio by my side and the tide chart in my free hand. By the time Tristan got home from work, I would come up with a plan for the evening. It was 6:30 p.m. and I was out the door and on a mission once again, telling myself, "*Now* I'll get that big one!"

After fishing all night without a hit, the weary feelings disappear just as the sun starts to light the sky. Splashes from bonito and false albacore become obvious on the surface of the ocean as they start to feed at daybreak. The stillness of a long, dark night comes to an end and the fever strikes. A newfound energy carries me into the morning.

A tide change, a wind shift, a rising or setting sun can swiftly change my feelings of disappointment into new energy that keeps me marching toward my next hoped-for monster catch.

Where is it coming from, this constantly renewed sense of hope that keeps me captive all the way through to the very last day of the Derby?

Last day of the Derby dream:

I get the hit I've been waiting for after decades of targeting a trophy striped bass. It's an incredible lunker for sure! It's an hour and twenty minutes before the final bell rings. I've timed my travel to get to the weigh-in just for this very moment. I land an amazing world-record eighty-nine-pound striper. (As the years slip by my dream fish gets bigger and bigger.) As I pull it from the surf onto the beach, I catch my breath and rise from my knees after chanting toward the heavens, "Thank you! Thank you! Thank you!" Adrenaline pumping through my muscles, I lift this monster as if it weighs a mere twenty pounds and gently toss it into my cooler in the back of my buggy. I speed toward the weigh-in and just thirty seconds before they hit the final bell, I drag my winner to the scale. Yeah, I win the Derby!

The nightmare:

The same fish, same time, same spot. The same dream—until I turn the key in my ignition. My fishmobile has gone dead! WD-40 doesn't do the trick. My CB radio is out of commission. I knew I should have invested in a cell phone. How to get to a phone, and should I call 911? Maybe they will send a cop or an ambulance to transport me to the weigh-in. The entire Vineyard knows how important the Derby is. Maybe I could drag my fish off the beach and hitchhike. That won't work, I'm too far from the road! No other human beings in sight! I'll never make it! I am overwhelmed with desperation. The final bell sounds.

I wake up in a pool of sweat, run downstairs, grab some coffee, throw my smelly lucky sweater on, grab some eels, jump in my buggy, and head for the beach to fish another day of the Derby.

17

PTFD
(Post-Traumatic Fishing Disorder)

IN 2011, GREG MYERSON, a fisherman from Branford, Connecticut, caught an eighty-one-pound, fourteen-ounce striped bass. It set a new International Game Fish Association (IGFA) all-tackle world record. When I read his account of catching that fish, I was imagining being in his proverbial shoes when he hooked it and played it to the side of his boat.

"I couldn't budge him at first," Myerson told *Field and Stream* magazine. "Then he took off on a real good run and I had to tighten the drag because he was burning line fast."

In another account, he said, "I felt the fish come out of the rocks, take a few long runs. Then I could see its huge dorsal and tail break the surface."

I could picture his net folding with the weight of the fish. What a feeling of relief and disbelief he must have felt once the fish hit the deck! I can only imagine what went through his mind when he put her to the scale. That fish changed his life forever.

Charlie Cinto never expected to hook a seventy-three-pound striped bass that day in the waters off Cuttyhunk.

Charlie Cinto on his way to weigh with his world-record seventy-three-pound striped bass in 1967. He slipped in the boat and cut his nose, but he's still smiling.

Charlie Cinto holds a record for that seventy-three-pound striped bass he caught while on a charter with Captain Frank Sabatowski off Cuttyhunk in 1967. I met Charlie at a Massachusetts Striped Bass Association (MSBA) sportsman show in the year 2000. He had just moved back to New England after spending many years in Florida. He told me that his dream was to be able to fish the entire monthlong Derby. Many years before, he had come to the Vineyard during the Derby with a small group of fishermen and rented a house, but he could only afford to stay about a week.

We own a small ten-by-ten-foot cabin, with electricity, located right behind our home. It is perfect for a tournament fisherman who only requires a clean bed to sleep in, a place to cook with a tiny refrigerator, a shower attached to the main house, and an outhouse. I invited Charlie to come for the Derby to fish with me, no charge. I was happy but surprised when he came and stayed the entire month.

He told me, "My friends said, 'You'll never keep up with her.'"

I learned that I have an off-island reputation for being a total fishing maniac. Charlie was seventy-one years old at the time and I was fifty-two. Did he keep up with me? Yes, he did.

Charlie is a legendary striped bass fisherman but never fished for bonito and false albacore. I tried to tell him to leave me when the sun came up, so that he could go and get some sleep. He insisted on sticking with me for hours chasing "little green torpedoes." I was by his side when he landed his first of many false albacore. Now here is a fisherman who has decades more experience than I have, and I was privileged to watch him catch his first of a species.

Fishing together most of the night and part of the daylight hours was an adjustment for both of us. I was not accustomed to fishing with someone every day of the Derby, since Jackie had passed almost ten years before. Charlie is from the days when most men felt that it was a man's duty to take care of a woman, and he was not used to being with such an independent gal.

The first evening we fished together, we were setting up two rods each with squid and putting them into sand spikes for a night of bottom fishing. Charlie, attempting to help me, was getting in my way while I was putting my bait on my hook.

I kindly said to him, "It's okay, Charlie, I got this." He made no movement to go back to tend his rods.

As I struggled to bait my hook once again, I repeated, "Thanks, Charlie, but I can do this."

The sun was going down and his body was blocking the view of my hook. The darkness was making it even more difficult to see what I was doing and I was having a hard time putting my bait on with his helpful hands in my way. Then I lost the grip on my rod and it almost fell in the sand.

I finally said, "Damn it, Charlie, will you just leave me alone!" I'll never forget the look on his face as he danced back over toward his own gear. He said, "Oh, yes ma'am!" but I could see he was confused. He's the kind of guy who bends over backward to help everyone. I love that about him, but during our fishing times, he was getting in my way, trying to help me do something I had been doing on my own for decades.

It took some time for him to understand that I know who I am. I know that I'm a woman, a mother, a wife, a fisherman, and I don't mind him opening a door or carrying a heavy load for me, but when it comes to fishing and getting my bait in the water, I do it on my own.

After spending hours on the beach together, we discovered that we are a match made in heaven. We were both born in January, both of Italian descent, both five foot something in height, and of course both striped bass fanatics. He has been an amazing friend and fishing partner for many years now. He stays busy making lures all year round. He has made a couple of special rods for me, and one of the lures that he makes, "proud popper," is one of my favorites.

We've all heard stories and have seen the photographs of the big fish that get landed, but what about those big ones that win the battle? There are many stories about the "one that got away," but for some mysterious reason, in more than thirty-five years of fishing, I myself had never lost a trophy-sized fish. I did lose one fish that was in the thirty-pound range one afternoon when I was fishing with Charlie.

One early June, he came to fish the spring migration with me. The Edgartown Great Pond had been opened to the ocean and a few thirty-pounders had been landed that day. Charlie had one on the beach and I was patiently waiting with my bait sitting nicely on the bottom, hoping for my turn.

I finally got the hit I was waiting for. My rod bent over and I set the hook. I smiled at Charlie and exhaled to enjoy the song of my drag screaming. Then, all of a sudden . . . slack line.

When I reeled in my slack, I had a little wiggly on the end of my line. No hook, no leader. I had lost the fish on my knot!

I had been using an improved cinch knot since Jackie taught me to fish, but I am always willing to try something new. That day, I was using a knot that Charlie invented.

If memory serves, he said, "Oh yeah, I lost a couple on that knot!" I started to growl under my breath. Now he said, "You just didn't tie it right."

I never used that knot again. I am pretty sure I am over that one by now—pretty sure.

The following day, the water was full of a heavy, thick seaweed that we call mung and it made it impossible to fish. As hard as we tried, for an entire tide of more than six hours, we could not get through the weed to catch a fish. It was frustrating because we knew that there were some big fish feeding underneath.

I consider anything over forty pounds to be a big fish, and I know that every fish I have hooked in that category, I have landed. Believe me, when you are in the surf, there is no doubt that you are battling a fish of that size. It's a little like suddenly being hooked to the bumper of a VW bug going fifty miles per hour.

Unlike Greg Myerson, I haven't had the opportunity to hook many fish that size, but I was fortunate enough to be fishing back in the 1970s when fifty-pounders were certainly a possibility. Twenty-eight- to thirty-two-pound fish were an average day's catch back then, and there were many fish between forty and fifty pounds to be had. Unlike today, we never talked in inches; it was always about pounds.

Traditionally, Martha's Vineyard does not have the most productive surf fishing in August. We call it "the summer doldrums." When the water temperature rises, the stripers seem to abandon the shoreline. Looking for cooler water, they take up residence farther away from the beaches, in the deep holes. Over the years I had not spent many summer nights on the beach looking for bass. My time was better spent in the daylight watching for splashes from breaking schools of bonito and catching bait for the freezer to use during the monthlong fall Derby.

I had been working for more than twenty-five years in my basement taxidermy shop, up to my elbows in fish guts. After I started a shore guide business in 2009, Vineyard Surfcaster, it was a new adventure for me to be out after dark with my clients, stalking striped bass during the warmer months of July and August. I normally fished hard during the spring and fall run of bass and then fished daytime for bluefish when the water temperature rose and the larger fish moved out from the shore into deeper water.

The 2011 fishing season was quite unusual. Fishing in the spring for striped bass and bluefish was slow. The new moon period in June, which is usually spectacular, did not happen. Not for me, anyway. We caught some nice fish, some of them weighing as much as thirty pounds, but not the usual migration of big bass.

Then, on August 9, 2011, I lost a really big fish.

I was fishing with my friend from Connecticut, Aram Berberian. We had worked together at the Home Port and Square Rigger restaurants many years ago, and although he fished summers on the Menemsha jetty when he was a kid, he had recently slipped over that line and gotten hopelessly hooked on surf fishing for striped bass. I love fishing with people who are newly stung by fishing fever and are enthusiastic about fishing new spots and breaking personal records. When Aram visits the Vineyard, we get together to do some fishing.

I had been doing fairly well at the breach at Norton Point and he had never fished that area, so we took a ride out in my Chevy Trailblazer.

When we arrived at about nine in the evening, a few of the regulars were already there: Bob "Hawkeye" Jacobs, Ralph Peckham, and Stevie Amaral. It was a rainy and cloudy evening, and thunderstorms were predicted. These are the conditions that excite me. The wind was blowing southeast at about twenty knots and it was difficult to fish. These were not easy conditions, but I had a partner in crime, so I figured, if he was willing to stay, we'd give it a try.

It was blowing hard. I switched lures quite a few times, but the wind was putting a big bow in my line and I couldn't feel any of them swimming through the water. I was going through all my containers of lures in the back of my fishmobile, but after casting my heaviest Darters, Bombers, and Danny plugs, not one of them felt right. The other fishermen must have been finding it difficult also, because one by one, they jumped into their buggies and headed back to Katama.

I finally put on a Stan Gibbs three-ounce light-brown-and-white swimmer, sometimes called a Bottle plug. Earlier that week I had been catching fish on the root-beer-colored Darter, so I knew if the bass were around they were probably feeding on squid. Brown and white seemed like a good choice. I caught my first forty-five-pound bass on a blue-and-white Stan Gibbs swimmer back in 1980 when the conditions were similar. At last I felt connected and I was *fishing*! I felt it hit the water, dig in, and start to swim.

By then everyone was gone except me and Aram. Steve's taillights were still fading in the distance when I had the hook-up.

Nice fish! It felt like it was in the twenty-pound range. I had it on for a while, but as I got it closer to shore I couldn't control it. All I could see was a splash of white water as it broke the surface and spit the hook. Damn, that was a nice fish—it is always difficult to get a good hook set when the wind is cranking and the water is agitating like a washing machine. "Oh, well," I thought, "no big deal, and now at least we know that there are some fish in front of us." I rechecked my drag to make sure it was tight enough to get a good hook set but loose enough to "let 'em run."

About a half hour later, Aram was back at the car looking to find a lure that would work best for him. I threw a nice long cast, and before I could feel my plug hit the surface of the water, I was on with a fish. I think my plug must have landed right in its mouth. I barely took a crank on my reel handle and *WHACK!* I screamed into the wind, "Aram, fish ON!"

This fish took off straight toward Nantucket. I heard the high-pitched *zzzzzzzzzzzzzzzzzzzzzzzzzzzzzzzzzzzzzzzzzzzzzzzzzz* as my line peeled off my spool. The sound of the drag was music to my ears. I knew immediately that this was a fish of a lifetime.

My heart started pounding and then my first thought was, "Oh my God, I am going to get spooled!" as the line was quickly leaving the spool on my reel. I then thought, "No, that won't happen. I have a fresh spool of 50-pound-test Power Pro braid on my Sustain 8000." That's about 350 yards.

After a long run of about 150 yards, the fish slowed for a few seconds and I was able to take some cranks to recover some of my line. I started to relax but then it took off again, straight out from the beach into the dark. Again, my drag sang as it stripped another 50 yards of line. Again it slowed, so I could recover some line and my spool started to fill once more.

My new ten-foot Century Stealth rod was bent about 180 degrees and my arms were tense with the weight of the fish. I was fervently

With a big one, 1989

hoping that, as advertised, this beautiful lightweight rod could handle the pressure of this big fish.

Then suddenly, my line went limp. It was gone! I couldn't believe it. *Gone.*

I felt like I had been kicked in the gut. I felt ill with disappointment. I reeled and reeled and reeled in my slack line until I got to the end. My 50-pound-test Power Pro had parted. Cut clean. No plug, no 175-pound-test Tactical Fishing Clip, and the 50-pound-test fluorocarbon leader was gone as well. My braid had parted, not frayed but a clean cut. All I could do was shake my head and utter one F-bomb after another.

What had happened? My mind started to sort through all the scenarios. Was it a shark? No way could I have had a shark on my line for that amount of time with a 50-pound-test fluorocarbon leader. A shark would have cut me clean at the hook on the first run. I have caught brown sharks up to eighty-five pounds from the shore and knew that it was not a shark. Could it have been a seal? Seals are not known to take long steady runs like that and probably would not have grabbed a plug the second it hit the surface of the water, especially at night. I had been fishing this area for weeks and had only seen an occasional seal.

Was my drag too tight? Possibly, but since I had lost a couple of nice fish the year before when they straightened my 3X hooks, I had learned to lighten up on my drag when using braid. Braid has no stretch to it, unlike monofilament, which has just a little bit of stretch. I had also switched to 6X hooks for occasions just like this. These hooks are six times stronger than a regular hook and should surely not bend no matter how large the fish is. I checked all my guides for any defect that could nick my line, but they were new and smooth. A nick in my guide could make my line break under the stress of a fish. There was no solution to change the outcome of losing this fish.

"Okay," I told myself, "take a deep breath and let it go."

What a fish. I am convinced that this was the biggest of my life. All those years I had been saying, "I never lost a big fish." Now I had a story of losing a *big* fish.

I am convinced that when it is your turn to catch a fish, you will land it no matter what you do wrong. I have seen it happen time and time again. I have seen fishermen land big fish with old line, rusty hooks, and rods and reels in terrible condition. I've seen them land fish with a drag way too tight or too loose. I've certainly landed fish many times that should have gotten away because of one thing or another.

I once landed two nine-pound-plus false albacore at the same time on Memorial Wharf. One was hooked in the mouth and the other fouled by his tail in my 12-pound-test line. Landing those two fish was pure luck. I know that when it's my turn to catch a fish, it will happen, no matter what!

So why was it that on that night as I was trying to fall asleep, I kept reliving losing that fish? In the morning, the second I opened my eyes, my thoughts were fixated on those few moments of hooking and losing that fish. For days after, I could not stop thinking about it, over and over again I was reliving scenario after scenario, before, during, and after that episode. I was begging the powers that be, "Please erase this moment from my mind and help me to let it go."

I started thinking that I was running out of time and might *never* in my life get another shot at a fish of that magnitude. I was getting depressed. I wondered if I might have PTFD—post-traumatic fishing disorder.

A few days later, I was talking with Tony Jackson, who also spends time on the same beach. Before I'd said anything about my traumatic evening, Tony said, "Justin Pribanic lost a *screamer* the other night!" He also said he had heard of a couple of other guys who had hooked into big fish and lost them. That got my attention. I blurted out my story to Tony. Suddenly I felt a little relief. "Maybe, just maybe," I told myself, "there are other really big fish out there and I still might have a chance of catching the fish of a lifetime."

There are very few fishermen on the beach late at night during the summer. I fish Chappaquiddick and Norton Point most of the time because they are the only beaches that I can drive on with my four-wheel drive. Ron Domurat is one of the surfcasters whom I see most nights. I asked Ron if he had ever experienced PTFD from losing a big one.

This is what Ron told me. He said about two years ago he had almost the same experience, in the very same place, and thought the same things that I thought. He said he could almost use my words. To this day, he still had trouble believing it was a striped bass.

When the fish hit, it felt pretty good and fought normally, and like many fish, it ran toward shore until it was about fifteen yards away. Ron said, "It then took off for about sixty yards but I turned it and regained about half of the line I had lost. It took off again on a slower second run of about thirty yards and I thought to myself, 'Wow, I've got a really good fish here,' but it didn't feel unusually heavy and I was winning the battle. I turned it again, again regaining about half of what I had lost in line. Then it took off on a run that I couldn't stop or even slow until my braid broke cleanly with about fifty yards left on my Van Staal 250. The final run was so strong and powerful, I could barely lift my eleven-foot Lamiglas much above a point parallel to the water. I kept saying to myself, 'This can't be a striper, this can't be a striper,' and I still have problems believing that it was. Once it took off for good, it never tired, and I can't believe even a world-record fish would not slow or tire during a run like that. Also, I never felt a tail slap, line rub, and the fish never slowed.

"At the time, it really didn't bother me all that much because I had so much trouble believing it was a striper. I've come up with theories and rationalizations that include hooking a decent fish that was grabbed by a big seal or a shark, or that it was in fact a big shark. But the more I think about it, the more I think that maybe, *just maybe,* it was something very special. And like you, with stocks crashing and my age working against me, I doubt that I'll ever get an opportunity like that again."

Ron continued, "But it wasn't the first big fish I lost. Two weeks after the 2008 Derby had started, I was on the north shore, waist deep in water and throwing eels on an early-morning falling tide, with the wind howling out of the southwest against the tide. On my fifth cast I had a solid pickup and hooked a huge fish that made a hard run down current. I finally turned it and was working it toward me almost parallel to the shore. When I finally got it to within about thirty yards of me, the 8/0 Gamakatsu hook inexplicably pulled out. I was sick. It was the biggest striper I had ever had on. Scott Tompkins won the boat that year with a fish just over forty pounds. I'm guessing this fish was in the forty-five- to fifty-pound range. This is what I wrote in my logbook: 'I was shaking and had to sit down. I couldn't even fish any more that night. I went on to have a good Derby and won the senior division with a twenty-five-pound fish but the loss of that fish and what might have been will haunt me until I leave this planet.'"

Ron is not new to surf fishing and I believe him when he says a fish was probably close to fifty pounds.

I asked Charlie Cinto if he had ever lost a really big fish and been tortured by it.

He said, "You had to remind me."

Sounds like another case of PTFD.

18

Bad Luck, Good Luck

WHEN I FIRST BEGAN to fish the surf, my rods were made of fiberglass. Before fiberglass, most fishing rods were made of bamboo or hollow steel. When graphite rods came on the market, we all thought they were the best, most sensitive, lightweight but strongest rods ever. One of our fishing buddies, Steve Amaral, knew a guy in Quincy, Massachusetts, who made custom graphite rods, so in 1979, Jackie and I asked Stevie if this guy could make us each a custom rod. They cost about $150 each. That was big money at that time, especially for a waitress.

Oh, how I loved that fishing rod. It is an eleven-foot graphite and I can't tell you how many big striped bass, bluefish, and weakfish I caught on it. I would use it to cast my lures into the ocean for hours on end. With that rod I could throw a great distance and could outcast many of the men who fished by my side on Chappy. When Jackie passed away in 1990, I inherited his eleven-foot graphite rod, the twin to mine.

Technology stayed the same for over thirty years, until some new composite rods came into play. The new graphite composite rods are lightweight but at the same time strong. In comparison, my old eleven-foot graphite feels like I'm casting a stiff, heavy tree branch! No wonder my body now suffers from a worn-out spine and neck pains. The bursitis in my right shoulder is probably a result of casting that eleven-footer for four to six hours at a time. Currently when casting for hours I use a ten-foot Lamiglas or Century Stealth. They are both much easier on my arms and both cast a large lure a great distance, without expending much energy. I now use my old eleven-foot graphite rods for fishing bait on the bottom, not for throwing a lure.

Quansoo is a stretch of beach on the south side of the Vineyard, at the mouth of the Tisbury Great Pond. Thanks to the island's prevailing southwest wind, there are usually tremendous rolling waves that crash on the shoreline. Most of the forty-plus-pound fish that I have caught came from this stretch of beach. Quansoo just might be my favorite spot to fish—but then I think that my favorite spot is wherever my feet are.

It was the seventieth annual Martha's Vineyard Striped Bass and Bluefish Derby. The fishing was not very productive. The water temperature was still around seventy-four degrees and I think that the fish were just not feeding before beginning their migration to the south. I decided to go to Quansoo and fish bait using my old graphite rods.

I parked my fishmobile and walked over the small bridge that crosses over the creek and onto the path leading through the dunes. I had made a little cart to help carry my rods, bait, and sand spikes, and especially to carry fish back to my fishmobile if I caught a big one. I call this cart Sooie, after Quansoo. I built it from my landscaper husband's old spreader. I rebalanced the handle, added rod holders, and let all the air out of the tires so that they could go through soft sand. It carries buckets of bait and sand spikes and tackle bags and, most important of all, the fish that I decide to keep for dinner or weigh-in.

I pulled Sooie straight out to the beach and set up my rods. Although it was mid-September, it was still beach weather. There were about ten people gathered around a campfire.

I drove my sand spikes into the sand about twelve feet apart. These sand spikes were made especially for me by Charlie Cinto. They have a long spike that I drive down about two and a half feet deep. They are made from a heavy metal and they're extremely strong, so they can hold tight if a large fish hits my bait.

I baited one of my hooks with a fresh butterfish that I had snagged that morning in Edgartown harbor. Then I chucked it as hard as I could into the ocean, set the rod in the sand spike, and baited the other rod with fresh squid that I had caught the night before. With both my rods baited, I checked my reels to make sure my drags were set just perfect to fight a fish. I had brought a little folding seat with me and settled down on it to wait for a strike.

I stay close to my rods at all times and check my bait often. There is nothing worse than fishing with no bait. Sometimes the crabs will clean the bait off my hook without even a little wiggle of the tip of my rod, and some nights I go through a ton of bait just trying to keep my hook baited.

The people who were sitting around the campfire offered me some s'mores. I enjoyed hearing them laughing and chatting as the darkness came.

I was once again checking my rod with the butterfish on the hook. I walked close to the surf and reeled my bait in. I turned around to get a fresh bait from my bait bucket and noticed an empty space where my other rod had been standing in the sand spike. My rod was gone! The sand spike was lying on the sand and the rod was *gone*!

My beautiful thirty-five-year-old graphite rod had disappeared into the surf. I had a sick feeling in my stomach. I shined my flashlight into the surf and walked up and down the beach looking into the water, but it was not to be found. I must have been making a ruckus, as the campfire group came down to see if I was okay. I was almost crying as I explained to them that my rod was gone. I couldn't believe it had been pulled into the ocean within seconds.

I figured that it had to be a large striped bass to have the strength to take the rod and pull the sand spike down. All my years of fishing and all the big fish that I had caught with that rod rushed through my mind. I was sick. I was kicking sand and muttering F-bombs.

Unbelievable. What terrible luck I was having. I am emotionally connected with that rod.

I rarely leave the beach when I have a supply of fresh bait, so I decided I might as well stay and keep fishing. Maybe I would get lucky enough to catch a fish. I finally settled down and accepted that I would never see that rod again. I was nervous, though, and stayed standing a few inches from the only rod I had left.

About a half hour later I was checking my bait once again. Just as I was retrieving my line, about ten feet from shore, it felt like I'd hit something. It didn't hook whatever it was. No, it couldn't be—could it? I reeled my line in and then lobbed my hook back into the surf and slowly jerked it back, dragging it on the bottom of the ocean. Yes, it snagged something once more. I caught it. I carefully cranked the handle on my reel and noticed that my line was attached to another line, and that was attached to a fish! I slowly and carefully dragged a thirty-inch striped bass onto the beach. It was covered with weed. I looked at its mouth, under the weed, and there was the hook from my rod that was still in its mouth. I was screaming with joy. The campfire people were once again lined up on the beach behind me. I grabbed the line and slowly and gently started to pull it, saying, "Please don't break, please don't break." There was so much line at this point, I had thirty-pound monofilament line all around my legs. "Oh, great," I thought, "now I'm going to trip and get pulled into the ocean and drowned, tangled with my own fishing rod." A nice man from the crowd started to help me so that I would not trip on the snarl of monofilament and fall into the surf. He was coiling all the excess line that I was pulling in from the abyss. I was slowly and carefully pulling and pulling. Then the tip of my fishing rod appeared out of the surf, and as I pulled, my beautiful old rod came back to me. I was finally able to grab the rod and it was complete: rod, reel, line, and that weed-covered thirty-three-inch striped bass on the end of the line. It felt like a miracle. I got my rod back.

That year, as in past years, the Massachusetts striped bass bag limit was one fish per angler per calendar day. My quota for the day was lying on the beach, and it was beyond being able to be released alive. It didn't take me long to count my blessings. I thought about how my luck was running and decided that if I continued to fish, my next cast would probably hook the fish of a lifetime. Since I had a dead fish at my feet, to keep it would be breaking the state law. I packed my gear, carried the fish to my fishmobile, and headed for home. It wasn't a contender for the Derby, but Tristan and I were happy to have fresh striped bass for dinner.

19

The Grand Slam

THE GRAND SLAM is awarded to the angler who weighs in the heaviest aggregate weight of the four species of fish in the Martha's Vineyard Striped Bass and Bluefish Derby. The four species are striped bass, bluefish, bonito, and false albacore.

I have always considered myself a bass fisherman, but I have evolved into what Derby participants call a "slammer." Winning a shore grand slam is more difficult than catching the biggest fish and winning one of the major prizes. A shore grand slam is the most prestigious award.

I would explain a slammer as "one who chases four species of fish from daybreak until sunset and then from sunset to sunrise again. These fishermen do not have enough sense to go home to bed or sit down to a proper meal." A slammer's diet usually consists of coffee and candy bars.

One of the benefits of living on an island is that I can always find fishable water. No matter which direction the wind is blowing or at how many knots, whatever the time of day or night, there is a chance of catching a fish, somewhere. I can also find a productive tide by just moving a few miles up or down the beach. One disadvantage to fishing the shore compared to fishing from a boat is that I can never find a good enough excuse why I should not go fishing. It's a quality problem.

If I fished from a boat, the darkness or a mighty wind might jeopardize my safety. That would be good reason to stay away from the water. My safety is not usually compromised when I surfcast with my feet on the shore. I've caught some really big fish during the most intense storms.

The Vineyard has a reputation for being one of the most productive fishing areas in New England and it attracts fishermen from all over the world. We have many target species from scup and black sea bass to large bluefish and striped bass. Although we have lost some of the access to the coast due to locked gates that protect trophy homes being built near the water, we still have public access to many great fishing spots.

The grand slam has become my Achilles' heel. Until 1986, Atlantic bonito were plentiful in our waters. I could easily catch as many as six a day during the warm months of July, August, and September. False albacore became a presence around the Vineyard in the mid-1980s. By the early 1990s false albacore up to eighteen pounds were arriving in huge numbers. Since they compete for the same food source and because they are larger and stronger than bonito, when the albies arrive they seem to push the bonito away from the shoreline. The boat fishermen have no trouble finding bonito, but for the shore fishermen they have become scarce. Because of this scarcity, each year when I participate in the Derby, I swear that I will fish only for stripers at night and leave the bonito and albies to the daytime fishermen.

Trouble is, I just haven't figured out how to do that. After I have fished for striped bass during the predawn hours when the sun peeks over the horizon and the "funny fish" start to feed on the surface of the ocean, the ruckus that they make is just too tempting to ignore. Both bonito and albies travel in large schools that feed on small schooling baitfish. Least terns take advantage of the small bits of wounded silversides or sand eels that get chomped up by the feeding fish. It is obvious when they have trapped some bait and I can easily spot the splashes on the surface of the water. I *should* go home to bed after being up most of the night, but somehow my energy level perks up and I then spend hours chasing these little speedsters.

My proudest award was in 1998 when I placed second for a shore grand slam. The first-place winner, Bob Marie, beat me by only a small margin. A few days before the end of that Derby I actually had my first-place bass in my hand, but before I thought it through, I released it. With the Massachusetts state law being a one-bag limit, we could only keep one fish per day. I thought that I had found a school of big fish. After releasing it, I never got another fish that night.

Danny Stiles was a short distance from where I was fishing. I knew it was Danny because his thick New York accent traveled through the darkness. The following morning, he weighed in a bass that weighed about twenty-eight pounds. I think my fish was about the same size, and if so, it would have put me about five pounds over the first-place winner. I still have nightmares about the moment I set that fish free. I bought a BogaGrip after that so that I could weigh the fish right out of the water. As the years pass and the fishing gets more challenging, I sometimes feel that that was my last opportunity for a first-place shore grand slam.

Currently the shore grand slam has never been won by a woman, so one of my goals is to be that woman. Second place is an incredible accomplishment, but it's not first. No other woman has ever been on the shore grand slam leader board. I should be content with second place and all the times I have had my name up on the slam board, but I'm not.

During the 1995 Derby, I was bottom fishing alone on South Beach. I was fishing a squid on one rod and an eel on the other. Suddenly both my rods were active and there was a school of fish in front of me. I caught a couple of nice fish. I got one bass, about a twenty-four-pounder, on the squid. I threw it back, but the next one to hit my eel I kept. It was almost twenty-six pounds. The Massachusetts state law has changed many times over the years, and this year was once again that we could only keep one fish per calendar day. It was before ten o'clock in the evening, so I left the beach and drove to weigh-in. I called my friends Hawkeye and Ron McKee and got them out of bed to join me. I said, "Get up, the fish are here!" That year, the three of us buddied up, so I wanted to share the information with them. I thought the school of fish would stay, but they fished for a few hours and never got a hit. I could not take another fish until after midnight, so I slept in my fishmobile and asked them to wake me after twelve. By about one in the morning they had run out of bait, and although I tried to encourage them to go back to the dock to get more squid, they opted to go back to bed. Neither of them fished eels at the time. I had a few not-so-fresh squid left and a couple of eels, so there was no sense in offering them my bait.

Now, alone once again, I threw the squid out as far as I could and lobbed the eel close to shore. I always place my rods at an acute angle and only halfway down into my sand spike. I learned to do that because in the years when the fish were mostly always big, I had a difficult time getting my rod out of the spike.

I had settled down and was sitting on my bait bucket when I heard my rod, the one baited with the eel, lose its tension and fall into my sand spike. I knew immediately that a fish had picked my bait up and swum toward me. I grabbed the rod and started to crank the handle as fast as I could to catch up with the slack line and whatever was on the end of it. Once I caught up to it, my rod bent, and I felt the weight of a large fish.

It was swimming parallel to the beach heading east in the surf. I started to crab-walk down the beach as fast as I could, without tripping over my feet in my wader boots while retrieving my line and keeping a taut line to the hooked fish. I needed to get the fish in front of me, so I could gain control of it. After a long walk down the beach, I finally could see a large striped bass belly flash white not far from the shore. I felt us both getting tired. I held my rod sideways and low to the beach and kept my line as taut as I could so as not to give the fish any slack or opportunity to throw my hook from its mouth. Those last moments are a dance with the surf as it pushes the spent fish in toward me and then the wave recedes and pulls the fish back into the ocean. I waited for a wave to push the fish closer to shore. After a couple of attempts and working back and forth in the surf, a final wave picked up the exhausted fish and pushed it toward my feet. I had landed a beautiful 41.35-pound striped bass.

It was another example of how the largest fish took my eel instead of the squid. Jackie always said, "You might catch more fish on squid, but the bigger fish go for the eels." It also proved that you don't need to cast a long distance at night as large bass feed close to the shoreline and right into the wash.*

Now I had a 41.35-pound striped bass weighed in, plus a bluefish that weighed about seven pounds, and a ten-plus-pound albie, but not one bonito. One four-pound bonito would have put me in first place for shore grand slam.

I have been a contender year after year, and most years I have had more poundage than the leader, but without the bonito. Pursuing those little green torpedoes has become an issue for me. I feel like I'm in bonito prison. I have a saying, "Without a bonito, I have nothing." That's Derby insanity.

For twenty-five years, Greg Skomal was our resident marine biologist on Martha's Vineyard. Although he moved off-island, he's still on the Derby Committee. He does an extraordinary job of creating charts to compare the number of all four species that Derby participants have brought to weigh-in each year. He helps us with scientific data to figure out issues that might come up as the species and the environment change each year.

In 2006 only ten bonito were weighed in from the shore during the entire Derby. The following season was better, but still only fifty-one were recorded. In a more recent year, five shore bonito were weighed in; that was followed by a relatively big year with thirty-three. In 2016 only *one* bonito was landed from the shore. Considering how many fishermen are targeting them each day, these numbers prove that it's just not my bad luck but that the bonito are scarce. Every person who weighs in three species from the shore has the same dilemma. So why do I think I will be one of those lucky anglers to get a bonito? I don't know the answer to that question, but I do know that I am not getting any younger.

---

* The wash is a heavy sea wave that breaks into white foam on the shoreline.

Bonito usually precede the false albacore returning to the Vineyard from their migration from the south. By late July or early August, I start keeping an eye out for birds diving. Their splashes indicate where fish are feeding. It's before the Derby begins, so I set the alarm for five in the morning because sunrise is when they are the most active. I love to take a predawn walk on a beach, casting and retrieving my lure, hoping for a hit from a bonito or albie.

Once the Derby begins and I am staying up late night after night it becomes more difficult to stand on a jetty or beach and wait for a shot at one. There are many advantages to fishing a dock or pier, especially when you are suffering from "vertical deficiency" because you've been up all night.

The drawbacks to fishing from a public boat dock are the crowds of tourists that gather around each day, the boats and ferries coming in and out of the harbor, and the tall barnacle-encrusted pilings that scrape your line if you accidentally rub up against them with a fish on the line. Everything from grocery carts to bicycles are lying on the bottom, and when hooked, they break our lines. Eleven months of the year Memorial Wharf functions as a boat dock. During the Derby the town looks the other way as everyone parks, illegally, three cars deep. This has been happening for generations.

Up until the mid-1980s, the waters around the Vineyard were teeming with all kinds of bait—big sand eels, menhaden, and mackerel to name a few. I never used a keeper because I could almost always snag bait to live-line. Over the last twenty years I have seen a serious decline in the bait. There are no more big pods of sand eels, and just a smattering of mackerel and menhaden, and even the silverside population seems to have subsided. Even the squid are becoming scarce. Fortunately, the butterfish still seem to escape their many predators along the East Coast and arrive here in thick schools.

I try to get to the dock as early as I can to fill my keeper before the bait dissipates with the rising sun and the boat activity in the harbor. Once I have my keeper filled with butterfish or squid I can sit on the edge of the dock and soak live bait, waiting for a pickup, and try not to fall asleep. I always used a five-gallon bucket with a tight-fitting lid. I punched holes all around it, attached a rope to the dock, and let it drift over the edge with my live bait. It was not easy on my back each time I had to lift it out of the water for fresh bait.

When I am on a mission and targeting four species of fish, my buggy gets overloaded with gear, and that five-gallon bucket took up too much room. I figured out a better keeper. It's my nature to make, rather than buy, what I need. This new keeper is easy to travel with and much easier on my back.

I use a collapsible leaf bag made of a heavy nylon material. I burn lots of holes all around it with a hot soldering iron, then I run a heavy string through the middle of long, thin, buoyant foam floats called Wacky Noodles. I secure them around the top of the keeper with plastic electrical cable ties. I attach a heavy rope from the top of the keeper so that I can tie it to the dock or pier. When I throw my keeper into the water, the Wacky Noodles keep it afloat. I use a long net to scoop out one bait without disturbing the rest. Collapsed, my bag is only about eight inches high and twenty inches wide. It dries fast and can be packed in my fishmobile more easily than a bulky bucket or bait basket.

On the roof I have homemade rod racks. They hold two ten-foot graphite rods, one for throwing plugs and one rigged for slinging eels; two eleven-foot rods for fishing bait on the bottom; a seven- or eight-foot rod rigged to cast light lures to bonito and false albacore; a heavier rod about the same length and my Shimano bait runner reel with twenty-pound braid for live-lining bait from the dock; a six-foot rod rigged with a sabiki (a sixteen-inch leader line with a number of small hooks in a row) for catching mackerel or herring; and another with double trebles for snagging butterfish. I have a six-foot light rod rigged with a squid jig. That's just basic rods to get me through a day. I would love to have the time to do some fly fishing, but I can't even conceive of adding more equipment at this point. When my fishing buddy Charlie Cinto joins me, he comes in my fishmobile and that doubles the number of rods. It is an impressive arsenal of gear.

Now inside the fishmobile I have plugs, plugs, and more plugs. I pack a bag with larger plugs for fishing the south shore. Some for throwing with light gear and then those big wooden swimmers for nighttime bass fishing. Darters, Danny plugs, Needlefish, Bottle plugs, and Bombers. The variety of fishing lures to choose from is mind-boggling.

Over the last ten years, there have come to be more homemade wooden lure makers. When I attend a New England sportsmen's show, although I own more than I will ever need, it's hard to resist some new handmade wooden lures. Some of these are beautiful works of art, made for collecting only. The cost can be upward of thirty dollars each and I would think twice about throwing them into a rocky, weedy ocean, in fear of never seeing them again.

My son's cast-off school backpacks work just fine for carrying my fishing gear. Most beaches on the south shore have an intense rolling surf. For this bigger water, I need some heftier lures so I can achieve more distance with my casts, especially with a fifteen- to twenty-knot southwest wind in my face. This bag has the same variety of plugs as my north shore bag, but they weigh two to three ounces. I bring some swimmers, Darters, and Poppers, and in the daytime I include lead heads and metal spoons and jigs.

Darter lures. Left to right: Black handmade wooden Darter by Connecticut Surfcasters Association president Rob Cohn; pink and yellow handmade hard plastic Darters made by Jim Fraser; blue, purple, mackerel, and black commercial Darters made by Gibbs Lures.

Bombers and Redfins, swimming lures that I use for nighttime bass fishing. The lures with the red gill marks near the eye are Redfins. They are made by the Cotton Cordell company. The others are Bombers. They are made by the Bomber company.

I have a bag packed with lures for walking the north shore. This bag usually carries an array of swimmers weighing one to two ounces. For the calmer, flatter water of the island's north shore, I use a lighter lure because it can be more difficult to fool the fish in calm water, and a big moon night tells me to find some rocks to target hiding fish.

Although I have a four-wheel-drive vehicle, the access has become restricted of late and I can reach certain places only by walking. I have a bag packed for walking at night with all my live-eel-slinging rigs, which include circle hooks and extra leaders. I try not to forget a rag. A separate and smaller pack for daytime walks is packed with everything I need for casting to albacore and hopefully that elusive single bonito.

Charlie Cinto lives with his wife, Annette, in Plymouth, Massachusetts. He is a retired ironworker, and although he is now ninety years old, he spends most of his time in a small room in the back of his home that he calls his "Man Cave." It's an organized and well-equipped shop where he makes handmade lures and fishing rods

Charlie Cinto Magnets, so named because they attract fish. He makes them from half an ounce to four ounces and in many different colors. I have caught all four target species on them.

and stores his personal collection of lures and fishing gear. He makes wooded poppers and swimming plugs on a lathe and paints them by hand. He makes molds to pour lead into and created a lure called the Magnet. The three-quarter- to one-ounce Magnets are perfect for bonito or false albacore and the two- to three-ounce are irresistible to striped bass and bluefish. He also makes lead heads for bouncing on the bottom of the ocean, and each season he comes up with a new idea for a lure that attracts fish. He sells some in the local tackle shops, but he gives the majority of them away. I have been one of the lucky recipients, and since meeting Charlie I have buckets filled with lures just like the ones I coveted when I first started fishing. I give many away to my friends and new anglers in hopes that one of Charlie's lures will get them started in the recreational sport of fishing.

Naturally, I can set off on foot when the conditions are perfect for lightweight plugs, then have a twenty-knot wind start blowing in my face when I'm a mile from my fishmobile and need heavier plugs!

On the backseat of my vehicle I have a container with a headlight and extra flashlights and little Lumi Lights to tape onto the end of my bottom-fishing rods. Pliers, fillet knife, a scaler, plastic bags, electrical tape, Band-Aids, and a scale. Another area of my backseat carries my waders, belts, rubber boots, heavy socks, extra sweaters, raincoat, and favorite fishing hats. Let's not forget a pile of sand spikes that I made from PVC pipe to keep my rods out of the sand while changing lures.

Ed Jerome and I were fishing during the Derby a couple of years ago and we got into some huge bluefish. We each kept a few, all between nine and eleven pounds. One of Ed's bluefish got on the overall board for a couple of days; it weighed more than eleven pounds, and when he weighed it in, it was less than a pound from the grand leader. We were a good distance from the car with close to seventy pounds' worth of fish. Thanks to my cart, Sooie, we had no problem getting all the fish to the cooler and all our gear back to the car in one trip.

One last important tool I carry is a hand saw. In the off-season I do a lot of trespassing. I access some of the most productive fishing spots by driving down long, bumpy dirt roads. "No Trespassing" signs are meant for summer visitors and I don't pay much attention to them, especially during the Derby. After so many years, many of the caretakers of these properties know that I am sneaking around in the middle of the night. Sometimes, after a big storm, I am met with downed trees and branches blocking my path to the ocean. I have worked up a sweat just to get to my fishing spot, sawing a small tree or branch that lay across the road.

When so-called normal people see fishermen driving around the Vineyard with all our artillery loaded on our vehicles, they might think this is over the top. I swear I need every little thing that I have packed in my fishmobile.

Between Tristan and me, my vehicle is the most functional car that we own and the one that we use when we make a trip off-island. I'm not happy when I need to unpack all my toys and turn it into a family car.

20

The Dory Man:
In Pursuit of Skilligalle

IN 1979 I WAS WORKING at the Home Port Restaurant in
Menemsha. It faces west across the creek toward Lobsterville. The
walls were crowded with mounted Fiberglass replicas of fish and
the tables were frequently occupied by fishermen, recreational
and commercial, local and nationally known. It was not unusual
to serve dinner to well-respected island fishermen Kib Bramhall
and Spider Andresen and turn to have John Travolta or Richard
Dreyfuss at the next table. Kib and Spider were affiliated with *Salt
Water Sportsman* magazine. I had only been fishing for a few years
at that time and I was like a thirsty sponge wanting to soak up any
information I could pry out of the fishermen who landed in my
station.

Among the regular clientele were David Tilton and his brother
Stephen, born in 1934 and 1936 respectively, who had been raised
among hard-core island commercial swordfishermen. Their father,
Alton, was a legendary island character. Alton's father, Welcome Tilton, was the brother of Captain George Fred and Captain Zeb Tilton.

The sculpture *Swordfish Harpooner* by Jay Lagemann, a landmark in Menemsha

All these Tilton men were celebrated Vineyard schooner captains, and they are all chronicled in published books.*

Back around 1980, David invited me and a couple of the Home Port waitresses to accompany him and his crew, including a spotter plane, for a day of swordfishing. The spotter, Jim Grundy, was from Rhode Island, and David's mate was Whit Manter. His boat at that time, the *Super Seesaw,* was a twenty-six-foot Mako.

We met in Menemsha, on the harbor at daybreak, and headed south from the Vineyard. We rode past Nomans Land, which is three miles off the south coast of Martha's Vineyard, and continued for another hour or so. This was my first boat-fishing experience of this magnitude. I was a little nervous but awed at the same time. I'm not sure now who the other waitresses were, but I do remember that David told us to watch the surface of the water to see if we could spot a swordfish fin. That was our job. I didn't know what that would look

* *Zeb: Celebrated Schooner Captain of Martha's Vineyard,* by Polly Burroughs; *Cap'n George Fred,* written by Cap'n George Fred himself.

like, but I wanted to be the first one to see it. I kept my eyes glued to the water, around the boat and toward the horizon.

The spotter plane circled above us, at times flying out of sight. David had contact with him by radio. We had been on the water for a very long time that day. The sun was shining and it was a beautiful, peaceful day. I saw seabirds different from any that I had ever seen before.

Suddenly, there was a commotion. I wasn't sure what was going on, but I knew enough to stay out of David's way. He ran out to the end of the pulpit on the bow of the boat. He had a harpoon ready to strike in his hand.

I heard the voice of the spotter plane come over the radio saying, "Ten boats!" "Nine boats!" "Six boats!" "Two boats!" "One boat!" and finally David threw the harpoon into the water. He then grabbed a big lead that weighed about twenty pounds and clipped it onto the line that was connected to the dart from the harpoon. Then these big orange balls went flying over the gunwale and into the water. Then—silence!

I thought he had missed the fish. Then I realized that he had struck the fish and it was swimming away from the boat, dragging the big floats and the lead weight behind it. David explained to us that the big floating balls and the weight helped tire the fish out before we could bring it to the boat. The balls keep the fish from sounding, which means going deep to the ocean bottom. Before the age of plastic, they would use empty wooden kegs. While we waited for that fish to give up, David and Whit prepared the harpoon, hoping for another fish that day, but we only got that one.

Once the fish's energy was spent, David and Whit retrieved the balls and then pulled the fish to the side of the boat.

I had no idea I was going to see such an enormous fish! I had never been so close to such an incredible sea creature. They leaned outside of the boat and bled it and cut the sword before bringing it on board. Once on board it was gutted and the fins cut. This, I learned, is called "dressing" the fish. We arrived back in Menemsha harbor with a fish that weighed over 350 pounds, dressed.

Being witness to David's harpooning a magnificent fish was an event that I will never forget. I wish I could remember more of the details of that day. It was a long time ago, and being young, I was probably less interested in what had just happened and was thinking more about what life had in store for me.

Within a few years of that day, and due to the new technique of long-lining, most of the swordfish have disappeared from our waters. Swordfish did not have a chance against long-lining. Fishermen will set out miles of lines with baited hooks and leave them in the ocean overnight. The following day they pull the lines back to the boat. Unfortunately, this technique of long-line fishing is prone to the incidental catching and killing of everything from undersize swordfish to dolphins, seabirds, sea turtles, and sharks. By the time they pull the lines in, most of the fish are no longer alive, and if it's a fish that can't be legally harvested, it gets thrown back in the ocean, dead. Long-lining has been banned along the Atlantic coast in some fishing areas but is still used today in many states and countries. Some fishermen have attempted to modify the size of the hooks and lines to be less destructive to incidental catch. Long-lining has helped fishermen to catch more fish, but it has upset the balance of our fisheries and the ecosystem. Sustainability has gone out the window.

It was quite a few years before David's and my paths crossed once more. We were having a little chat when I realized that he was an incredible source of swordfishing stories from his youth. By then I was writing fishing articles for *On the Water* magazine, so I wanted to record some stories about the days when the waters of New England were still teeming with large swordfish and I wanted a firsthand account of the daring men who pursued them. David consented to tell me some tales. He contacted Donnie Mitchell, who had fished with him for many years on David's dad's boat the *Southern Cross*. Born in 1926 in Quansoo, Chilmark, Donnie was the first dory man and cook on Alton's boat for many years.

David, Donnie, and I gathered at David's little shack on Menemsha harbor for an afternoon of tales from the "olden days" of swordfishing. As I listened to David recall the days of being out in the middle of the ocean in a twelve-foot dory when he was barely a teenager, with the responsibility of bringing a fish weighing hundreds of pounds up from the depths of the ocean, I had to remind myself to breathe. The whole crew was counting on him to hold on to the harpooned fish and stay with it until it could be brought to the mother ship.

David's father, Alton Tilton's boat, the *Southern Cross,* was forty-nine feet long. She was built during Prohibition as a yacht for reveling and offshore parties. At the end of Prohibition, she was found burning on a small uninhabited island off Buzzards Bay. It's thought that she was most likely destroyed for the insurance money. She was put up for auction and Peter Brant, from Nantucket, bought her and rebuilt her into a commercial fishing boat.

In 1950 the *Southern Cross* took her first trip to Georges Bank, east of Cape Cod, to fish for swordfish. Before that, Alton had fished off Nomans Land as early as the mid-1920s. The crew consisted of

The *Southern Cross*

Alton Tilton, 1968

Alton, the man with the harpoon, on the stand ready to strike a fish; Donnie Mitchell and David Tilton, the first and second dory men respectively; the wheelman, aloft to steer the boat onto the fish; and a mast header, whose job was to look for swordfish, staring under the surface of the water close to the boat all day. David said it took a good man to be a mast header because the temptation was so great to look out to see what everyone else was doing.

The only electronics they had were a magnetic direction finder and a ship-to-shore phone, so they could communicate with a Boston marine operator to call home or contact other fishing boats. The direction finder would give them a reasonable direction to the Nantucket Lightship, which had a certain signal, and might pick up a radio station in Portland, Maine. With the two signals they would draw a line on their chart and get a reasonable idea of where they were. There was no radar in those days.

Since electronic depth finders were not yet widely used, they used a sounding lead with 200 fathoms of heavy marked codfish line with fathom markers on it. When they wanted to know how deep the water was, they threw the lead overboard and waited for it to hit bottom. They then read the fathom mark and hauled up the line. By noting how many fathoms deep the water was, they could tell if they were getting close to a canyon. They knew if they went from 50 or 60 fathoms to 150 fathoms and couldn't feel the bottom, they had gone over the edge of the canyon.

When they fished on Georges Bank they fished between 50 and 100 fathoms. The coils of rope, called warps, were stored in old wooden bushel baskets, the kind that used to hold fruit and vegetables at the grocery store. They would cut the wire handles off the baskets, so the rope could run smoothly out of them. They were fishing with 100-fathom warps; with six feet to a fathom, that meant 600 feet of rope were coiled in each basket. Occasionally if they were fishing near the edge of the canyon, at a depth of 80 or 90 fathoms, when they were hauling it out from the dory, a fish would take them over the edge into deeper water. So in the back of the dory they had a "bender," which was another basket containing another 100 fathoms of rope. If they were getting close to the edge, the first thing they did was tie the bender onto the warp and there were two or three feet of rope attached to a wooden keg with a slipknot. If it became necessary, as they were getting taken over the edge, they could pull the slipknot and the rope would come away from the keg and they would then be working with another 100 fathoms of line. So they could be working with up to 1,200 feet of line with a fish. If a fish went down 200 fathoms into a canyon or over the edge, they would have 1,200 feet of line to haul back by hand.

The striker aimed for the side of the dorsal fin. The muscles in the back of the fish are where the strength lies. If you hit a fish and the iron is two inches under the skin, you can lift a fish that weighs 250 pounds without ripping the harpoon out. Underneath the hide it is extremely tough, but anywhere around the stomach it has no strength. Because of the way the harpoon is made, when it is buried beyond the iron it is hard to pull out. Once a fish was harpooned

Brass harpoon point

from the pulpit and the warp line was set, the dory man went out to retrieve the fish.

David explained, "When a fish is hit, and you start to pull the fish in, with the first pull you pull as hard as you can. If it is going to come loose, that's when it will happen. If it stays in at that point, you don't pull it that hard again."

David's first time in the dory alone was when he was about twelve years old. He had been asking his dad to let him pull a fish. He had already been working on the boat for a time and been verbally coached, so he knew what to do. Finally, Alton hit a small fish, about 150 pounds. He let David pull the fish to the dory. It only took about twenty minutes and David felt disappointed that it was not much of a fight. After that experience he spent many years pulling big fish as a dory man; he also became an expert boat captain and harpoon striker. Talking about his own children, he said he couldn't see putting his own boys into a dory in the middle of the ocean when they were that age. It was a very different time and these men were a very special breed.

They had life jackets in the schooner, but not in the dory. The best they had was the wooden keg that was attached to the rope that was attached to the fish. The dory was quite seaworthy, and unlike most other small boats, it could be tipped onto its side without capsizing,

David Tilton with his dog, Cassius

but mind you, dories were only eleven to fourteen feet long. When a dory man was in trouble, he grabbed on to the keg so he could float. When they were pulling a fish and a keg, getting caught in the warp line was always a danger. When the fish was swimming hard and strong, they had to stay clear to avoid getting a hand or a foot tangled. The only safety gear the dory man carried was a knife in case that happened and they went overboard. "Cutting the line would be a last resort, though, because, if anything, they didn't want to lose the fish," David said. "The big boat didn't want to pick you up out of the water if you lost the fish!"

When they prepared to fish Georges Bank, they carried one thirty-gallon and two fifty-gallon drums of extra fuel, and between twelve and fourteen tons of ice. They put 350 pounds of ice blocks in the bottom of the hold and then covered these with crushed ice. The ice would keep the fish cold for up to two weeks with no problem. They would dress the first fish they got and let them sit under canvas on the deck until the morning. Alton preferred them to be treated that

Rollers for pulling the rope attached to the harpoon

way because the fish were much more firm and solid in the morning after sitting out all night.

The hold was divided into pens. They would dig down through all the crushed ice to a pen and find the cake ice. Then they would lay down three fish and cover them with crushed ice, three more fish and more crushed ice, until they had nine fish to a pen. If they got fifty or sixty fish that averaged two hundred pounds each, that was a good trip. That would be over ten thousand pounds of swordfish.

David recalled a day when they had "ironed"—harpooned—a big fish. They were near the edge and had a dory out. Normally they would have let the fish go with the keg. A keg held eight gallons. The fish started to go down into deeper water and the keg was going down. As he watched from the mast, the keg went back and forth and down deeper and deeper until it burst.

He said, "That was a *big* fish! When the pieces of the keg came up there wasn't a piece much bigger than a toothpick left. Of course, we lost that fish! That didn't happen very often. Most of the time the fish didn't travel very far with the keg and it didn't go down very deep."

The dory man would stand in the bow of the dory. Rollers were used in the dory so that you could pull the line smoothly without pulling the iron out of the fish. The roller had a stem on it that was

Nippers protected the hands of the dory man when pulling a swordfish up from the depths.

dropped into a hole in the rail. They wore a "nipper" on their hands. It was a little band with a groove in it. If their hands got wet when they were only protected by a glove they ended up with blisters. Not so with the nipper.

One day when he was about sixteen years old, David was in the dory in a rough sea with big swells. The water was a hundred fathoms deep. David had been pulling and pulling on the fish as the dory bobbed up and down in the huge swells. He would gain line, then when the dory was swept on top of the swell he would have to give it back. The tide was moving so fast it felt like the fish was towing him. He gained and lost for quite a long time before finally Alton, "the old man," as David called him, came out on deck and yelled to him that he hadn't moved an inch in over half an hour. "The fish had mudded!" When a fish got himself into the mud, it became almost impossible to pull him up. Donnie joined David in the dory, and although that fish was "hell bent" to free himself, they got him. With two men sometimes it was possible to get a mudded fish.

Another time they had a mudded fish in shoal water off Nomans Land. David maneuvered the dory in circles to put another couple of wraps around the fish so that they weren't pulling directly on the iron. Thus he was able to get the fish out of the mud. "He was deader than hell, but we got him!" said David. This technique took a long time and a lot of energy but most times it worked.

On one trip, for seven days straight they lay in black fog so thick they couldn't see the length of the forty-nine-foot *Southern Cross*. Merchant ships called tramp steamers were cutting across Georges Bank where the fishing boats were working. Tramp steamers operate without a schedule, going wherever they are required to deliver cargoes. They could run hundreds of feet long. They were supposed to have a bow watch on them, and although they were supposed to blow their horns or whistles in the fog, most times they didn't. One of these freighters could strike a fishing boat without even feeling it. There was a fleet of big schooners that fished for swordfish out of Canada. A tramp steamer struck one that was 110 feet long. According to the story, the steamer turned around to see what had happened—and hit the schooner again. This time they sank it. The steamer still never felt it and wasn't convinced it had hit anything.

Alton's *Southern Cross* was only forty-nine feet long, so they stood a two-hour watch at night. Fortunately, when it was foggy it was also quiet, so they could hear the *thump, thump, thump* of the wheel when a steamer was coming. They would wake everyone up in case of an emergency. Starting the engine was out of the question because they wouldn't be able to hear the freighter if they did. So they looked at the compass, noted the direction, then looked at the clock, checked the direction, and somehow figured out which direction the freighter was heading. They had no communication with these ships. They did have a double-barreled twelve-gauge shotgun on board, and when one of these boats was bearing down on them they would fire two shots, fire up the engine, and head out in the opposite direction, as best they could figure.

I asked David if he was as terrified living it as I had been just listening to this story.

He said, "No." Then he added, "I had once been out in the dory when a steamer came close." Hair-raising! He had heard stories of guys who had to throw their kegs over and let their fish go so they could row the dory out of the way of an approaching steamer.

Swordfish head that broke through one side of the dory

With the technology that we have today, these incidents would never happen.

When the dory man had a fish on the line, they would get the dory over the fish to drive it down into a deeper depth. That made the fish work hard and tired it out sooner. David recounted, "I hadn't gotten the dory to the fish yet and I was cranking and coiling to beat all hell. The fish was coming to the surface with the line coming straight over the top of his head. Then, pow! The sword came through my bow as if the dory was made of cheese. The sword came right through both sides of the bow of the dory and right by me. Fortunately, it missed me!"

This is what's known as "getting plugged."

His brother Stephen got plugged three times during one summer. One fish came up through the coil of rope, and another hit through the bow. David was running the schooner that day and said he saw the dory go almost vertical in the air.

"I don't know how the hell he managed to stay in that dory," David said. "And then I saw him taking his clothes off and I thought, 'What the hell is the damn fool going to do?' The fish had made a big hole in the dory, so Stephen was stuffing his clothes in the hole. They went down to pick him up. That was the third time in one season that he had gotten plugged.

"You're so hungry at night and no one is even talking they are so busy eating," David continued. Then about halfway through the meal the old man, Alton, looked at Stephen and said, "What the hell are you doing wrong?"

"I don't know what you mean," said Stephen.

Alton said, "Well, you must be doing something wrong with the way you're pullin' these fish, you're irritating them. We can't keep stopping to patch these dories!" He was more concerned with the lost fishing time than with how close his son had come to losing his life. These fishermen were of a strange breed.

Donnie said, "I once got plugged three times in one day!" David was astounded and said that Donnie must have irritated the fish a lot more than Stephen did.

Donnie said, "I got one fish that came up through the bottom of the dory, hit my boot, and hit so hard it took a chunk out of the rubber!" Another time he had one come up and rip the sleeve of his woolen shirt, never touching his skin. Donnie never kept track of how many times he got plugged, but he certainly could recall "the one that damn near done me in!"

They were down south of Nantucket Shoals and had harpooned a big fish. It was harpooned right close to the tail. Donnie jumped into the dory. The fish breached and stopped and he pulled it up to him, then the fish breached and stopped again, and again he pulled it closer to him. The next time the fish went down, the line went slack and Donnie couldn't feel him. Then all of a sudden he came through the bottom of the boat. The sword pierced through a plywood patch five-eighths of an inch thick on the outside of the boat, through another patch on the inside, and up through the seat.

Donnie explained, "'Course my knees were on the seat and I went through the air like a torpedo! I came down and I landed on the swordfish in the water. The minute I landed on him I didn't want to get tangled in the line. Luckily he swam off and I swam away from the line. Then all of a sudden, I'm going down like a Coke bottle. I'm goin' down. It's getting dark and my arms are killin' me.

"I was thinking, 'What's wrong? Why can't I come up?' Then it comes to me that my boots and clothes are full of water! Down I went. The fright was horrible. Then I remembered when I was in the Navy they made us learn how to tread water and take our clothes off. As soon as I knew what was wrong, the fright left me, you know. I reached down to take my boots off. When I reached down to take the elastics off my boots, I went down even farther. Once I got them off, I came up like a whale and blew my dentures right out of my mouth. I reached over and grabbed hold of the dory. Willard Marden jumped into the other dory and rowed out to get me. The big boat came around and put out another dory to get the fish. We didn't lose him. It weighed 550 pounds dressed. A big animal! But to make this story a little"—here he paused and snickered—"funny."

Donnie continued, "The next morning, I had to get into the dory again. I had never been afraid in my life and I had had a lot of close calls. But this day I was scared, I was shakin'. I didn't have any boots. I had to wear Bjarne Larsen's boots and he was much bigger than me and I didn't have any teeth. I lost my false teeth and I looked like Andy Gump! So, we were on the way home and this friend of mine, Buzzie Snowden, who was on the boat, called ship to shore to my wife."

Buzzie told her, "Donnie got drunk in the barroom last night and got in a fight and lost his teeth." Donnie said, laughing, "She believed him. I came home feeling all sorry for myself and she was all mad at me."

Donnie later worked on one of the Larsens' boats, the *Christine & Dan*. Besides the Tiltons, the Larsens were the biggest swordfishing family in Menemsha. They were the high-liners of the harpoon industry—Bjarne, Debba, and the youngest, Louie Larsen, "Old Louie," as they called him now.

Donnie talked about those days. "When you fished with the Larsens you pulled the fish hard. When they were scarce, you took your time, but when they were catching a lot of fish, they wanted you to pull hard. That's your job in the dory. You could lose your job if you couldn't get these fish in."

The lightest ironed fish he ever saw happened when the fish were scarce. Alton had hit a fish and he hit it low. He put Stephen in the dory and told him to tend it easy. They thought the harpoon had gone through the belly. When he brought the fish in, the iron had gone through the pectoral fin and the knot had not gone back through the fin. So the iron was hanging free and he was pulling the fish in by its fin with the knot up against the fin. It took over two hours but he got the fish.

By the 1950s everything had started to change. They brought the dories in and had the bottoms covered with fiberglass. This prevented them from getting plugged. The fish would hit the dory and slide off. If you had a lot of weight in the boat it might come through, but that didn't happen often.

Even before long-lining took over, dory fishing was eliminated in favor of a new technique using a twenty-pound lead weight. The weight was snapped onto the line followed by one big plastic ball on the end of the warp line. They found that when they attached a weight on the line maybe fifty or sixty feet back, if the fish tried to come to the surface, the weight would pull it back down. But when a fish was trying to go down deep, with the ball, line, and weight, after about a half hour he would be pretty much spent. The lead on the line replaced the dory man. Donnie remembered the swordfisherman Jimmy Morgan's comment about this: "After all the work we did to pull in swordfish and to think that we were replaced by a stone!"

By the early 1960s Alton's boat had been sold, but he kept fishing for quite a long time after that with Jimmy Morgan, dragging for ground fish. David and Stephen had left the Vineyard to start a business in Minnesota. Donnie finished his last season on the *Luther* with "Turtle," Captain Harold Lawry. Bjarne Larsen died around 1968 and that's when Donnie quit. He was about forty-two years old.

For hundreds of years, Mother Nature controlled the days of harpoon fishing at sea. If it was overcast you couldn't see into the water, and if it was foggy you couldn't see far enough out to see the fins. All the fishermen started long-lining in the end. Donnie didn't like it.

When they long-lined, his job was to help set out the buoys; when they came back, he gaffed the fish on board and then he cleaned them. They caught a lot of small fish. Everyone had bad feelings about long-lining. Harpooned fish are better eating than long-lined fish because the fish are brought to the boat still alive and then bled immediately, whereas long-lined fish lie dead in the water for an indefinite period.

One of David's last trips out swordfishing was in 1983. He was fishing on the same boat that I had gone swordfishing with him on, his twenty-six-foot Mako, the *Super Seasaw*. They brought twenty swordfish into Menemsha that season. The commercial season for swordfish started in the middle of June and ended in the beginning of September. The average weight was 260 pounds dressed. The last day he took that boat out he ironed a yellowfin tuna weighing 130 pounds and a 186-pound swordfish. In 1986 he got his thirty-three-foot Fortier, the *Seasaw II*, and from that day on he has only seen two swordfish. He went down to the southern part of Georges Bank twice.

He said, "I saw one fish and missed the damn thing." When David said that, Donnie looked at him and they had a really good laugh with each other. I was honored to be witness of their trip down memory lane.

The Dump is about fifty miles south of the Vineyard. It is at an epicenter of warm-water eddies. These eddies that move in from the Gulf Stream are prime feeding grounds for many species of fish. The last fish that David got was out at the southern corner of the Dump.

Some sharks were feeding on the discards from a dragger. The swordfish was feeding on the baitfish on the surface. The crew saw the sword come out of the water chasing bait and then they saw him turn and go down under the water. As good luck would have it, the fish came up to grab a piece of hake, and just as the boat was upon it, David grabbed the harpoon and struck him. He hit him. The fish had a scar on its back where they could see that someone had stuck it before and lost it. That was his last swordfish. David stopped swordfishing mainly because the swordfish had disappeared. He still maintains his commercial license and keeps looking. There have been some reports of good swordfish being spotted south of the Vineyard lately. David is thinking about attaching his stand to his boat this coming season.

Stephen Tilton passed away on October 23, 2009.

Donnie Mitchell passed away on September 25, 2013. He was eighty-seven years old.

21

The Art of Taxidermy

THE WORD "TAXIDERMY" derives from the Greek words *taxis* (to move) and *derma* (the skin). The ancient Egyptians embalmed fish as well as humans, and sometimes placed embalmed fish and animals in burial vaults with the remains of important deceased people. Humans have been attempting to preserve beloved creatures since the beginning of recorded history. The challenge for a taxidermist is to preserve the miracles of nature in as near a lifelike form as possible.

In my own small collection of taxidermy books, there are some that date back as far as 1882. Although it's been said that "there are a thousand ways to skin a cat," my research suggests the process of skinning fish and animals has remained the same for hundreds of years. Most of the products used to tan and mount fish have stayed pretty much the same for almost a hundred years.

Taxidermy was primarily a secret art performed in cellars and barns around the old woodstove. It wasn't unusual for a taxidermist to put his tools aside and stop working when a visitor entered his shop. In the book *Taxidermy Without a Teacher*, copyright 1882, Walter P. Manton writes, "Well, here we are at last. Please turn the key in that

I mounted this forty-pound striped bass for William Kadison. William caught it from his dad's boat *Poco Loco*. David Kadison is no stranger to the Derby. He and his children have won many prizes with the trophy fish they have caught from *Poco Loco*.

door—to keep all inquisitive priers out—for the process into which I am about to initiate you is something of a secret, shrouded by the thin veil of mystery."

In the last thirty years, this secretive attitude has begun to change, much like the changes in the recreational fishing world. In the late 1970s and early 1980s the products began to improve. The poisonous chemicals and some of the materials and laborious techniques were being replaced by nontoxic and ready-to-use supplies. The arsenic trioxide and formaldehyde used in preserving and bugproofing were so toxic that after years of exposure many taxidermists died. Fortunately for today's taxidermist, nontoxic materials have taken the place of most of these toxic chemicals. Water-based acrylic airbrush-ready paints have replaced enamel and lacquer-based paints.

With the introduction of plastics and of course the changes in the last twenty years brought on by technology and the internet, the veil of mystery has been lifted. Once taxidermists started to share information about techniques and products, everybody's work improved. Finally the profession was moving forward.

Traditional materials used for "stuffing" fish ranged from moss and leaves, balsa wood, excelsior, and plaster to heavy papier-mâché or sawdust. The final creation was either too heavy to hang on the wall or so porous that it absorbed moisture from the air, which caused the fish to expand and crack. It was also difficult to end up with an anatomically correct fish. I refurbished a few old fish where the skin had been wrapped around a product that felt like cement. These fish were much heavier dead than they had been when alive. Today we can carve lightweight bodies from dust-free carving foam that is reasonably easy to handle, or we can order ready-made urethane manikins to match the exact dimensions of most fish. A wealth of learning tools are available these days. *Breakthrough* and *Taxidermy Today* are two of the major magazines for taxidermists and wildlife artists. Someone interested in becoming a taxidermist can also get valuable information from videos, supply companies, and taxidermy schools, as well as associations on the state, national, and international levels.

In the last thirty years many taxidermy schools have opened all over the country. Before this, unless an aspiring taxidermist could apprentice under a professional taxidermist, the only way to learn was from the few how-to books on the market or a correspondence course from either the Northwestern School of Taxidermy in Omaha or the Schmidt School of Taxidermy in Memphis. I have these booklets in my collection.

When I started to get interested in becoming a fish taxidermist in the early 1980s, Wally Brown was the first name to come to mind when talking about mounting a trophy fish. Wally had been one of the best-known taxidermists in the New England area for over fifty years. Born on April 13, 1922, he established his commercial taxidermy business in 1952, taking in both fish and animals. He did skin mounts of the fish in the beginning, but by the early 1960s he had become interested in fiberglass reproductions.

Thanks to Richard T. Fisher, maker of fiberglass boats and founder of the Boston Whaler company, Wally Brown got an opportunity to learn to work with the new product. While continuing to do his regular taxidermy, he went to work for Boston Whaler. He stayed there long enough to learn to work with fiberglass, gel coats, and resins. Once he started using the new materials and techniques, his reproduction fish caught on like wildfire. He became very popular up and down the New England coast and his work kept him very busy.

I knew of Wally Brown's work from the time I started fishing in the 1970s. Most of the trophy fish hanging on the walls of my fishing friends had been mounted by him.

I had been to his Cape-style house in Falmouth on Cape Cod a couple of times. In 1984, when Jackie and I took our Derby grand prize striped bass to him, he did fiberglass reproductions of both my forty-five-pound second-place fish and Jackie's forty-eight-pound grand winner. I wanted an actual skin mount but couldn't find a taxidermist who could perform that kind of work. I was also going to wait until I caught a fifty-pound fish, but this was the beginning of the moratorium on striped bass. These fish were getting scarce and I wasn't sure if this fish might be the last striped bass I would ever catch.

When I first considered learning to become a taxidermist, I called Wally and asked him if he would consider letting me apprentice with him. I told him I really wanted to learn skin mounting but I would love to work with him. He encouraged me to learn what I could on my own and said that I could call him anytime. I realize now that he must have been asked that question many times. I didn't realize it then, but he did me a favor by sending me on my way.

Many years later, while I was working on a story about Wally Brown for *On the Water* magazine, I went over to Falmouth and met with his son, Stephen. By then Wally was afflicted with Alzheimer's and was in an assisted-living home. I did have a few telephone conversations with him over the years, but I was never invited to see his shop until then. Being a self-taught marine taxidermist, he only brought a special few into his workplace.

He had worked in the basement of his house, like me and most every other taxidermist around the country. We went into the backyard and through a bulkhead to access the basement. I noticed the sandbox in his backyard that he used to mold fish. We walked down the stairs into the humble shop. The cinderblock walls felt damp and cold. Cobwebs now hung from the low ceiling rafters and covered the tiny windows. It was dark and cluttered with tools and materials that only another taxidermist would find familiar and interesting.

Unfortunately, I was not the first taxidermist to be privileged to tour his shop. His son, Stephen, told me that a taxidermist had come from New Jersey and purchased many of the paints, materials, molds, and unfinished fish blanks shortly after Wally's career as a taxidermist ended. He said I could make an offer on anything that was left and that I thought I could use. We walked cautiously, turning over piles of stored materials and unfinished fiberglass fish blanks. I was happy to purchase the airbrushes that he used to paint with. I left with a truck full of fiberglass fish in various stages of completion, supplies and materials, and an eight-foot skin-mounted dolphin fish that needed to be refurbished.

In 1985 I sent away for the Northwestern School of Taxidermy's correspondence course. They sent me a packet of booklets. My first lessons were on skinning and tanning birds. Until I finished those lessons, I was not able to go on to the next species, fish. Since I don't hunt, I had a dilemma: how to find birds to work on. I thought about asking my neighbor Billy Diaz if he could shoot a pigeon for me with his slingshot. He once threw a beer across the Tashmoo channel to me with his slingshot. It landed at my feet and did not even suds over when I opened it. He is a crack shooter with that thing. I never did get a bird to practice on.

Studying the lesson booklets was frustrating, and learning from them seemed pretty close to impossible. After struggling through the primitive black-and-white sketches of the insides of birds and fish, I decided to pursue the next avenue.

I had conversations with many of my fishing friends about my desire to become a skin taxidermist, and everyone was supportive. Jackie Coutinho gave me a book called *Fish Mounts and Other Fish Trophies* by Edward Migdalski. Jackie had also had some interest in learning to mount his own fish. I talked to Kib Bramhall and Spider Andresen while I was serving them dinner at the Home Port Restaurant. I respected their vast involvement in the recreational fishing community. They thought it was a great idea.

Finally, I mentioned my idea to a fellow fishing friend and entrepreneur lure designer, Arnold Spofford. He graciously invited me to his home with his wife, Ellen, where I talked with him about my interest in learning to become a taxidermist. He was also supportive and thought it a good idea. He gave me some of his sportsman magazines that had the addresses and telephone numbers of taxidermy schools around the country. The closest one to the Vineyard was in Pennsylvania: the Pennsylvania School of Taxidermy. I contacted the school and explained that we did not have many wild animals on the Vineyard, but we have a large fishing community. I told them I wanted to specialize in fish and I also wanted to learn to mount the actual skins. They typically didn't allow anyone to learn just one species, and the full seven-month course, which included birds, fish, and mammals, cost about $20,000. Since I was supporting myself and my home on my waitress wages, it was not possible to come up with that kind of money or take seven months away from my job. They were flexible enough to let me enroll in the two-month fish course, and they also encouraged me to sign up for the business course.

I borrowed $2,000 from my parents to help with tuition and housing. In January 1987, my future husband, Tristan, drove me to the snowy hills of Ebensburg, Pennsylvania, then returned to the island, where he stayed in my house, stoking the coal stove and feeding my dog, Rita, and my cat, R.P. (Rita's pet).

I am fortunate that I was able to get a formal education in traditional fish taxidermy. I brought some small bluefish from home and purchased a few fish from the school. I came home with my first ten fish completed. In a short time, I learned the basics that would have taken me many years to learn if I had not been schooled. Now it was time to open shop.

I cleaned up my basement and set up a workspace with a few scant tools that I needed to get started. I had been freezing some fish that I had caught to practice on. I had Bob Post's winning bluefish, my first paying job, and it terrified me. Other than a few hand tools, I needed to order a few hundred dollars' worth of supplies. The largest purchases I needed were a chest freezer and a compressor to run my airbrush for painting.

I kept my waitress job at night. Will Holthum, my boss at the Home Port, in Menemsha, bought the Square Rigger restaurant in Edgartown, and when the Home Port closed for the winter, the waitresses who were year-rounders began to work nights at the Rigger.

It was a struggle, skinning fish all day and waitressing at night. I found that when I cut myself, which I did quite often, lemon was not the best choice to rid my hands of fish smell. I read in one of my taxidermy magazines that toothpaste did the trick. It worked for a while, but by the end of an evening of waitressing, my hands, with many Band-Aids on the fingers, also reeked of fish smell!

I thought that if I had my own business, I would be able to go fishing whenever I wanted. Since I had missed the Columbus Day blitz because I was working at the Home Port, becoming my own boss was top priority. I didn't realize that when you own a business you have less time to do the things you love. If I did not do the work, it did not get done. No calling a substitute to take my place.

When spring came, the fish came flooding into my shop. Johnny Hoy, local blues singer, brought me a fifty-pound striped bass that he caught. That was the first big bass I ever mounted. It is a tremendous responsibility working on someone's prize trophy fish. I shed many tears and had nightmares about that one fish, but through all my struggles, I got the job done. In the end he was happy.

I kept my waitress job for the next three years. At that point, I told my husband I could not do two jobs anymore and had to take a chance to see if I could earn a living on taxidermy alone. During most of the years of my taxidermy career, I could never financially make ends meet. To subsidize my income, I did a cleaning job on Saturday mornings for a rental turnover, during a couple of summers I worked as mate on Ed Jerome's boat, the *Wayfarer*, I wrote articles for local magazines, and eventually I taught fishing workshops and became a surf fishing guide. It was a juggle to keep all my balls in the air. Luckily, Tristan's landscaping business paid all the household bills. The money I earned I used to pay for my secondhand fishmobile and all my personal living expenses, but there was not much left over.

Today, most taxidermists order ready-made urethane manikins to match the approximate dimensions of the fish they are working on. I worked with many species of fish that most taxidermists around the country are unfamiliar with. Other than striped bass and bluefish, most saltwater fish are so difficult to skin out and mount that most taxidermists won't touch them. Bonito and false albacore have few to no scales, their skin is fragile, and it is difficult to scrape all the meat away from the thin skin without tearing it. Supply companies don't offer manikins for bonito, false albacore, sea robins, scup, black sea bass, or many of the other saltwater fish that I am asked to mount. Luckily, when I went to school, I learned to carve my own lightweight manikins from a dust-free carving foam.

I'm not sure when fiberglass reproductions started to replace skin mounts. One of the largest companies in the country, Pflueger, was started as a small taxidermy business in Florida by Al Pflueger in 1926. At some point they made the transition from skin mounts to fiberglass reproductions. I will guess that it was around the same time Wally Brown went to work with Boston Whaler to learn to work with fiberglass. Today they sell reproduction fish all over the world. I am among a small handful of taxidermists who specialize in saltwater skin mounts. Compared to fiberglass reproductions it's a laborious job. Each fish, from a trophy catch to a child's first, is labor-intensive and not very lucrative.

Although I do mostly skin mounts, when I first started my business I had to learn the molding process and fiberglass work to mount sharks and some other special projects. I taught myself how to cast fish in fiberglass. The amount of work that goes into the molding process is also tedious. Plaster can be very difficult to work with, and just preparing the fish to be molded can take close to a full day of work. A plaster mold can only be used once. With Bondo and fiberglass resin I can make molds that can be used many times without losing the quality of detail. Now that Wally Brown is out of business, I have refurbished and repaired many of his fiberglass reproductions.

Taxidermy is not a common profession, but many people over the years have told me that when they were young they wanted to be a taxidermist. It was not on my list of things to be when I grew up. Female jockey, folksinger, nun, and artist, but not a taxidermist. In 1988, if I had not married Tristan, who runs a successful landscape business, I would not have been able to stay in business for thirty years and keep my house or a decent car on the road.

A few years before I went to taxidermy school, I attended a seminar off-island in Chicopee, Massachusetts, on taxidermy. It was held by a professional taxidermist named John Rinehart. Someone asked John if he thought the profession would ever die out. He replied, "As long as man has an ego, the taxidermist will be in business." Over the years, that Rinehart quote rang through my mind from time to time. Was I providing a service that was prompting anglers to harvest more fish, and was my work helping to stroke man's ego?

About three years into my business, I started to question the decision I had made to become a taxidermist. I began to think that I might be part of the problem of the decline of the fish that I loved so much. I do believe that most sportsmen are conservationists at heart, understanding that we should not use up our natural resources and accepting that we need to do our part to preserve today's declining species for future generations.

A girlfriend of mine came to visit with us for a few days with her boyfriend, named Patrice. He is an African shaman who came to the Vineyard to teach a seminar on shamanism. I was attracted to his spiritual values and felt great respect for him. I took him on a tour of my basement taxidermy shop. After showing him the many fish I had preserved and the process of skin mounting fish, I asked him what he thought about what I was doing on a spiritual level.

He said, "Whenever someone tries to imitate nature's artwork, it is the greatest compliment you can pay to God." I felt a sense of relief and came to believe my life's work is morally acceptable. At the end of the day, I am humbled, because as hard as I work on re-creating God's beautiful creatures, I know I can never make these fish look anywhere near as perfect as their original maker. Becoming a fish taxidermist

Spike Lee outside my shop with the striped bass he caught aboard Buddy Vanderhoop's boat, *Tomahawk*. Mounted by Island Taxidermy Studio.

has opened my eyes to the detailed beauty of every species. There is a special joy in working with Mother Nature's original and perfect art.

I had the pleasure of mounting fish for the actor Jim Belushi and the filmmakers Spike Lee, Leslie Cockburn, and Michael Mann. A blue claw crab I preserved and mounted in a diorama-like setting was presented to the Clintons while they lived in the White House.

I took in striped bass up to sixty-six pounds and preserved many fifty-pound-plus fish that will remind the anglers of the day they caught their trophy. But the most rewarding fish I worked on were the many "first fish" caught by small children. I run into grown men on the street who tell me they still have the fish that I mounted for them when they were kids.

I've heard it said that "to be a taxidermist, you need to have a weak nose and a strong stomach." I guess I fit the bill. I've spent the last thirty years up to my elbows in fish guts, but it was a labor of love.

I have shown my work in island art galleries—Louisa Gould Gallery in Vineyard Haven and Scrimshaw Gallery in Edgartown. Tom DeMont, owner of Scrimshaw, sold many of my Wildlife Art pieces before he passed away in 2011. He was a fan of my work and helped

Jim Belushi in my studio with the striped bass I mounted for him. He too caught it on board Buddy Vanderhoop's *Tomahawk*.

me bring my work from commercial quality up to what I call "art gallery worthy."

I am now retired, and although I am not taking on any new work, I have about three years of unfinished work in my shop. Not customer work, but fish that I was going to use for my own artworks. My best advertising was to hang my work in the tackle shops. Now that I have gathered back all the work that was hanging in four tackle shops here on the Vineyard, one in Nantucket, and two on Cape Cod, I have a larger collection of fish than I even imagined.

I met with the Martha's Vineyard Historical Society in early 2018. They purchased the old marine hospital on Lagoon Pond Road in Vineyard

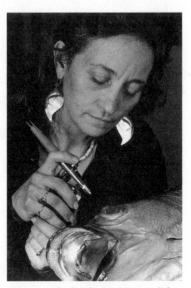

Photograph taken by Mark Lovewell for Robert Post's book *Reading the Water,* 1988. Airbrush painting a fifty-pound striped bass.

Fly by Night, mounted by Island Taxidermy Studio

Haven and refurbished it. The new museum opened to the public in March 2019. The best of each species of my taxidermy work is now on permanent display so that generations to come can enjoy a close-up view of many of the fish taken from the waters of New England. I can't think of a better ending for my career in taxidermy, my "thirty years of being up to my elbows in fish guts."

22

The Squeaky Reel

AFTER FISHING THE SHORELINE for many decades it's become second nature for me to drive alone down long, desolate roads in the darkness to access some of the best fishing spots. Many evenings, from May through November, I fish North Neck on Chappaquiddick Island. To get there I board the three-car ferry *On Time* near Memorial Wharf in Edgartown. When I exit the boat, especially during the busy summer season, I can feel the peace and solitude wash over me the minute I drive onto the tiny island called Chappy.

About two miles down Chappy's only paved road, I turn onto North Neck Road. I weave my way along the bumpy dirt road and park my fishmobile in the small Land Bank public parking lot, which holds about five cars.

I take plenty of time to make sure I have everything I need to fish for a few hours before I head up the shell-covered single-lane path toward the Gut on foot. The path leads to a steep set of stairs down to a small slice of beach. Climbing the stairs is such a chore that I only want to do it once, hopefully after I catch a big fish.

Clothed in chest waders cinched with a tight belt for safety, a

The stairs leading to the Gut via North Neck on Chappaquiddick Island

hooded sweatshirt, and my lucky fishing cap, I wear a second belt that keeps my pliers handy around my waist, and to light my way, a headlamp around my neck. My backpack is ready with extra hooks and leaders, a rag, a tape measure, a bottle of water, and my rope if I intend on keeping a fish. Last, I carry my precious eels in a bag with an ice pack.

On this particular night there was no moon. It was so dark that I had to walk very slowly on the slippery round rocks near the water's edge. The parking lot had been empty, and I couldn't see any lights as I scanned up and down the beach. I was casting and retrieving my eel, ever so slowly. I was relaxing in the darkness but tensed with the anticipation that any minute I would feel the tug from a large striped bass.

Suddenly a figure appeared out of the darkness. My heart skipped a beat, but calm returned when a gentleman's voice said, "Excuse me, would you mind if I oiled the handle on your reel?" He held up a tube of Penn lube.

I had become oblivious to the fact that my old reel was squeaking away with every crank of the handle, and I gladly accepted his offer, so we could both enjoy the silence and tranquility of the night. I told him I thought that I was alone, and I apologized for disrupting the peace and quiet. He smiled as he squeezed a few drops of oil onto my reel handle, turned, and disappeared once again into the darkness of the night. Yes, peace and quiet.

23

Trash Fish to Gourmet Cuisine

ALL OVER THE GLOBE, stocks of many of the most palatable fish species are being depleted, and for about a third of these most desirable fish the populations have totally collapsed. In the forty years that I have been involved in the fishing community, I have seen technology advance to the point where the techniques we use to harvest fish from the ocean have become destructive not only to the targeted species but also to the by-catch and the ocean habitat that is vital to the fish's survival. In a short time we have changed from harpooning and small-boat single hook-and-line fishing to long-line fishing and the use of huge factory trawlers and purse seine ships. Gone are the massive schools of cod that sustained New England for centuries. The huge schools of menhaden that are crucial to the diet of most of our large ocean fishes, from whales to striped bass, are being depleted by a small fleet of large industrial factory ships that harvest hundreds of millions of pounds annually and reduce them for omega oils. Our high-tech harvesting methods have harmed many species like the swordfish, and more recently the popularity of sushi has put even more pressure on the tuna family.

Not being able to replenish the fish that we take from the sea has become a problem. I don't know the answer to this dilemma. Maybe if we as consumers develop a taste for what have been considered "trash fish," we can take some of the pressure off the more popular species and allow them to recover from overharvesting. In 1944, fishermen and fish markets started using the term "trash fish" for fish considered less desirable for any reason. This included by-catch—fish swept up accidentally with targeted species—and those whose meat is more difficult to separate from the bones. "Rough fish" means more or less the same thing.

When I went to the Home Port Restaurant for the annual Dukes County Fishermen's Association dinner, I learned that the new owners, Bob and Sarah Nixon, were changing their whole philosophy of serving dinner. They wanted to support the local fishermen and farmers by offering fish and meat that is in season, and were coming up with ways of serving some of the foods that we unfairly think of as not suitable for gourmet dining. The appetizer of braised bluefish with clams and squid was delicious. The entrée was a whole gutted black sea bass that was served with the head, fins, and skin. We did need to work a little harder for the meat, but it was worth the effort. I have successfully cooked many black sea bass myself, but this meal was outstanding.

Theodore Diggs, an innovative chef who at one time worked at the Home Port, is obviously a lover of nature and the environment. He told me that Americans are adopting the rituals of the Europeans and becoming much more aware of where their foods are coming from. They are embracing a new attitude about serving food and becoming aware of the bonding and communication opportunity around food. He noted that "by-products" such as liver, tongue, cheeks, and marrow, along with scup, skates, and other "trash fish," are finding their way into mainstream dining. The public is beginning to see that when prepared properly, these foods that in centuries past were only eaten by the poorer classes are simply delicious. He added, "I think the waters are the next necessary frontier in this trend towards valued proteins." He believes that the more we utilize "trash fish," the better it will be for the environment.

My brother Paul and I are baby boomers born right after World War II. Although our mom was an English war bride and our dad was of Italian descent, we were raised on the basic American diet. Since both of our parents worked, we had simple meals of meat, potatoes, and a vegetable or salad. Fridays were the exception: on Fridays we always had fish.

When we were young, on Saturday afternoons, Paul and I would spend time with our Sicilian grandparents in their little second-story apartment in Lawrence. They had come to America in the early 1900s as young children and ate the foods that their families had eaten in what my grandmother called "the old country." Their home had a wonderful aroma of Italian cooking. The air was thick with simmering spaghetti sauce, homemade Italian sausage and meatballs, fried breaded veal cutlets, and the dreaded tripe and octopus.

My grandmother Natalina, our Nana, always wore a housedress, black shoes with a fat high heel, and of course an apron. I can still picture her with a wooden spoon in her right hand, her snuff-stained fingers always smelling of garlic. My grandfather, whom we called Nanu, sat at the head of the little metal-topped table with a gallon of red wine, waiting for her to serve him his afternoon meal. I will never forget some of the exotic and scary foods we witnessed him ingesting. Tripe and octopus come to the forefront of my mind.

"Eeewww! Nanu is eating octopus!" My grandmother was trying to coax us into trying it, but as soon as it touched my tongue I was sure that it was something that I did not want to chew. I can still feel the suckers on the tentacles. We were typical American children.

As a shore angler I have used squid, eels, mackerel, butterfish, and many other edible species for bait. Squid has long been used as bait but is now offered at many restaurants. I find them a most fascinating creature. These marine cephalopods are composed of two fins, a mantle, a head, eight arms, and two tentacles; squid come in three hundred species and are found all over the world. Squid can be caught around the Vineyard with a small lure with two layers of sharp hooks at the base. The lure is "jigged" up and down through the water until it attracts a squid. The squid grabs the hooks with its tentacles and is lifted out of the water into a bucket. On the Vineyard, in the spring and then again in the fall, if you go to a lighted dock at night, you can more than likely catch some squid. In the last few years we have been seeing a decline in the squid population as well. No one seems to know or be able to agree on why the squid are not as plentiful today as they were a few years ago. Are they also being overfished, or is it a natural cyclical event? Are the dogfish or other predator species eating all of them? Have their spawning grounds been destroyed or compromised? I do know that while I am fishing at night anywhere along the south shore of the Vineyard during our fishing season, I see the lights in the distance from too many commercial draggers offshore, taking squid.

In my more than twenty-five years as a waitress, I never served squid. Now calamari has become a popular item on the menus here on Martha's Vineyard and around the country. The first time I ordered it in a fine restaurant, I felt uncomfortable with the fact that I was about to eat bait! It was difficult to enjoy the same morsel I offered to striped bass. In time, though, I acquired a taste for it and now I love it and serve it to my family cooked in many different ways: baked, stuffed, sautéed in olive oil with garlic, or breaded and deep fried.

My aunt Angie has always loved eating calamari. She taught me to make what she calls "black sauce,"* a rich and tasty tomato sauce with squid ink that she serves over pasta. In the markets squid are sold without the ink sac, so when I am loading my bucket with squid for bait, I always put some aside for my aunt and my own family.

Lobster is another baitfish that became a delicacy. I sometimes wonder who was the first human who wanted to eat a lobster. I imagine someone saying, "That looks so delicious. I can't wait to eat it!" as the lobster is snapping both of its claws trying to sever a finger. There is culinary evidence that the ancient Greeks and Romans enjoyed lobsters. The British, especially those who lived near the shore, held them in high esteem long before they were accepted in the New World. In America lobster was considered poor man's food. Servants in colonial

---

* See the recipe for black sauce in "Favorite Fish Recipes."

America were known to negotiate agreements specifying that they could not be made to eat lobster more than twice a week. Lobster was so plentiful in New England that people walking the beaches after a storm might report finding thirty- to forty-pound lobsters in piles washed ashore. In the 1880s Americans started to acquire a taste for lobster, and now it is prized—and expensive. Today, commercial permits to fish for lobster are strictly regulated, and those lucky enough to hold those permits work very hard to keep up with the demand.

Lobster was once so plentiful in the waters near Martha's Vineyard that it was used to catch striped bass. The "gentlemen fishermen" of the Cuttyhunk Fishing Club, established in 1864 when some New York millionaire businessmen bought land on Cuttyhunk and built a clubhouse, discovered that they could catch striped bass using lobster as bait. Just like today's fishermen, they fished among the rocks that surround the shores of Cuttyhunk, but instead of wooden swimming lures they used lobster tails.

There were bass stands built out from the Cuttyhunk shoreline to provide access to where large striped bass feed among the weed-covered rocks that shelter the smaller fish, crabs, and lobsters they prey upon. Young local fishermen, called chummers, were hired to do the messy work. Each angler had his own personal chummer, who would carry a gunnysack filled with bait to the end of the bass stand before sunrise. He would then scatter a concoction of chopped-up fish such as menhaden, eel, and lobster into the water to attract the striped bass. After the angler had finished a large breakfast at the clubhouse, he would join the chummer on his assigned stand. The chummer would bait the hook with a large piece of lobster and take the first cast before handing the rod to the angler. He was paid one dollar for each fish landed, but if the fish was very large the payment was more. At that time lobster was a delicacy for striped bass but not for human beings.

On our vacation in Sicily, I learned more about how tastes can change. Although Italy, just like America, has been affected by over-fishing, in the streets of Palermo we strolled past appetizing market displays of fresh fish. Fillets of swordfish, bonito, and mackerel took a backseat to what we call trash fish in this country. There were layers of scup-type panfish, an array of anchovy-size tidbits, and many kinds of tiny whole fish that I could not identify. Fresh octopus and a few different species of squid and cuttlefish were plentiful. Every restaurant had calamari and octopus on the menu, and my favorite souvenir is a package of dried squid ink that I found in a grocery store.

There are many species that are still plentiful but have not yet made it to our dinner table. These include the northern sea robin, dogfish, skate, and butterfish. I have taken and eaten many sea robins. Although they are not very attractive, they are delicious. Despite their prehistoric bony heads, the meat on their body is a mild white fish that is moist and actually resembles lobster tail as it curls when it's sautéed in butter. I've heard it referred to as "poor man's lobster."

Sand sharks, also known as dogfish, have been used in England for fish and chips for decades. Although I have hooked many skate and dogfish, I have never kept one to eat. These are among the many fishes that Teddy Diggs had served at the Home Port. Apparently you can cut scallop shapes out of the skate's wings; Teddy has been successful with his own skate wing recipes. Skate are the by-catch of fluke fishing. Usually the fishermen cull the skate and throw them back into the ocean, but most of them don't survive because of the way they are handled.

Butterfish start showing up around the Vineyard in the summer when the water temperature reaches seventy degrees. I use them for bait to catch bluefish, bonito, and false albacore, but when I have extra, into the cast-iron frying pan they go! The name butterfish is perfect because they melt in your mouth and have a light creamy flavor. They're usually less than nine inches long so filleting is not practical. I remove the entrails, head, and tail, roll the body in a bit of egg and then flour and spices, and sauté them. The scales are so small and soft that they don't need to be removed. It's a bit more work to eat them compared to a fillet of a larger fish, but they are scrumptious and worth every bit of picking.

The ocean that surrounds the Vineyard and the whole eastern coastline has so much delicious healthy food to offer us. By utilizing these treasures we not only support our local fishermen and farmers economically but also make a positive step in rebuilding some of the damaged ecosystems. I believe that when we support the people who have traditionally given to our community for generations, we make a better life not only for ourselves now but also for our families of the future.

24

Pass It On

THE NORTH SHORE OF THE VINEYARD, rich in historical legends and tales, has an atmosphere of mystery and intrigue. This rocky, sparsely developed shoreline, interrupted by a few pond openings, ranges from the Gay Head Cliffs at the farthest southwest tip of the island to the northwest corner of West Chop. When the northwest winds blow, the gnarly roots of cedar trees, scrub oaks, and pines, along with a scattering of flora and fauna, hold the fragile eroding banks from sliding into the sea.

So many magnificent fishing stories have been written about characters whose lives started from this stretch of coastline, starting with Moshup of ancient Wampanoag legend. As I cast my line toward the chain of the Elizabeth Islands, I often think I can feel, lurking in the shadows of the eerie bank behind me, the souls of some of these fishermen, like "Cap'n" George Fred Tilton and his brother, the notorious Captain Zeb Tilton, or Captain Norman Benson of Lambert's Cove.

When I first got hooked on surf fishing and before I owned a four-wheel-drive vehicle, this was the shoreline that was most accessible to me. Compared to the arsenal of fishing gear that I own today, I started with an inexpensive rod and reel, some hooks and weights for bait fishing, and a few lures. A hooded sweatshirt and a pair of hip boots were sufficient to keep me dry on the north shore.

After decades of surf fishing, naturally my gear has become much more sophisticated, and most of the time I feel safe, secure, and quite comfortable. I love wandering the beaches under the stars, rod in hand. On occasional moonless August nights, phosphorescent material lights up the ocean and I can watch the wake that my lure makes as I retrieve it through the surf. It hardly matters if I catch anything, but I always have hopes of maybe bringing home a dinner or even landing the fish of a lifetime. I've had some nights, though, when, cloaked in darkness, especially under the new moon, I've felt the hair on the back of my neck stand straight up. I call this having the "heebie-jeebies." Occasionally, my imagination still gets the best of me when I hear the wind rustling through the trees, rats or skunks scampering back and forth, or an occasional deer running full speed on the beach behind me. I have seen and heard bats flying around the tip of my rod, attracted to the sound of the whipping motion.

One night on Chappy, alone as usual, I was casting into the darkness. Suddenly I spotted a large black mass in the water off to my right. Could it be a large boat adrift and heading my way? The black shadow got larger and closer to where I stood on the beach. My heart started to pound in my chest as it came closer and closer. I was thinking that maybe it was a huge commercial ship gone astray. Then it got bigger and darker and so close that I jumped back from the water!

At that moment, I looked over my left shoulder. A vehicle was coming down the beach, its headlights shining on me and casting my shadow on the water. I had literally been afraid of my own shadow!

After all these years, I have learned to identify most of the strange noises and shadows in the dark. As spooky and creepy as this shore of the Vineyard can be, it's my love for the elusive striped bass that keeps drawing me back. Striped bass weighing close to sixty pounds and enormous loner bluefish like those taken by fishermen of old can be found off north shore beaches like those at Cedar Tree Neck,

Makonikey, Paul's Point, and the Brickyard. I have learned that the larger, wiser striped bass are apt to leave the cold, deep holes where they hide during the daylight hours to feed just a few feet from the shore in the night.

When the glacier formed the Vineyard and the Elizabeth Islands more than eighteen thousand years ago, huge boulders were deposited along what is now called Vineyard Sound. Massive rocks, within casting distance from the beach, show only a portion of their greatness at low tide. I can only imagine what lurks below the surface of the water. These rocks not only provide hiding places for the larger fish but give the tiny baitfish security as they school between the seaweeds and shellfish that cling to the rocks.

I have found that one of the most productive techniques of fishing these boulder-strewn waters is a slow retrieve with a surface-swimming lure. After casting over and over again as far as I can out into the darkness and then slowly retrieving my plug so it leaves a wake through the maze of rocks, I can become mesmerized under the stars. The mystery of what lurks behind one of these boulders is only revealed when, in the stillness of night, I feel the sudden massive tug on the end of my line. Then the battle begins. As adrenaline pumps through my body, I am reminded why I am out here in the dark when "normal" human beings are tucked into their warm beds.

One evening during the Derby my fishing buddy Charlie Cinto and I had cast our fresh bait out into the ocean and were sitting on our bait buckets waiting for a big fish to find our offering. We had a good wind and tide, so our plan was to spend the night fishing the bottom and chatting away the hours until the sun rose. We were in a fairly secluded area and rarely did we see other fishermen.

As the sun was setting we heard some voices coming down the path through the dunes to the beach. Three teenaged boys came chatting and laughing down to the water. They told us that one of their moms had dropped them off and they had the same plan as we did, to fish all night. They did not know they were in the proximity of a living legend, Charlie Cinto.

We teased the boys, saying, "There will be no fooling around tonight, it's Derby time and we mean business!" To our surprise, they were all tucked into their sleeping bags and were asleep by eleven o'clock!

We caught some nice striped bass that night and kept one each so that we could bring them to weigh-in. We quietly sneaked past the boys and dragged the fish back to the car and into the cooler full of ice. That year, Massachusetts state law had a two-fish bag limit, so we quietly went back to our rods and buckets and continued fishing.

As the sun peeked over the horizon and the boys awoke, they came running up to us to ask if we had caught any fish. Trying not to smile at each other, we assured them, "Naw, you didn't miss a thing!" Their mom came shortly after, and they gathered up all their belongings and left.

About a year later, on the same stretch of beach, I came across those same young men. Dick's Bait & Tackle's annual Memorial Day weekend tournament was on, it was late afternoon, and I was going to target some striped bass once the sun set. These boys were on the jetty during a bluefish blitz, struggling to land some big ones. They didn't have any steel leaders and kept getting cut off by the big toothy bluefish, losing the fish and their gear. I'll never forget how one of them looked at me with wide eyes and asked, "Hey, lady, can you help us?" I reached into my tackle bag and gave them some steel leaders. I was having fun helping them land their bluefish.

They left when it got dark. I ended up catching one nice bluefish weighing over nine pounds, and to my surprise it placed second in the tournament. I had striped bass on my mind, so I didn't really put much effort into hooking a bluefish. Later I realized that maybe I could have caught a first-place winner.

A little later that summer, on the same beach, I met one of those boys. Both of us were fishing alone. We struck up a conversation and I soon discovered that he was the grandson of a man I knew very well many years ago, the late Ed Warsyk. Ed lived on the Lagoon in Vineyard Haven and was a regular coffee customer in the early days of the Black Dog Tavern when I was a waitress. He was the person who planted the fishing bug into his young grandson, my new friend Ben Scott, by taking him fishing on his boat.

Ben and I bonded immediately, and we spent many hours fishing together that summer. He had just turned eighteen and I was in my fifties, but I loved searching the beach for fish with him and being with him when he landed his first shore striped bass. His enthusiasm was contagious. He seemed like an old soul and felt like a peer. His thirst to learn all about fishing reminded me of myself when I was young. His mind, a little sponge, absorbed and enjoyed my tales from the "old days of fishing." He shared stories of fishing with his grandfather, Ed, and I shared stories of my journey of learning to fish for striped bass with my mentor, the late Jack Coutinho.

Now, especially when Charlie Cinto is fishing with me and as I cast my offering into the surf and around those ancient boulders on that northern side of the island, I smile. Melted into one moment in time, I am feeling the ancient souls of great fishermen from the past, reflecting on my wonderful twelve years of fishing with Jackie, enjoying the company of an eighty-year-old legend, and feeling the excitement for all the firsts my new friend Ben will experience. The presence of this rocky shore reminds me that my decades of millions of casts and retrieves is but a blink of the eye. I feel so grateful to be a woman who found her passion for fishing on this venerable island of Martha's Vineyard.

When the sun is setting and I'm standing at the water's edge after a hard day in the real world, I have the feeling that all is well, and I feel at one with my maker. Have I come full circle?

When I think about those early years when I was learning to fish, I still wonder why I kept at it so persistently. When I wasn't scared out of my mind, I was dealing with tangles in my line and leaks in my waders and wondering what species of creature was going to attack my bait.

I often think, "What is it about fishing that has possessed every part of my being and why?" Is it because it brings me in close contact with nature? Is it because I love to walk on the beach under the stars and the moon? Or is it the sun, the wind, the rain in my face?

Maybe it's the social game we fishermen play? The sneaky thinking trying to outwit nature and other fishermen? Is it the hunter-gatherer in me that loves to cook and share a meal of fresh fish that I caught myself? Is it the love of the fish itself? Thinking at first that they all look alike and now seeing that, like humans, every individual fish is unique. Is it the challenge of the hunt and the long hours of finding and catching them?

I deeply feel the ultimate paradox of wanting so badly to hook and land the biggest fish in history, but then I see myself standing over a magnificent creature and feeling compassion for all the years it evaded other fishermen, and I make the decision to set it free.

I don't understand the hold over my entire being that the act of fishing has on me. I do know that it's become a part of me, and like my dear friend and inspiration Charlie Cinto says, "As long as I can put one foot in front of the other, I'll be fishing."

25

Losing Another Fishing Buddy

ROBERT JACOBS, better known as Hawkeye, passed away on May 8, 2016, after a battle with lung cancer. When I think of him, "unique" is a word that comes to mind. A bit eccentric and quirky. Not a malicious bone in his body. A brilliant man who was amazed when he discovered that my dogs understood what I was saying to them.

He asked with a confused look on his face, "He knows what you are saying?" I answered, "Yes, Hawk, dogs actually understand some vocabulary." He was not fond of dogs or kids, but he tolerated mine.

I met him sometime in the 1970s. He was originally from New York and worked in Boston for many years. He came to the Vineyard during the summers to work as a taxicab driver. We met when Duane took a job driving a cab. We socialized with a group of cabbies.

It was 1977 and John Best, another cabdriver, and I asked Hawkeye to take us fishing. He loved to fish, and when he had time, in between poker games, softball, and driving a cab, he went fishing.

He picked us up in his maroon 1968 Plymouth. He rearranged his belongings and fishing gear that filled the seats just enough so that

John and I could sit. He drove us about a half hour from Vineyard Haven to the Gay Head Cliffs. That area can be one of the most treacherous fishing spots on the island. Crashing surf and slippery boulders everywhere. Not the best choice for a couple of novice fishermen, especially in the dark.

As soon as we were on the beach, without a word, Hawkeye waded out into the abyss and left us on the beach to figure it out for ourselves. We both knew the basics of surfcasting, but neither of us had a clue as to what we were doing in the dark! That's what it was always like when you went fishing with Hawk. You better be prepared, because once you got to the water's edge, you were on your own.

Thirty years later, when John and I reminisced about that evening, John said he remembered that the wind was blowing so hard that his lure was landing behind him. I can remember that it was so dark, I was terrified, and I was having a difficult time standing up waist deep in the water as I was getting pushed around by the rolling surf. I could barely cast my lure and my leaky waders filled up with water. I was uncomfortable as my soaking-wet feet sloshed around in my wader boots. In my early days of fishing, I could only afford inexpensive waders and they never held up for more than a couple of months before they sprung leaks.

Hawk was nowhere in sight and the only thing that brought me comfort was a bottle of brandy in my wader pocket and knowing that John was struggling with me on the beach.

When I joined Hawkeye in his Plymouth, most of the time we broke down on the way home when we fished up-island. I laugh now, but I wasn't amused then.

John didn't pursue fishing after that night, but since no other fishermen would take me, from time to time I would join Hawkeye. We fished together many times over the next forty years and became close friends.

Hawk may have appeared to be a disheveled, absentminded professor type of guy. I used to say to him, "Hawkeye, your brain is a storehouse of useless information." But he was a master of numbers. He had an analytic mind that drove me and his other friends crazy at times. He remembered everyone's license plate numbers and knew where they parked their cars to fish. He remembered the weights of his fish and the years they were caught. He remembered the weights and dates of my fish, ones that I had forgotten about.

I had many remarkable times with Hawk, fishing together or having a typical one- or two-hour phone conversation. I always waited until after noon to call him because he was a night owl. He slept until at least 11 a.m. His personality would flip between a helpless child and a brilliant man. We could talk fishing, politics, and life in general, ad infinitum. My ear was sore when we finally hung up the telephone. I would say, "I gotta go now," but then our conversation went on and on. He was more like a brother to me than my brother.

Between 1991 and 1993, after I lost my mentor, Jack Coutinho, Hawk and I fished the Striped Bass and Bluefish Derby together. I felt a huge hole in my life after being so close to Jackie for over twelve years. I felt sad and alone while fishing on the beach, but it was difficult to fish with just anyone.

Hawk was living in Boston and was only able to fish here on the weekends, until he took his vacation the last two weeks of the tournament. Our fishing relationship worked out because Tristan and I had just become foster parents to Christopher, so my weekends were limited. I could put in more time hunting for fish during the week, so when he came on Friday night I could tell him what was going on. He could spend the weekend fishing, so when he left on Sunday night he could fill me in with what he found, or didn't find.

Not only during the Derby but all through the fishing season, we spent many hours casting into the Rip at Wasque Point on Chappy, live-lining herring at the herring run, walking the north shore, or sitting on our bait buckets chatting, waiting for a fish. Tristan and Hawkeye had sports and stamp collecting in common. When we invited Hawk over for dinner, I enjoyed cooking for two guys with healthy appetites.

Later, we took Ron McKee into our fold. Ron lives in Maine, and we noticed him fishing the beach at Norton Point on the south shore. He would walk long distances because he didn't have a four-wheel drive. He impressed us with the strength he had to carry so much gear to a beach that was usually accessed by four-wheel-drive vehicles. As we watched him not far from where we fished, Hawk would remark, "How can that guy carry so much stuff?" We saw him drinking out of a huge thermos and then at a second glance, he was looking out of his binoculars. He always carried two ten- or eleven-foot bottom-fishing rods, sand spikes, a bucket of bait, and a loaded backpack. We started to offer him rides.

Ron told us many tales of catching fifty-pound bass in Maine. He impressed us. At that point, Hawkeye had never landed a forty-pounder and I had never broken my record of forty-five pounds. We were secretive, but after much discussion we agreed that we could trust him and turned him on to some of our secret spots. Fishing on the Vineyard for many decades, we had the advantage of knowing little nooks and private areas that most off-island fishermen couldn't find.

Hawk was in the city during the week, so I fished alone most of the time and Ron needed a ride and I could use the company. I invited him to join me in my fishmobile. He became a good friend for many years.

We became the wild threesome! Three compulsive fishermen who didn't have enough sense to go to sleep. We lit the fire under each other. Hawk gave Ron a room to stay in when he came down from Maine, and in trade Ron helped Hawk maintain his bachelor home. They became teammates and called themselves "the Rusty Hooks."

Hawkeye hoarded small bluefish fillets in his freezer and they sustained his diet all winter. Bluefish does not have a long shelf life and they don't hold up well in the freezer without tasting oily. He insisted on describing how delicious his frozen bluefish fillets tasted, night after night. Yuck. I begged him to stop talking about them as I don't find them at all palatable. But every time we talked, he ended our conversation by saying, "I had the most delicious frozen bluefish last night." I would say, "Hawkeye, you are so annoying!" I can still hear him saying, "I take pride in being your most annoying friend." He worked hard to hang on to that title.

It was difficult for Hawk to take a passenger in his beach buggy because he had his own method of organization. Some would say it looked like clutter, but he knew exactly where everything was and could get quite upset if anyone moved his things—rods, buckets of lures, nets, everything you find in a tackle shop and more.

I'll never forget the night that the big migrating bluefish arrived and we planned to meet at the Rip on Chappaquiddick. It was in November and all the Derby fishermen had left the Vineyard and not many island people were still fishing the beach. As I was driving over the dunes, I saw the smoke. Lots of billowing black smoke rising over the dunes. I knew immediately that it was Hawkeye's Jeep. For weeks before this incident, whenever I got close to his vehicle, I could smell the fumes coming from his gas tank. I had tried to get him to pay attention to the fact that his Jeep reeked of gas fumes, but he found *me* annoying. Hawkeye was not one to fix something before it totally broke.

As the flames continued to consume his vehicle, he jumped inside to rescue his fishing rods and lures. I could see that it was going to blow any minute. Minutes after he exited the burning Jeep, the gas tank blew up. He thought his lures were safe from the fire, but the flames ended up jumping about twenty feet into the dunes and caught some of his buckets of lures on fire. They melted into the sand.

I was so angry with him and said, "We can always replace your fishing gear, but we can never replace you." I gave him a ride back home. He was traumatized by the entire event.

By the 1990s not many fishermen still used the Penn 706 reel. It was notorious for making a grating sound each time you turned the handle. He couldn't sneak around with his bailless reel. That sound carried in the dark of night and gave up his secret spots. You could hear him from North Neck all the way to Cape Poge Gut, or on a quiet night, a good quarter mile down the beach.

How can we ever forget those baggy Gralite waders? With no belt! If he had ever been knocked over by a wave, without a belt around the waist of his waders, he would have been dragged under the water. He wore the Gralite waders long after technology changed and neoprene and lightweight waders came on the market. Gralite waders were made of a PVC product, and were especially large and baggy and could easily get filled with heavy ocean water. The chance of getting back on his feet would have been slim. I would get angry with him and would tell him, "I'm not going to your funeral if you drown without your belt on!" My threat didn't work and he never in his life wore a belt around his waders.

I could go on forever with memories of my friend Bob Jacobs— our trip to Cabo San Lucas, our secret fishing spots with names that only we understood, Gordons, Dreamers, and Far Side, to name a few. Then his annoying brotherly behaviors that made me want to scream. My brilliant friend could make me laugh till my belly ached and he could bewilder me as I listened to his interpretation of how to scientifically catch fish. He was a one-of-a-kind guy, kind and compassionate but with his own unique perspective on life.

As the cancer was making him weak and sick, he would say to me, "I don't want to go, I just want to keep fishing."

I could relate to the way he was feeling. In 2001, I was diagnosed with hepatitis C. The doctor told me that although I didn't have any symptoms other than fatigue, my liver had been infected with the hepatitis C virus for more than thirty years, and they started me on a forty-eight-week treatment with interferon immediately. I was not sure if I was going to live through the treatment, which felt like a daily chemotherapy. Fortunately, I am one of the lucky ones, and today I am cured.

Hawkeye's ex-girlfriends loved him, as did his brother, Donald, and many of his cousins and aunts. They all came from off-island to spend those last days with him.

When he was sick, we talked about what it might be like if he did die, although we tried to hang on to every little bit of hope. He felt that there was nothing for him after this life. He said, "It's like when I come out of anesthesia, I have no memory, it's just nothing."

Hawkeye working at Dick's Bait & Tackle in Oak Bluffs

I told him I don't know, but it seems to me that there is an energy that exists after we drop these old decrepit bodies. Some call it a soul.

A couple of weeks after my friend passed, Dick's Bait & Tackle's Memorial Day weekend tournament was renamed in honor of Hawkeye, who loved fishing that special weekend and for many years placed on the leader board.

I joined the tournament, and although I rarely get sick, that weekend I came down with something that took my energy. I slept most of the day. Late in the evening on Saturday, I dragged myself out of bed and was sitting in the living room in my rocking chair.

Then I got the urge. I told my husband, "Tristan, I'm going to grab some eels and go take a few casts." I keep my eels alive in the basement in a bucket of water with an aerator, so I have fresh live eels to use each time I go fishing.

I still had my jammies on. I put on heavy socks and pulled my knee-high boots on. Then I slipped a hooded sweatshirt over my head and over that a weatherproof top. I put a few eels in a bag with an ice pack and headed out. Driving down the long dirt road, I was talking to Hawk. I said, "Come on, buddy, we're going fishing. Let's get a big one." I trudged my way to the water's edge, and three casts of my eel later, I landed a 26.8-pound striped bass. That fish won the tournament. It had nothing to do with me. I felt Hawkeye's spirit was with me. I shook my finger toward the heavens, saying, "See, Hawkeye, I told you!"

I hope there is a hereafter where his spirit can connect with the big ones that he pursued.

His absence has left a big hole in the fishing community on Martha's Vineyard. Hawkeye, 1947–2016.

26

How to Catch a Fish:
Rules and Exceptions

DURING THE FISHING SEASON, I teach "Learn How to Fish" workshops. It's amazing to discover how many men, women, and families have lived on this island for generations and want to but don't know how to fish. I practice the Chinese proverb by the philosopher Lao Tzu: "Give a man a fish and you feed him for a day; teach a man to fish and you feed him for a lifetime."

I meet one or more students at a beach and lead a three-hour hands-on workshop. I share with them the techniques that took me years to learn on my own, starting with tying knots, learning how the drag works, maintaining gear, techniques on casting, and reading a tide chart. After three hours of instruction I say, "With all this said, the only way I know how to catch fish is, keep your line in the water."

Through all the decades that I have fished I have seen just about every tried-and-true technique be contradicted.

Rule: Don't shine lights on the water at night. It spooks the striped bass and they will leave the shallows for deeper, darker waters.

Exception: One night, Jackie and I were fishing the Edgartown Great Pond opening. They had just opened the pond to the ocean and we knew the bass would show up. The sun was setting and it was getting dark. There were quite a few other fishermen there. I remember Stan Popowitz being there. He still tells tales of that night because it was the night he caught his first-ever striped bass.

A fisherman drove up behind us and pulled out a large Coleman lantern. When he turned it on it lit up the whole beach. Just as the fishermen started to cuss at him, screaming, "Turn the damn light out," the fish hit! He never turned the lantern off, but it was one of the best striped bass nights ever. Jackie and I laughed about it for years and talked about how amazing it was to catch bass at night and be able to see everything we were doing. A rule broken.

Rule: Always use the freshest bait you can find.

Exception: When fishing live bait from Memorial Wharf, we work hard at using a fresh bait. When it stops swimming, we toss it back in the water and replace it with a fresh one. We had a good run of tinker mackerel. Tinkers are young mackerel that bonito and false albacore can't resist. We always like to use the mackerel that are under eight inches. They are a perfect mouthful.

One of the dock regulars, Cheryl Welch, stopped by to do some dock fishing. Cheryl was not one to be on the dock at 4:30 a.m. She was more casual about her Derby fishing and arrived hours after most of us established our territory for the day. She came with some frozen mackerel. Frozen bait can work at times, but of course fresh is more desirable. She reached into her plastic bag and pulled out a mackerel that was close to a foot long. Much bigger than most of us would consider using. Usually when a bait is spent, and the eyeballs fall out and the stomach falls apart, it's time to change bait. Cheryl fished that bait long after its time. The eyeballs fell out and the sockets were all that was left in the head. The stomach split open and the entrails were hanging out. As we lined up patiently waiting for a fish to pick up our fresh live-lined bait, can you guess who caught the biggest bonito that day? Cheryl. Another rule broken.

Rule: If you want to catch a fifty-pound striped bass from the beach, fish after the sun goes down.

Exception: I was fishing the Wasque Rip on Chappy. It was a bright, sunny August afternoon and the four-wheel-drive vehicles were lined up enjoying the summer day. Next to each vehicle were blankets, beach chairs, grills, umbrellas, and sand spikes armed with fishing rods ready in case some bluefish came to feed. It felt more like a family day than a serious fishing trip.

I was kicking back, biding my time, waiting for the sun to get low, when most everyone would leave and hopefully some bass would come to the Rip.

When I fish alone I need to stand near the water casting, so I will know if a fish comes by. The best part of fishing the popular Wasque Point Rip is that someone always has a lure in the water. The fishermen take turns throwing lures. Once a few decide to stop and go back to their buggy to take a break, another angler will give it a whirl.

No one had a hit all day. I was sitting in my beach chair, watching. It was the summer doldrums. Then I noticed a commotion down the beach. I could see that someone had hooked a fish. I walked down to see what was happening, just in time to see a man land a huge lunker striped bass. The fish obviously weighed more than fifty pounds. The fisherman who landed it was a novice. He looked at it and said, "What is it?" I said, "It's a striped bass. In fact, it is a beautiful striped bass. It's the one that most fishermen spend a lifetime in search of." Obviously, without having any experience, he had landed a fish of a lifetime. Unbelievable and almost not fair!

Rule: Always use light line for bonito or false albacore. Never use a steel leader or snap swivels. These fish are keen-eyed and shy away from heavy terminal tackle.

Exception: It was Derby time and I was fishing bottom bait, targeting bluefish. I was using a six-inch butterfish cut in half, on a heavy 7/o hook, with an eighty-pound-test steel leader attached to thirty-pound monofilament line. To my surprise, I caught a bonito that won second place grand overall in the 1985 Derby.

Rule: Striped bass feed in the dark of night. New-moon nights are the best times to tempt a bass out of hiding. Metal lures work best for daytime fishing. They reflect the sunlight and are usually fished with a fast retrieve. They are not the best choice in the dark. Point Jude offers metal lures with a painted black finish. Every experienced fisherman knows that black and purple are good choices for night bass fishing.

Exception: In 2008, the Derby offered an optional two-member team competition. Ed Jerome, Derby Committee president, and I became teammates. We called ourselves "the Wayfarers," after his charter boat. I had been mate on his boat during that summer and we fished together on the beach whenever I could talk him off the boat.

One evening I found a pod of fish feeding close to the beach on the south shore. This memorable night broke all the rules. I typically do not like fishing under the full moon, and there have been times when on a bright night I have opted to stayed home. It's been documented that stiped bass are nocturnal feeders. Most anglers who target striped bass fish in the dark of night. When a full moon lights up the water, it's more difficult to tempt a keen-eyed striper to take your bait. I have also been taught that big stripers are lazy, and it is better to find them in a swift current. They take advantage of using less energy to feed. When the current is running fast, they can open their big mouth and suck up baitfish as it gets tossed around in fast-moving water. I also believe that the most likely places that could hold fish are structure, that is, big boulders, jetties, or a sandbar. Structure gives fish the opportunity to trap bait, so any structure can be a perfect spot to target feeding fish. I was in a spot with no apparent structure, a full-moon night with no cloud cover, and a low tide with a current that was barely moving.

I don't know why I decided to throw a plug in that spot, but I could hardly believe that with each cast, the second my lure hit the water, a striped bass grabbed it. I usually don't count fish, but I know I landed more than forty fish that evening. Each was a respectable thirty-five to forty inches. They all weighed fifteen to twenty pounds.

Every so often another fisherman would pass me. When I saw lights coming down the beach, I pulled my line in and stood near my car, attempting to look bored.

Even my close friend Hawkeye passed me. He came up from the left of me, stopped just long enough to complain, "Full moon, low tide, no wind, sucks." He drove on. I felt a bit guilty, but, after all, it was Derby time and we were not teammates that year.

Then Phil Horton stopped. He likes to chat. We both complained about the lousy conditions, "Full moon, low tide, no wind, sucks."

Phil did not leave, and I was anxious to get my line back in the water before the fish moved out. Finally, I put my rod in the rod holder on top of my buggy and desperately attempted to look disgusted, but, trying not to be rude, I started to remove my waders, saying, "Might as well go home, there won't be any fish around tonight." Phil finally drove on. As soon as his taillights were out of sight, back to work. I pulled up my waders, grabbed my rod off the top of my fishmobile, and headed to the shoreline. The fish were still there and once again as soon as my plug hit the water a fish grabbed it.

I was busy landing fish, measuring, and then quickly releasing them, hoping for a fish larger than forty inches. Since I had a bass over twenty pounds already weighed into the tournament, I did not want to take another one unless it was significantly larger.

A while later, more lights were heading my way from the opposite direction. It's Hawkeye, returning after trying to find fish beyond me on the beach. I once again stopped casting and was trying to act discouraged and ready to leave. As soon as he drove away, once again, the second my plug hit the water, another forty-inch fish. An amazing evening.

Suddenly, I had a fish hit my lure much harder than any of the fish I had already landed. I suspected it was upward of thirty pounds. My knees went weak and my heart began beating out of my chest. I fought the fish right up close to the beach when suddenly my line went slack and the fish swam to freedom. I gasped with disappointment. My line didn't break, and I still had my plug. I wondered what went wrong. I noticed that one of the points on my treble hook had been straightened out. Recently I had switched from using mono line to a braided line called PowerPro.

Monofilament was invented by DuPont in 1938. Mono line is made of nylon and it replaced heavy braided Dacron. The early monofilament was stiff and difficult to use. Two decades later, in 1959, DuPont introduced Stren, a thinner and softer monofilament line. For the next forty years, most every fisherman used monofilament fishing lines.

Then came the introduction of PowerPro braid. It is a thinner, smoother, slicker ultra-strong braided line. Mono has a bit of elastic stretch, but the new braided line has only a fraction of that stretch. Thus the contact with the fish is more direct, and I quickly learned that the tension was strong enough to straighten out my hook.

I rechecked my drag. I loosened it a bit, so it pulled from the spool with a little less tension.

I was praying.

"Oh PLEASE, give me another chance."

A short time later, after catching and releasing a few more fish, I had another opportunity to land a fish that could potentially place in the Derby. Once again, as soon as I played it close enough to shore, I felt that sinking feeling as my line again went limp. I checked my lure and the same thing. It had straightened out one of the prongs on my treble hook.

I learned that night that since the braid has no stretch, no forgiveness, I needed to adjust my drag and modify my technique of landing a fish. After fishing with the same line for decades, it was a difficult adjustment. I found I was losing more fish using braid than I ever did with mono.

Hours had passed and now the bite subsided. I left the beach, empty-handed but smiling after an epic night.

I called Ed as soon as I got home. I said, "You're not going to believe this but . . . " I told him my story of the more than forty fish in that one spot, full moon, no tide, no clouds, no current. He agreed to join me the following night. I was not sure if the night would be repeated. It was.

Ed and I, side by side, landed and released fish after fish. Our very own striped bass blitz. As we looked at the water's surface, it didn't make sense, because it was so calm it looked like a sea of glass. We could not believe what we were experiencing.

After an hour or so of fishing and not seeing any other fishermen, I noticed a man walking toward us. He was not wearing waders. He had bare feet and shorts. A dead giveaway that he was new to the game. He must have walked a long way because we were on a stretch of beach that was usually accessed only by four-wheel drivers. It was unusual to find anyone walking that far from civilization, especially late at night.

He walked right up to me and to our surprise said, "Hey, I've been watching you guys from down the beach. I have not had a bite, what are you using?"

"What are you using?" I asked. He came back with, "A Deadly Dick."

"Oh yeah, that'll work." It was Derby time and I naturally did not want to tell him what lure we were fishing with.

We were using black Darters. We were retrieving them slowly. They weigh three and a half ounces and they are floating wooden lures that when reeled slowly swim on the surface. Deadly Dicks are made of solid brass with a nickel plate to give them shine. They quickly sink to the bottom of the ocean, so to make them swim you need to retrieve them fast. The Deadly Dick the man was using weighed about three-quarters of an ounce and is a small lure usually used to target bonito and false albacore. This slender shiny metal lure reflects the sunlight and imitates a small forage fish like a silverside or sand eel.

He must have felt that I didn't want to have a long conversation with him because, thankfully, he turned around and walked out of sight.

Ed looked sideways at me and said, "You dirty dog."

I smiled. It was just a little fib and I'm from the "days of yore" and thought it was rude of him to ask. You never ask a fisherman what they are using, especially when they are catching fish, and especially when it's Derby time.

The next morning Ed and I were at the weigh-in. This same guy ran up to me thanking me for telling him to use the Deadly Dick. He said he had never weighed a fish into the tournament before and he had caught his first twenty-pound fish. He ended up with a daily prize.

Although I had given him some misinformation, he must have fished close enough to that school of fish to catch one. I was happy that he had caught his personal best on the lie I told. It wasn't the first time that a lie I told ended up working for someone.

Now I'm thinking about breaking one of my own rules and some night I might use a Deadly Dick for striped bass.

How *do* you catch a fish?

The longer I fish, the more exceptions to the rule I witness. These are only a few examples. My advice is, just go fishing, use whatever lure you have. Don't let it stop you from trying because you feel like you don't know how to do it. You never know when you might catch a fish of a lifetime. Do learn to tie a good knot, since you never know and do not want to lose a nice fish on a bad knot.

27

A Glimpse of My Maker

ONE EARLY SPRING, I was fishing the pond opening between West Tisbury Great Pond and Quansoo beach. Quansoo faces south, and with a strong prevailing southwest wind, most of the time there is a good surf rolling onto the beach. I caught a striped bass and was in the process of releasing it. I was in a kneeling position in the wash close to the edge of the water while taking the hook out of the fish's mouth. The undertow as the water is pulled out again is a strong current that can be dangerous, and I was blindsided by a wave that knocked me off balance. I recovered and was able to stand up, but it scared me. I could get pulled under, and now that it's more difficult for me to pop up from a stooping position, I should be wearing a flotation device.

In 1994, the Derby Committee gave each committee member a bright red Stormy Seas inflatable vest. Stormy Seas Life Jackets was founded in 1993 by Helen Moore, who was motivated to save lives at sea when a family member almost died on the west coast of Tasmania, Australia. I questioned Derby president Ed Jerome as to why those of us who do not have a boat need to wear one. I had been fishing in the surf for close to twenty years at that time and never felt a need to wear a flotation device. Ed told us, "Whether you're fishing from a boat or on the shore, wear it, and you better not drown without it on." The Derby wanted to send a message to fishermen about the importance of safety. The vest was a bit cumbersome, but I got accustomed to wearing it and realized that in some situations it was not just an accessory but a necessity. I thought it might not save my life, but at least they would find my body bobbing in the morning.

After several years, my Stormy Seas vest had worn out and the zippers were no longer functional. I cast it aside and forgot about it until that day I had a scare in the wash at Quansoo. I decided that I'd better replace it.

The choices for personal flotation devices, known as PFDs, had come a long way since my Stormy Seas vest. After some research, instead of a full vest, I purchased a Cabela's inflatable suspender. It's lightweight and small so that it doesn't hinder my mobility. If I was to fall in the water, I can pull a string and it will inflate and keep my head above the water. I started to wear it most every time I went fishing, but especially when I fish alone at night in big surf.

In late October or early November, bay scallop season opens in the saltwater ponds. I fish in the Lagoon in Vineyard Haven. A family shellfish license allows me and Tristan to dig for quahogs (softshell clams), and to dip net for bay scallops. Each town determines what day of the month the season opens and the bag limit for each licensed shellfisherman.

Bay scallops are typically found in the shallow waters of bays and estuaries along the East Coast. The peak season is during the fall, and the first few days after it opens is the best and most productive time to get them. Once the season is opened to commercial fishermen, scallops get more difficult to find.

The first days after the town opens the season to family permits, anywhere between twenty and fifty shellfishermen can be seen in the ponds up to their waists in water armed with dip nets, a peep sight, and a floating basket. A peep sight is used to see the scallops among the weeds as they sit on the bottom of the pond. I constructed a homemade "peeper" out of a large black plastic plant pot. I cut off the bottom and replaced it with a round piece of Plexiglas, then sealed it with silicone caulk. The black plastic helps cut the glare of the sun-light and I find it's lighter than the traditional wooden peep sights. The peeper is pushed under the surface of the water, and by putting my head down into it, I can locate and with my net scoop up the scallops. The scallop net handle is six feet long. This length is needed so that I can scoop up the scallops before they see me and swim away and before my feet push up any silt, hindering visibility. The opening of the net is about nine inches and it is thirty-two inches long. I scoop many scallops into the long net before I pull them out of the water, put them in my floating bushel basket, and check them for size.

The bay scallops shell can be up to three inches in diameter, but the muscle, which is the edible portion, is on average about a half inch wide. The size of the shell is not an indication of maturity. The mature scallops, or "keepers," can be distinguished from the imma-ture scallops, or "seeds," by a little ridge called a growth ring that extends laterally across the shell. The ring is generally visible, or you can detect it by running your fingers down the shell and feeling the nub. Along the outer edge of the bay scallop shell are thirty to forty bright blue eyes. Each eye has a lens, retina, cornea, and optic nerve, enabling it to see movements or shadows and to detect predators and dip netters. To swim, they clap their shells together using their muscle, which propels them through the water.

October 28, 2016, was the first day of bay scallop season in Vineyard Haven. I always try to buddy up with another dip netter, so I called my friend Ted Collins. It's safer to go with another person. I met Ted in the parking lot behind Wind's Up on Beach Road not far from the Lagoon Pond drawbridge and the boat landing. During the summer Wind's Up rents stand-up paddleboards, kayaks, sailboats, and windsurfers, but now the business was closed, so we had a place to park with easy access to the pond.

Ted and I pulled on our waders and prepared all our scalloping gear. After getting into my waders, I secured my belt. Then I tied my peep sight and floating basket to my wader belt with ropes so that they wouldn't float away from me with the moving tide and wind.

I learned to leave my cell phone in the car after ruining a couple by getting them wet.

I grabbed my long-handled net, and when Ted was ready, we walked together into the Lagoon. It was a cold and windy day. I never thought about wearing my inflatable suspenders. We were in the pond, no big surf, and I usually only walked in water up to my waist. I didn't think there was any danger.

Scallops move around by swimming close to the bottom of the pond. On the first day of the season, it takes time to find what section of the Lagoon holds the most bay scallops. We could see a few scallopers in the distance across the other side of the pond toward Hines Point.

I bent over to put my head down into my peeper, searching. About forty-five minutes had passed and I had only found about a quarter bushel of scallops. That's not a very good load for the first day of the season. I started getting cold and the wind had picked up. Seeing the scallops, even with a peep sight, becomes more difficult when the wind is blowing the water surface. My exposed hands were getting cold. I looked up from my peeper and I couldn't see Ted. I was the only one in that area of the Lagoon. I had been walking around with my head in my peeper and I assumed he had given up and gone home. It was not like him to not tell me, but I was cold, and I was not getting many scallops, so I decided to leave. I could see there were still a few people way in the distance, on the other side of the Lagoon. I headed back to the parking lot. I found out later that Ted was one of those people.

About twenty-five feet from shore, I stepped into a deep hole. My feet could not reach the bottom. I was close to shore, so I didn't feel panic. Then the water went up to my chin and I could feel cold water pouring into my waders. I started kicking my feet as hard as I could.

I realized I was in trouble. I was hanging on to my floating basket and kicking, but I wasn't moving. Something was holding me down and I couldn't figure out why I was not making any progress. I attempted to push with my net pole, but I couldn't reach the bottom. Then my pole got tangled in the rope of my peeper. I lost my grip and I watched the pole as it slowly drifted under the water. My peep sight had tipped on its side, filled with water, and sunk to the bottom of the hole while it was still tied to my belt. I was anchored to the bottom.

I struggled to turn my head to look behind me. I could see another scalloper about a hundred feet away, walking in my direction. I started to scream, "Help, help!" I wasn't sure if anyone could hear me. I screamed again but my voice sounded weak. I was kicking my legs as hard as I could and yelled a few more times.

Screaming into the wind was wasting my energy, so I thought to myself, "Don't panic." I turned my attention to the grasp my cold hands had on my basket and tried to keep my head above water. Even with a tight belt and a splash coat on top, my waders were filling up with ice-cold water. I could feel my legs getting heavy and kicking was becoming more difficult.

After a few more minutes that felt like an eternity and kicking my heavy water-filled legs, suddenly something let go of me and I began to move forward. I hung on to my basket and kicked my way to shore.

I crawled onto the mud on the shoreline. It took some effort, but I stood up. Then I started to shake. My knees went weak as I pulled off my beanie hat. It took all my strength to pull my splash coat and my heavy water-soaked sweatshirt and wool sweater up over my head. I threw them in a wet pile on the mud at my feet. My waders were full of water, but I was able to pull them down and get my feet free. My wool socks were soaked and felt like they weighed five pounds each. I pulled them off my freezing-cold, waterlogged feet. I gathered up all my wet clothes and threw them into the back of my fishmobile. I noticed Ted's car was still there and found out later that he had worked his way over to the far end of the pond toward Hines Point. He said he thought I had seen him walking across to the other side. He apologized.

My peeper and net were nowhere to be seen. I left my basket with the few scallops in it on the shore and jumped into my car and started the engine. Now I was shaking from head to icy toes. I was chanting, "Thank you, thank you," as I reminded myself to breathe.

I was too cold and shaky to call Tristan on my cell phone, so I called him when I got home. I briefly told him what happened. I told him that I had lost my basket, peeper, and net. They were somewhere in the bottom of the pond in a deep hole behind Wind's Up.

I jumped into the shower and shook. As I ran hot water over my head and body, it hit me that I had come close to meeting my maker. Then panic hit me, and I began to vibrate. I felt weak and could feel my heart racing. I had to remind myself again to breathe and told myself, "You're okay."

Tristan went back for my basket and ran into Danielle Ewart, the shellfish constable, and the commercial fisherman Billy Sweeney at the boat landing not far from the hole behind Wind's Up. In 2010, Danielle became the first Vineyard woman to be named shellfish constable. Her expertise is in shellfish restoration projects and she had worked summers in the Martha's Vineyard Shellfish Group hatchery. She is passionate about her job and takes it seriously. Danielle waits for each person to get back to shore and you better believe she will check your basket. She examines the contents of each basket while teaching about the subtle difference between a keeper and an illegal take.

Billy got into his boat and recovered my sunken peeper and net from the hole. Billy delivered them with my basket of scallops to my house. Danielle and Billy spend almost every day on the Lagoon, and they told me that they thought everyone knew that there is a big, deep hole behind Wind's Up. They said something about the hole and the keels on the sailboats. Just in case I was not the last one to know, they tied a big floating orange warning ball in the hole. Billy told me that there are many deep holes in the pond and he had gone over his head many times. I said, "Once is enough for me." From that day on, when I go dip netting for scallops, I always wear my inflatable suspenders and I have a whistle on it to call for help.

As I think back over that day, I remembered that when I tied the rope from my peeper and basket onto my belt, I noted that it was not a very secure knot. It is a blessing that my knot let go. If not, I think I would have drowned.

After getting my body warmed and calmed down, I shucked the quarter bushel of scallops from my basket and we enjoyed a delicious dinner of baked stuffed bay scallops.

Favorite Fish Recipes

THERE IS A GROWING environmental movement to support eating local. Concerned folks want to help heal the earth from all the decades of our taking more than it can replenish. Aiming toward a sustainable lifestyle, they are purchasing local, seasonal foods from environmentally friendly farms and buying fish that are caught or farmed in a sustainable way. By keeping animal product consumption to a minimum, we can be part of that movement. Since we on Martha's Vineyard are surrounded by the ocean, eating fish that we catch ourselves can not only be rewarding but can also be a way for us to do our part to try to balance the ecosystem.

There has been a disconnect by consumers from the food that we buy in the markets, whether meat, fish, or vegetable, and where that food originated from. Today, more people want to get in touch with where their food comes from and how it is handled.

It can be disturbing to some people when we explain how those fillets of fish, so rich in omega 3 oils, reached their plate tasting so fresh and delicious. I understand that it can be difficult for someone who is new to catching and keeping their own fish to learn how to clean a fresh-caught fish. The pleasure of knowing exactly where the fish's meat came from and when it was harvested, and the pride of catching it yourself, outweighs the handling process that can seem cruel from the outside. To ensure that you are eating quality fish, you should plan ahead on how you will clean it, keep it cold, and transport it home to your kitchen.

When I teach workshops I provide my students with information on handling the fish they catch and teach them how to fillet.

Bluefish

I'm often asked for my favorite recipes. I must admit, I am not a gourmet chef. I seldom have the time to toil over a complicated recipe. I believe the best fish meals start with fresh fish and the biggest crime with any fish is *overcooking*. Bluefish have a reputation of tasting oily and fishy. When I hear people say "I don't like bluefish," I know they have never eaten fresh, properly handled bluefish.

Fish is more appetizing when it is handled with care from the moment it comes from the ocean. If you don't have time to take care of a fish to keep the meat from spoiling, thank it for the pleasure it gave you in the fight, and then release it.

When I land a bluefish that will be eaten, I immediately bleed it by cutting through the gills, under the throat. I've found that by using a pair of snippers, I can reach in under the gill plate and snip the main artery. I put the fish, head down, in a bucket of fresh cold water from the sea. This lets it bleed and keeps the meat firm, and it is believed that it removes some unwanted toxins from the fish before it is filleted.

As soon as I have finished fishing, I immediately fillet the fish that have been bled. I have a setup on the tailgate of my fishmobile to help me facilitate this chore. I scale them and fillet them. I'm in the habit of leaving the skin on. When we were selling to the markets, they preferred it that way. Fresh bluefish fillets look much more desirable in the glass case with the shiny blue-green skin side up. Plus, it holds the fish together much better if you decide to grill it. Bluefish does

My home-built stone smoker

not have a long shelf life and does not freeze well. I always cook my catch within the first three days. When it is frozen, the oils take over and spoil the flavor. I prefer to serve it fresh on the dinner table rather than store it in the freezer.

Smoking it before it goes in the freezer is a way to keep it preserved without compromising the bluefish flavor. I have an attractive stone smoker in my backyard that Duane built for me in 1978. You can purchase an electric smoker or make your own out of anything from cardboard to an old refrigerator. Smoking any fish or meat is an ancient technique that helps to preserve the flavor and gives it a longer shelf life. I like to smoke four to six fish at a time. Massachusetts allows each recreational angler to keep up to ten bluefish per day. I only keep four to six fish for smoking. Eight to twelve fillets are more than enough to fill my smoker.

My Smoked Bluefish Recipe

8 fillets

- 2 cups kosher salt
- 2 cups brown sugar
- 1 bay leaf

- 1 tablespoon ground dry mustard
- 1 teaspoon ground black pepper
- ¼ teaspoon cayenne pepper
- 1 tablespoon dry oregano
- Whole allspice
- 3 fresh garlic cloves
- 5-pound bag wood chips for smoking

Curing the fillets: Mix 1 cup of the kosher salt in ¾ quart of hot water; this is an 80 percent salt solution for a good brine. Add 1 cup of the brown sugar.

When completely dissolved, add enough water to cover your fillets. When the water is cool, place the fillets in a non-aluminum container. A stone crock works great for me, but any large glass container will work. To make sure the fish is submerged in the brine, put a dish on top and weight it down with a cup of water, or a clean rock.

Place in the refrigerator to brine for 24 hours, then drain the brine and rinse the fillets in cold water. It's now time to add flavor to your fish. You can dry cure it or place it in a marinade. I like to dry cure it for a few hours. I mix 1 cup kosher salt with 1 cup of brown sugar. Add 1 teaspoon of ground black pepper, 3 crushed garlic cloves, 1 tablespoon dry oregano, 1 crushed bay leaf, 1 tablespoon of dried mustard, and ¼ teaspoon of cayenne pepper to give it a little kick. You can personalize the cure using your own selection of spices. Rub this mixture on each fillet.

Let the fillets sit on a rack for 3 or 4 hours, then rinse off the cure and pat the fish dry with paper towels. If you don't do this, they will be too salty. Place the fillets back on a greased wire rack. I leave the skin on, so I lay them skin side down. Leave enough space between them so that they do not touch each other and to let the air circulate around each fillet. Let them sit in a cool place for another 4 to 6 hours while you get your smoker ready. When a dry, glossy film forms on the surface, they are ready for the smoker.

I run an electric extension cord from the house out to the bottom of the smoker to a large electric frying pan. I fill the pan with wood chips. I buy commercial wood chips. I like using cherry, hickory, mesquite, or apple chips.

The electric pan will start the chips smoking. I adjust the heat so that it lets them smolder, refreshing the chips when needed. I leave the fish in the smoker until the surface turns golden. This usually takes 6 to 8 hours. Once the fish is finished, it can be refrigerated for at least three weeks or frozen for a few months without compromising the flavor.

I met Terry Soares in the 1970s while she was visiting her daughter Cheryl, who was living on the Vineyard at that time. Terry's parents are French Canadian but settled in the seacoast town of New Bedford, Massachusetts. That's where Terry raised her family. She was always creative in the kitchen and never used a cookbook but created her own recipes. I have not seen Cheryl or her family for many years, but her mom's recipe is still one of my favorite stuffing recipes for bluefish.

Mrs. Soares's Baked Stuffed Bluefish

Allow ½ pound of bluefish fillet per person.

- 2 stalks celery, chopped
- 1 tablespoon chopped onion
- 3 tablespoons butter
- 1 package Pepperidge Farm herb stuffing mix (or rough-cut fresh bread crumbs with 1 teaspoon sage, ¼ teaspoon basil, and ½ teaspoon dill)
- 1 cup cooked rice

- 1 fresh orange
- 1 fresh apple, peeled and chopped
- 1 chicken bouillon cube
- About ⅛ cup chopped fresh parsley
- Salt and pepper to taste

For the stuffing, sauté the celery with the onion in 1 table-spoon of the butter in a skillet.

Melt the remaining 2 tablespoons of the butter in a 2-quart saucepan, then mix in enough of the stuffing to cover the fillet and the cooked rice.

Add the sautéed celery and onion to the stuffing.

Grate the peel of half the orange, then add the juice of the whole orange into the stuffing with the zest.

Add the apple. Moisten with chicken bouillon melted in hot water or chicken broth. Season with chopped fresh parsley and salt and pepper to taste.

Cover the fillet with the stuffing/rice mixture and bake in a 350-degree oven for approximately 20 to 30 minutes, until the stuffing is golden on top. Since everyone's oven is a little different, I suggest keeping an eye on it to make sure it does not get overcooked. The sweetness of the orange, apple, and celery enhances the bluefish flavor.

When I come home from a day or night of fishing, I separate the fish we can eat in a few days and then wrap the remaining fresh fish to distribute to friends and neighbors. My neighbors Kevin and Patty Begley have benefited from my fishing obsession for years. Patty shared with me her amazing recipe for using leftover bluefish.

Patty's Bluefish Cakes

After filling up on all the fresh bluefish you and your family can eat, sort through those left over and separate out all the best. I discard the skin and the very dark meat from the center of the fish.

- Cooked leftover bluefish
- 1 potato, boiled and mashed
- 2 garlic cloves, chopped
- ¼ cup finely chopped onion
- 2 tablespoons chopped fresh parsley
- 1 tablespoon dill
- ¼ teaspoon oregano
- ½ tablespoon Old Bay seasoning
- Milk (optional)
- 1 egg, beaten
- ½ cup cornmeal, flour, or panko
- ¼ cup olive oil or butter

Mix the fish with some boiled mashed potato. Add the garlic, onion, parsley, dill, oregano, and Old Bay seasonings. You can add some milk if the mixture is too dry.

Form into cakes. Dip in the egg wash and lightly coat with a little flour. Sauté in olive oil until golden brown. The fish is already cooked, so they won't take long.

Serve with cocktail or tartar sauce and lemon.

These cakes freeze well also.

Striped Bass

Since the striped bass is a species of concern and overfishing, pollution, and unfair techniques of harvesting them have left them more difficult to find, I keep only a few striped bass throughout the season. When I do keep one for the table, here are a few of my favorite recipes.

Striped Bass with Pasta and Homemade Pesto

This recipe is perfect for a quick meal for your family or when you entertain and need to serve a crowd.

I grow my own basil, but you can purchase bunches in the grocery store.

- 3 cups fresh basil leaves
- 8 garlic cloves
- ¼ cup pine nuts, walnuts, or almonds, or a combination
- ½ cup fresh parsley leaves
- ¾ cup grated parmesan cheese, plus more for serving
- 1¾ cups extra-virgin olive oil
- 1½ pounds striped bass fillet
- 1 lemon
- 1 pound of your favorite pasta (linguine, fettuccine, or vermicelli work well with this recipe)
- Salt and pepper to taste
- White wine (optional)

For the pesto, pack the basil in a food processor.

Add 4 of the garlic cloves, the pine nuts, parsley, and Parmesan cheese.

Blend together and then slowly add 1 cup of the olive oil. Blend until the mixture is smooth. This is enough to last many meals. I package it up in small containers and freeze them for later use.

Then I fillet a striped bass, skin it, and cut it into 1-inch chunks. Add the juice of the lemon and some ground pepper to the fish and let it sit. Cook the pasta and set aside.

Heat the remaining ¾ cup olive oil in a heavy skillet on medium-low. Add the remaining garlic cloves, chopped. When the garlic is soft, turn the heat up to medium-high, and when the pan is hot, add the chunks of striped bass. I sometimes add a splash of white wine. Turn them while cooking for only a few minutes, until the fish is opaque. Pour the fish and olive oil mixture onto the pasta, and add the pesto and more grated cheese on top. Salt to taste.

Serve this dish with a garden salad and it is a perfect meal even for a crowd.

Oven-Poached Striped Bass

Striped bass is a whiter, milder fish than bluefish. It holds up better than some fish to freezing, but we are spoiled and usually fill up with fresh-caught fish during the season, so I don't stockpile any in the freezer. If I freeze any fish or bait, I use a vacuum sealer. It's a wonderful tool and will lengthen the freezer life of any food.

In Massachusetts, the minimum size to keep a striped bass is twenty-eight inches. If I do keep one, it is usually over forty inches in length and the fillets are quite thick and can dry out when baked.

- ½ cup white wine
- Juice of 1 lemon
- 1 teaspoon whole peppercorns
- ¼ cup chopped green onion or chives
- A few pinches fresh parsley, dill, or other herbs
- Striped bass fillet (½ pound per person)

In a saucepan over high heat, mix together 1 cup water, the wine, lemon juice, peppercorns, and green onion. Add some fresh parsley, dill, or any fresh herbs you love.

Once it boils, reduce heat to low and simmer for a couple of minutes to infuse the flavors, then pour the liquid into a baking dish.

Place the thick fillet of striped bass in the liquid, skin side down. Cover with foil.

Bake on the center rack in a preheated oven at 325 degrees for approximately 30 minutes. If it is still translucent, leave it until it becomes opaque white. When the fish separates and slides when pushed with a fork, remove from the oven.

As always, I time each meal by keeping an eye on it.

Cold Striped Bass with Sour Cream Dill Sauce

Sour cream dill sauce is amazing served on cold poached leftover striped bass. When I worked at Helios, a Greek restaurant, this is a recipe that we served. It is a perfect dish during a summer heat wave when no one wants to be in a hot kitchen.

- 1 cup sour cream
- ¼ cup mayonnaise
- ½ teaspoon salt
- ¼ teaspoon pepper
- 4 tablespoons chopped fresh dill
- 1 tablespoon lemon juice
- 1 tablespoon drained capers

Mix all ingredients together in a bowl and refrigerate for at least 1 hour before serving over chilled poached striped bass.

Squid

My father's sister, my godmother and aunt, Angie, and her husband, Freddie, were the cooks in our family. All our holidays were spent around the long table at Auntie Angie and Uncle Freddie's house. Wonderful Italian aromas of frying homemade sausage and meat-balls, simmering tomato sauce, baking fowl, and shrimp scampi filled the air. Meals that lasted most of the day were served each holiday, followed by cannolis and pastries and card games with lots of wine and spirits, well into the night.

One of my favorite plates was the homemade pasta and cheese ravioli. The rich tomato sauce was sometimes enhanced with squid ink. This dark red tomato sauce is called black sauce.

When Tristan and I visited Sicily in 2010, it was the first time we saw squid ink recipes on the menu—black sauces, pasta, rice, and risotto.

When I clean a fresh squid, I carefully cut the sheath to find the ink sac. The ink is contained in a tiny metallic-silver teardrop-shaped

I found a package of dehydrated squid ink in a grocery store. Luckily, I can catch my own fresh squid, but you can purchase it on the internet.

Bill Waggaman—visiting from Bear, Delaware—
with his first jigged squid. After a successful night
of striped bass fishing on Chappaquiddick, I took
him squidding off the piers in Edgartown.

sac. I remove the sac and put it into a bowl with a couple of tablespoons of water. With a fork, I crush the sac to open it, and the water
turns inky black. This is what I add to my tomato sauce. I have found
that two sacs are plenty. More than two and the flavor becomes too
strong. It is difficult to explain the flavor. It is not fishy, it's just *rich*,
and the ink turns the sauce a rich, dark red color.

This is my black sauce recipe, passed down from my family.

Black Sauce

- ½ cup olive oil
- 1 onion, finely chopped
- 2 garlic cloves
- 1 28-ounce can crushed tomatoes
- 1 28-ounce can tomato puree
- 1 6-ounce can tomato paste
- 1 teaspoon each of dried oregano, basil, and thyme

- 1 bay leaf
- 2 tablespoons sugar or some type of sweetener (my aunt will add some crushed canned carrot in place of sugar)
- 2 sacs (about 2 tablespoons) squid ink
- Fresh squid (2 medium; optional)

Heat the oil in a large pot over medium heat. Simmer the onion and garlic until translucent. Add the crushed tomatoes, tomato puree, and tomato paste and 2 cups water.

Add all the spices and sugar and the squid ink.

If you have some fresh squid, cut it into 1-inch pieces and add them to the simmering sauce. Simmering squid for a long time makes it tender and adds even more flavor to the sauce.

Simmer the sauce for at least 1 hour on low.

Serve over your favorite pasta and top with freshly ground Parmesan cheese.

Bay Scallops

On the Vineyard we can fish for bay scallops only in the late fall and winter months. I usually get enough for Tristan and me to enjoy some meals through the winter and a few pounds to give away for Christmas gifts. In late October, with the Derby ended, as soon as they open the season, I pull my waders on once again, walk into the Lagoon in Vineyard Haven, and use my dip net to scoop them up. By early December it is too cold for me. The commercial fishermen are better equipped to fish all winter from their boats with scallop drags. Sea scallops are very different not only in size but also in flavor from bay scallops, which are relatively tiny. They are as small around as a nickel and not larger than a quarter. Sea scallops are three times larger. Bay scallops are more delicate and taste best if they are not overcooked, so be prepared to serve them a few minutes after they hit the pan. Because these tiny bivalves are sweet and tender, a quick sauté in butter or olive oil with a splash of white wine and a hint of lemon is a perfect way to serve them. Our favorite is baked stuffed scallops.

Baked Stuffed Bay Scallops

- 6 tablespoons butter, plus 2 tablespoons melted butter
- 20 Ritz crackers
- ¼ cup panko
- 1 tablespoon fresh chopped parsley
- ½ tablespoon dried dill
- ¼ teaspoon fresh ground black pepper
- 2 garlic cloves, chopped fine
- 4 tablespoons grated Parmesan cheese
- 1 to 1½ pounds bay scallops (¼ pound per person)

Preheat the oven to 400 degrees.

While the oven is preheating, make the stuffing: Melt the butter in a small saucepan.

Put the Ritz crackers in a plastic bag and roll a rolling pin over them until they are reduced to small crumbs. (I like to use Ritz crackers. They have a buttery, salty flavor that is great with any stuffing for fish.)

Add the crumbs and the panko to the pan.

Add the parsley and dill, black pepper, garlic, and Parmesan cheese.

Place the bay scallops in an ovenproof casserole dish brushed with 2 tablespoons melted butter. Cover the scallops with the stuffing mix and then cover them with a cover or tinfoil. Bake for approximately 7 minutes. Then remove the cover and bake a few more minutes, until the stuffing is browned. Do not overcook.

Herring

Although the Atlantic herring are not as abundant as they once were, in December some large schools will still come into Edgartown harbor. Hawkeye and I spent many evenings as the sun was getting low jigging our sabiki rigs for these Atlantic herring. These are the only species for herring we are allowed to harvest. We have worked in my basement until midnight, filleting them and preparing them for pickling. It's worth the work, and attractive jars of pickled herring make great Christmas gifts.

This is a recipe that I have developed over the years.

Pickled Herring

Catch the herring (12 is plenty but 20 is better), scale them—the scales wipe off easily with the edge of the fillet knife—and carefully fillet them. This is time-consuming, but there is such a little bit of meat on each fish, and I like to get it all. Wash the fillets under running water and then soak them for 48 hours in cold water and ½ cup of kosher or canning salt. Do not use iodized table salt.

The brine prevents the herring from getting mushy.

- 12 to 20 herring fillets
- 1 large onion, thinly sliced

Brine

- 1 cup kosher salt
- 1½ cups brown sugar or 1 cup pure maple syrup
- 1 teaspoon peppercorns
- 4 crushed bay leaves

Bring 2 quarts water, the salt, and the sugar to a boil for 10 minutes to dissolve the salt and sugar. Add the peppercorns and bay leaves. Refrigerate this brine until it has cooled. Place your fillets in a large glass bowl or crock (do not use an aluminum or metal container) and pour enough of the brining solution over them to cover completely. I place a plate on top to keep them under the solution; the salt will make them float to the top. Refrigerate for 48 hours.

Pickling Solution

- 1 part water
- 1 part vinegar (you can use either white or cider vinegar; I like a combination of the two)
- 4 bay leaves
- 1½ teaspoons whole allspice
- 1 teaspoon mustard seed
- 1 teaspoon whole peppercorns
- 4 garlic cloves

Remove the fillets from the brine and run them under cold water once more. Pat them dry with paper towels. Wash and boil your jars to sterilize them.

Cut the fillets into 2-inch pieces.

Layer the chunks of herring with sliced onion into the clean jars. I like to use red onion, but either red or white is fine.

Combine all the pickling solution ingredients and fill the jars to the top with the pickling solution. Refrigerate for at least 4 days before serving. Serve with sour cream and crackers.

Although this recipe is delicious, I have experimented with different flavors. If you like it hot, you can add a dried hot chili pepper. I sometimes add some sliced fresh ginger to give it a little kick.

You can add dill and even a little sliced lemon.

Sea Robin

Sea robin are sometimes considered trash fish and most anglers throw them back. When I started my taxidermy business in 1987, I offered to mount a scup to present to the child who caught the largest during the Martha's Vineyard Bass and Bluefish Derby's Kid's Day Derby. Then I noticed that the smaller children seemed to be more successful at catching sea robins, and I decided to switch and mounted a sea robin instead. Wouldn't you just know that for the next six years, not one sea robin was caught! For many years the large sea robins seemed to disappear. Eventually I went back to doing a scup. Since 2007, the sea robins have returned, and large ones are being caught by anglers targeting striped bass and bluefish.

When my nephews, Tommy and Joey, visited me from New Hampshire when they were young, I took them fishing. They wanted to keep every fish they caught. I warned them that any legal-sized fish they kept, we would eat. It was mostly large sea robins. I learned to cook them at that time.

They have a hard, prehistoric-looking bony head with many sharp points sticking out. Getting past them is the difficult part. The body, protected with a tough skin and small hard scales, contains the edible portion. The meat is solid white with a delicate taste. They are delicious. Sometimes they are called "poor man's lobster." If you keep a sea robin, it should measure at least twelve to fourteen inches long tip to tip, to make it worth the effort of preparing it. Lately I have caught some up to seventeen inches long.

Sautéed Sea Robin

Carefully remove the fillets from each side of the back of the sea robin. Discard the head, tail, and fins. After removing the meat from the backbone, lay the fillets flat skin side down and run a sharp knife between the meat and the skin. Discard the skin.

Melt 2 tablespoons of butter in a pan. I use a cast-iron frying pan. Put the entire tail meat into the hot butter. It will curl up like a lobster tail. Add some salt, pepper, and lemon to taste. Serve with rice and vegetables sautéed in olive oil and you have a gourmet meal.

White Perch

The white perch has a silvery, greenish-gray body that varies from black on its elevated back to whitish on its belly. The white perch is not a true perch but belongs to the bass family. White perch usually grow to about seven to fifteen inches long and rarely weigh more than a pound. They favor brackish water, but they can sometimes be found in freshwater in coastal areas. Their range is as far south as South Carolina and north to Nova Scotia. Here on the island, they spawn in brackish water in the early spring. I catch them in the back of the Tisbury Great Pond at a public access spot called Sepiessa. I'm not big on fried food, but battered and fried white perch is one of my favorites. Since the fish are spawning when I catch them, I take only a few at a time. Three fish is more than enough for our small family.

Pan-Fried White Perch

· 6 white perch fillets
· 1 egg
· ⅛ cup milk
· ½ cup flour
· Pinch of paprika
· Salt and pepper to taste
· ¾ cup mild vegetable oil or olive oil

Beat the egg and milk together in a bowl large enough to fit a fillet.

My catch from one evening at Sepiessa in West Tisbury Great Pond

Mix the flour with the paprika and salt and pepper to taste.

Heat the oil in a large frying pan. (I use a cast-iron skillet.)

Dip the perch fillets in the egg wash and then into the flour mixture and carefully place them in the hot oil. Brown on both sides.

White Perch Salad

Leftover white perch is also delicious served cold. Make sure there are no bones in the leftover fillets. A perfect sandwich for a quick afternoon lunch.

- Leftover cooked white perch
- 1 stalk celery, chopped
- 1 small onion, chopped
- ¼ cup mayonnaise
- Squirt of lemon juice
- Salt and pepper to taste

Mix the fish with the celery and onion, then add the mayonnaise, lemon juice, and salt and pepper to taste.

These are the recipes that I use. Like I said, I am not a gourmet cook and don't have an enormous amount of time to toil over complicated recipes. In twelve-step programs there is a saying, "Keep it simple," and I like to apply this to my everyday life.

Recipes from Fishing Friends

I asked some of my fishing buddies if they could send me some of their favorites. Some of these are simple and some are more time-consuming, but I guarantee they are worthwhile to try.

BOB LANE

I have been friends with Bob Lane and his wife, Jill, for more than thirty years. He preceded me as the president of the Martha's Vineyard Surfcasters Association. We have fished together in tournaments and just for fun. All 250 pounds of him ventured with me in my blow-up kayak in pursuit of striped bass in Menemsha Pond. Bob has started a program of collecting useful sundries, gifts, and clothing that he packages up and sends to men and women serving in Afghanistan, Iraq, Bahrain, Japan, and on an aircraft carrier in the Pacific. This is Bob Lane's simple but delicious recipe that can be used for any white meat fish.

Pistachio-Glazed Fish Mediterranean Style

This recipe is simple but delicious, designed for busy people who want to eat healthfully but do not have time to cook a meal with complicated ingredients.

- 1 cup shelled pistachios
- 2 tablespoons olive oil

- 1 garlic clove
- ½ pound of fish per person

In a food processor blend the pistachios, olive oil, and garlic until smooth and the consistency of peanut butter.

Spread the pistachio blend evenly over fish fillets.

Bake at 400 degrees or grill without turning.

Serve with a garden salad and rice.

MIKE STIMOLA

I met Mike Stimola through Bob Lane. Mike and Bob are fishing buddies. Tristan and I have become close friends with Mike and his wife, Rosemary. Mike is a well-known photographer (https:// michaelstimolaphotography.com/portfolio), and Rosemary publishes books for children and young adults (www.stimolaliterarystudio .com). We celebrate each New Year at their home in West Tisbury.

This is a recipe from Mike. He said in his message, "As you know, so much of cooking is less about the absolute time frame and more about knowing your ingredients."

Grilled-Baked Black Sea Bass

- 1 pound black sea bass fillets or steaks
- 2 tablespoons olive oil, plus more for drizzling
- 1 tablespoon basil pesto (see page 266), or more to taste
- 1 large fennel bulb
- 1 large sweet onion
- 1 large zucchini
- 2 large tomatoes

- 1 tablespoon salted butter
- Salt and pepper to taste

Light the grill and heat to high.

Prepare the fillets: Make an aluminum foil cooking pouch large enough to accommodate all the fillets. Drizzle fillets with olive oil, then salt and pepper them. Brush on just enough basil pesto to coat the fillets.

Seal the pouch by folding the edges, bottom over top layer (I use a double layer of foil about 15 inches long under the fillets and a single layer on top).

Prepare and cook the vegetables: Thinly slice the fennel bulb (not the stalks) and onion and place in a saucepan with 2 tablespoons of olive oil (you can retain some of the fennel fronds as a garnish). Sauté, covered, over medium heat until they are just getting soft. Stir occasionally.

Meanwhile, slice the zucchini lengthwise into ¼-inch-wide strips and cut the strips in half.

Quarter the tomatoes and cut each in half again.

At this point, put the pouch of fillets on the grill and reduce the heat to medium. Cook for 10–12 minutes. Cooking time will vary with each grill.

Add the zucchini and tomatoes to the sauté pan when fennel and onions are just getting soft. Add the pesto (use more if you want to intensify the flavor) and butter, and blend in. Lower the heat and cook, uncovered, until the tomatoes and zucchini are just soft. Salt and pepper to taste.

Cover, turn off heat, and wait on the fillets.

Plating and serving: When the fillets are done, open the pouch and plate the fillets. Dress each with the vegetable topping. If desired, garnish with fennel fronds.

You can serve this dish with a side of white rice preceded by a simple salad of arugula, tomato, and goat cheese with lemon vinaigrette.

LISA BELCASTRO

I met Lisa when I was invited to join Cynthia Riggs's Wednesday writers' group. She is a Christian romance novel author. Among her many writing awards, her book *Shenandoah Dreams* won the 2015 Christian Small Publishers Association Romance Book of the Year. We have become friends and we fish together every chance we get.

Basil Dijon Bluefish

- · 4 fresh bluefish fillets
- · Juice of 1 lemon
- · 4 tablespoons butter, softened
- · 1 garlic clove, minced
- · 1 tablespoon coarse country Dijon mustard
- · 4 tablespoons basil leaves, chopped
- · Salt and pepper to taste

Place the fillets skin side down in a glass baking dish. Squeeze fresh lemon juice over each fillet.

In a small bowl combine the softened butter, garlic, and mustard. Spread the mixture generously atop each fillet. Sprinkle the chopped basil over each fillet. (I love to use lemon basil fresh from the garden as well as traditional basil.)

Refrigerate for at least an hour.

Fire up the grill and cook skin side down to start.

Serve hot off the grill. Salt and pepper to taste.

SHIRLEY CRAIG

I met Shirley and her husband, Phil, at Wasque Point. She was one of the few other women who dared to join the lineup with the guys during a bluefish blitz. Her husband, the late Phil Craig, was the author of popular island mysteries starring the fictitious character J. W. Jackson. Phil and Shirley collaborated on a cookbook, *Delish*. This recipe was not published in her book.

Almond-Crusted Fish Fillets

- Olive oil for coating the pan
- 4 tablespoons mayonnaise
- 2 tablespoons honey
- 3 teaspoons Dijon mustard
- 4 fish fillets (striped bass, bluefish, fluke, or cod)
- ½ cup ground almonds

Preheat oven to 350 degrees.

Mix the mayonnaise, honey, and mustard together.

Place the fillet in a pan coated with olive oil.

Spread half the mayo mixture on the fish. Sprinkle half the ground almonds on top and pat down into the mix. Turn the fillets over and repeat on the opposite side.

Bake for 15 minutes or until the fish flakes easily.

ED JEROME

Ed Jerome, president of the Martha's Vineyard Striped Bass and Bluefish Derby since 1986, was a retired principal of the Edgartown grammar school and also a writer. He collaborated with the artist Ray Ellis, writing two books about the Derby.

Ed and I were close friends and fished as teammates, the Wayfarers, from 2008 until 2014. During the fishing season, he was the captain of his charter boat, the *Wayfarer*. On September 18, 2018, during the seventy-third annual Derby, Ed was in Sengekontacket Pond gathering clams for his much-loved Linguine and Clam Sauce recipe and had a fatal heart attack. Weeks before he died, he shared this recipe with me to be included in this book.

I was fortunate enough to be working on duty at the weigh-in station the morning of the day Ed died. Ed came to the station, as he often did, and spent two hours talking to those of us who were there: to me, the weigh-in staff, tourists, and fishermen coming in for their morning coffee or to claim their daily or weekly awards.

His widow, Maryanne, told me that the last image she has of Ed is of him standing in the doorway of the weigh-in chatting with me. Maryanne calls me his "fishing wife." I am honored. He enriched my life and the lives of thousands of island children, friends, family, and Derby participants. Here is Ed's recipe:

Martha's Vineyard Clams and Linguine Italian-Style

Clams and linguine for the purist. Hardshell clams on Martha's Vineyard are called quahogs by Native Americans. As a result, in New England, that is the word of choice for hardshell clams. The smaller quahogs are called little necks or cherry stones.

Quahogs and linguine are best when you dig the clams yourself, and they are easier to open with a clam knife after a day in your refrigerator's crisper.

Clams and their juices should be separated with meats in one container and the juices in another, free of any particles of the shells. The meats should be ground fine in a small mixer and put aside to be cooked later. This recipe serves six.

- 1 pound linguine or angel hair pasta
- 18 large clams, ground, with juice reserved
- 6 to 8 ounces extra-virgin olive oil
- 8 to 10 garlic cloves, chopped
- Approximately ½ cup lemon juice
- 8 tablespoons butter
- Handful of chopped fresh parsley
- 10 little necks
- 1 loaf garlic or French bread

Heat the extra-virgin olive oil in a large saucepan, add the garlic, and cook for approximately 1 to 2 minutes. Do not overcook the garlic. Add ¼ cup of the lemon juice and raise heat to medium-high. Add your ground quahogs, bring to the boiling point, and simmer for 5 to 8 minutes. Reduce heat to medium and add the butter, constantly stirring with a wooden spoon.

Add the remaining ¼ cup lemon juice, a handful of chopped fresh parsley, and 10 opened little neck clams to use as garnish. Continue stirring with the spoon until a frothy white color shows in the mixture. Keep this mixture over medium-low heat for another 10 minutes, then on low to keep warm.

The final touch is to pour the clam juice into the water that is used to boil the pasta. Add the linguine and cook, watching it closely so it does not overboil, because the natural salt in the clam juice boils faster.

A loaf of French bread or garlic bread goes to soak up all the delicious broth.

Fishermans
Mess Halibut Stew Italienne
— queha's Chowder.
Sort

2 lbs. fish	1 c. white wine
1 clove garlic minced	½ c rice
¾ c chopped onion	2 T olive oil
½ c chopped green pepper	2 t salt
1 c " celery	1 t Ital herbs
1 c t.j	⅛ t pepper
2 cans tomatoes	½ t worcestershire
	green veg
	2 T parm.

MARGHEE BARROWS

Marghee Barrows and I were the closest of friends in the years we both worked at Helios Greek restaurant. I waitressed and Marghee cooked and baked in the kitchen. After Marghee moved away from the island, I didn't see her for about thirty years. We found each other through Facebook and have reconnected. When I asked Marghee if she had any fish recipes that she would share, she laughed and told me that just the night before she was using a recipe that she got from me many years ago. She sent this photo of the original recipe. I had forgotten about it. My dad, Gus Messineo, was the originator of this recipe. I used to use it all the time and am so happy to have it once again. It is fantastic.

Mess's Halibut Stew Italienne

In a large wide, deep pot, heat on low 2 tablespoons olive oil. Sauté the onion, green pepper, and celery till translucent. Add the garlic and watch carefully that it does not overcook.

I use a pot large enough that delicate fish and veggies will cook evenly. You don't want to damage them by stirring too much.

Add the cans of tomatoes. I like the whole peeled tomatoes. I break them up a little with my hands so that they are not so large but still stay chunky. Add the rest of the juice from the can.

I leave out the cup of tomato juice and use chicken, vegetable, or fish stock instead.

Then add ¼ cup white or red wine. Add salt and pepper to taste, and a dash of Worcestershire sauce. Add dried oregano and thyme or fresh herbs from your summer garden. Two tablespoons of tomato paste are good also, for depth of flavor (fancy foodie talk).

Simmer awhile, 15 minutes, and taste and adjust seasonings. When good to go, add in green vegetables, such as sliced zucchini or broccoli or both, or use frozen peas as they are easy and beautiful. Then add in 2-inch chunks of any fresh white fish: striped bass, haddock, cod, fluke, or a combination. You can use shrimp or scallops or whatever you have. If using thin, delicate fish like summer fluke or winter flounder, put in at the last minute of cooking since it cooks superfast.

I like to make rice separately in a pan or my rice cooker. If you put the uncooked rice in the soup, it will soak up all your beautiful stock. When everything's ready, I put about ½ cup cooked rice in a bowl, then gently spoon fish, veggies, and broth over the rice, making sure everyone gets a little of everything. Add a squeeze of lemon, maybe a drizzle of good olive oil, a sprinkling of chopped parsley, and since this is Italian, some Parmesan cheese. (Food Network people have a fit when you serve fish with cheese, but I love cheese on everything and this is how my dad liked it and it is his recipe!)

Serve with good French bread on the side for dipping into the broth, extra lemon wedges, and butter for the bread. Yum.

I sometimes make this with potatoes and skip the rice. Clams also work well with this recipe. Steam them separately and when they start opening put them in the soup. Each time I make it, it's always different, but so good each time.

Acknowledgments

I WOULD LIKE TO THANK the fishermen who have inspired me to write this book. I am grateful to the members of the Martha's Vineyard Striped Bass and Bluefish committee who volunteer throughout the year for the success of this nonprofit organization's fishing tournament. Not only have they donated more than $30,000 each year to our high school scholarship program but also the tournament has enriched my life and the lives of so many fishermen from all over the world for more than seven decades.

I am hoping Jackie Coutinho and fishing teammate Ed Jerome are watching me in the surf from the afterworld. I thank them for the years they fished with me in search of the elusive striped bass.

I would like to thank Victoria Wilson, vice president and senior editor of Knopf. This book would not have been a reality without her professional guidance and her invaluable editing and publishing expertise. I am profoundly grateful for her patience and her generosity in working with this first-time author.

I am forever indebted to Jenny Seward for her emotional support in my recovery. Jenny also started the ball rolling when she suggested that her childhood friend Vicky Wilson might be interested in my story.

I am grateful to Rosemary Stimola for her loving support, friendship, and generosity in sharing with me her expertise in the publishing world.

Heartfelt thanks to photographer and fishing buddy Mike Laptew for the hours he spent with heavy camera equipment capturing me in action with a fishing rod and lure.

Thanks to Ben Scott, photographer and talented fly fisherman, for his friendship, sharing his many photos, and capturing the image used on the jacket of this book.

I thank all the editors and publishers of *On the Water* magazine for encouraging me to write despite my claim "I'm a fisherman, not a writer."

Special thanks to Susanna Sturgis, for her meticulous editing.

I am eternally grateful to my best friend, Martha Abbot, for decades of love, support, long talks, and dog walks. She always makes me laugh when I feel like crying.

To Carla L. and Susie P. for all the years of emotional and spiritual support. Through their guidance I have learned to live life on life's terms. They told me, "Hang on, because you cannot even imagine what life has in store for you, if you stay sober, *a day at a time.*" I could not have imagined that I would become a first-time mother, a surf fisherman, a well-respected member of our community, and a writer. They gave me hope and encouragement.

I thank Maryanne Jerome for trusting me to be her husband Ed's "fishing wife."

I thank my husband, Tristan Israel, for all his love and support. I'm grateful to him for his hands-on help raising our special-needs adopted son, Christopher. Also, I thank him for taking over my parenting responsibilities for a month each year. He became "Mr. Mom" and the master of the microwave, which allowed me the time and energy to give my undivided attention to pursue my passion of fishing eighteen hours a day, for five weeks each year, during the Martha's Vineyard Striped Bass and Bluefish Derby. I am thankful to him for trusting me to wander the beaches alone, or with strange men, and show no jealousy or doubt my commitment to our marriage.

I am grateful to the island of Martha's Vineyard and the bountiful waters that surround it. The Vineyard enveloped me, keeping me safe while I pursued my passion.

To *Morone saxatilis,* the striped bass; during my quest for this elusive fish I gained a profound respect for the fish itself as well as an appreciation for all that it has contributed to my life.

My literary journey changed when I was invited to join the Wednesday Writer's Group held in the cozy living room of the eighteenth-century Cleaveland House, owned by Cynthia Riggs. I thank them for reassuring me when I expressed all the self-doubt that comes naturally to a recovering substance abuser.

Most of all, I thank my higher power, for protecting me and allowing me to survive years of drug and alcohol abuse. Each day, like my friends and family who prayed for me, I pray for those who are too sick to pray for themselves. I'm grateful for the privilege to enjoy each sunrise, sunset, and the surprising pleasure from each tug of a fish, large or small. Most of all, I am grateful for the gift of sobriety.

Bibliography

Cole, John N. *Striper: A Story of Fish and Man.* New York: Atlantic/Little, Brown, 1978.

Fred, Cap'n George. *Cap'n George Fred.* Edgartown, MA: Dukes County Historical Society, 1969.

Holder, Charles Frederick. *The Log of a Sea Angler: Sports and Adventures in Many Seas with Spear and Rod.* Boston and New York: Houghton Mifflin, 1906.

Karas, Nicholas. *The Complete Book of the Striped Bass.* New York: Winchester Press, 1974.

Manton, Walter P. *Taxidermy Without a Teacher.* Boston: Lothrob, Lee & Shepard Co., 1882.

McDonald, John. *The Origins of Angling.* New York: Lyons & Burford, 1957.

Messineo, Janet. "Derby Dames, Women Who Stay Out All Night." *Vineyard Style Magazine* (Fall 2000): 28–33.

———. "In Pursuit of Swordfish: The Doryman," *On the Water Magazine* 10, no. 12 (April 2007).

Migdalski, Edward. *Fish Mounts and Other Fish Trophies.* New York: John Wiley & Sons, 1981.

Neumann, Conrad. *Up-Island Poems: Tales of a Life on Island & Sea.* Menemsha, MA: Up Island Books, 2017.

Post, Robert. *Reading the Water: Adventures in Surf Fishing from Martha's Vineyard.* Chester, CT: Pequot Press, 1988.

Schmidt, Alfred C. *Personal Training in Taxidermy.* Memphis, TN: Schmidt School of Taxidermy, 1937.

Index

Illustration Credits

All other images courtesy of the author.

This boo...obe Cor-
poration...rst cut by
Claude C...Geoffroy
Tory and...although
he introd...him that
we owe t...is letters
a certain...eator an
immediat...ce.

Berryville, Virginia

Designed by Christopher M. Zucker

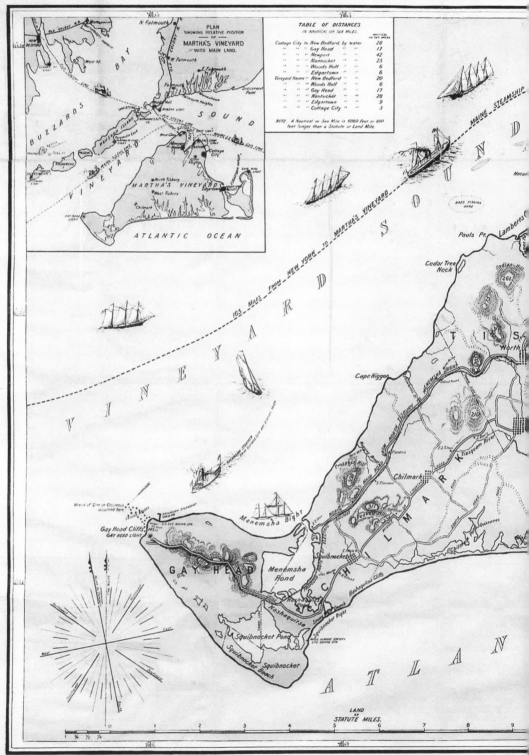

PUBLISHED AND COPYRIGHTED BY G.W.ELDRI